GW01071941

Watercolours

&

Weevils...

...a light-hearted look at ex-pat life...

Mary Colbeck

ISBN 978-0-9572772-4-3

Published by Scallop Shell press

29 Derby Road,
Caversham,
Reading.
RG4 5HE

DEDICATION

This is dedicated to the memory of Pat, who always wanted to 'make a difference' – and did.

Please forgive any problems with sequencing: I'm editing this some years later, and I've had to fill in one or two gaps from memory. Senior moments being ever-more-frequent, there must inevitably be some anomalies. Some of the entries are diary-style, some written from memory as a narrative, but the journal doesn't necessarily need to be read sequentially anyway – just dip in and out and go with the flow. Please also be aware that I wrote as I found the different locations at that time: I am quite sure that local conditions and the different political situations have changed since then, Egypt, of course, being a case in point.

Very many thanks to Alan for his patience and help with the PC, to Linda for help with proofreading, and last, but definitely not least, many thanks also to my publishers, Lindsay and John for their patience, support, hard work, and suggestions.

CONTENTS

The Background

I suppose the real start of the story was back in the summer of '97, when Pat and I were having a quiet coffee in the summer-house of our garden in Reading. No, maybe that wasn't the start: maybe it was way back in the sixties when I went to work in Germany, helping run a bookshop for the troops in BAOR. I don't know what made me do it: - no-one I ever knew had ever worked overseas before – wow! How brave was that! The only time I'd been abroad before was to Austria on a coach-trip. It was in British Army of the Rhine that I met Pat who was a regular British soldier, serving there as a photographer. From Germany he was posted to Aden – he was there for the Withdrawal – and I worked another two years in Germany before coming back to work in London. It was five years later that we actually got married when he was posted back to UK.

With Army postings we moved around mainly the South of England and Germany again, and Pat took every opportunity to study in the evenings, until eventually, after twenty years' Army service, he was commissioned into the then Educational Corps. He served five years in the Corps until his Commission ended, which is when we moved to Reading. For many years Pat continued to study in his own time, starting with an HNC, and working up to an MA and Fellowship in what was then the Institute of Personnel Management - not bad for someone who I'm fairly sure was dyslexic, had largely been ignored by the teaching staff at school, and who'd left secondary modern school at sixteen with just five GCE's. I was, and am, very proud of him.

So, there we were, in the summer of '97. Pat and I were sitting in the summerhouse (the lovely lady from whom we'd bought the house had kindly left us said summerhouse but insisted for some reason on taking with her a rickety old coal-house) having a quiet coffee in the sunshine. I particularly remember the day because of the sunshine…

Pat told me that his company, Foster Wheeler (FW), the global Engineering Procurement and Construction contractor, where he was the Training Manager, had offered him a two-year posting to Oman, (in the Persian Gulf, for those whose geography is as shaky as mine is. I failed GCE Geography in spite of a beautiful essay on the Swiss coast-line. Take your time, just think about it.) I digress. As is my wont. First the good news: he'd earn a lot of money. Then the bad: it was unaccompanied. Very bad news. We'd been happily married for twenty-six years and had no desire to be apart, but it was a unique opportunity to make some money, and with a mortgage and two teenage children, we decided to give it a go.

Off he went to Oman. It wasn't an easy time for either of us, but especially for him, out in the desert miles away from anything that constituted civilisation, but he survived – we both did. He loved the Omani people with whom he worked and, as always, he saw potential in each individual, and helped give them the opportunity to succeed. He was always good at that. They were very fond of him.

I'd have loved to visit him in Oman, but when he had leave he wanted, and needed, to come back to UK to see me and our two lovely children, Gerry and Ben. We decided that when he finished the contract I'd go out and have a holiday there with him, but it was not to be, as his contract finished sooner than expected, and we didn't have a chance to do what we'd planned.

Anyway, given one successful field posting behind him, we shouldn't have been surprised when, on coming back to UK, he was offered a second overseas posting – this time accompanied – great! Where? The Philippines! I have to admit to very mixed feelings – I loved where we lived in Reading with our large garden; we had a great circle of friends, and I'd been having Bel Canto singing lessons with Anthony, a local music teacher for several years... (Bel Canto, literally 'beautiful singing – is the Italian method of classical singing - well, I did my best!). A small group of us travelled every week to local retirement homes giving concerts to the residents.

I'd also qualified as a mature (very!) student as a Teacher of English as a Foreign Language, and specialised in English for Business and Industry. I had loads of work, and loved my students. I knew I'd miss all this, but I wanted to be with Pat, and I'm so glad that I did go with him... Pat was to start as Admin Manager until the 'real' Admin Manager took over, when he would expand his duties to include Sustainability and Training – both very dear to his heart... Pray continue dear reader:

The Philippines - The Start of the Adventure...

We'd arranged to fly out for the Millennium: if the boffins were to be believed, computers would crash (even more than usual) and planes would fall out of the sky. Call me a wimp but I wasn't too keen on that idea, so we opted to fly out a couple of days in advance. Pat's boss had kindly authorized a couple of days' stay in a posh hotel in Manila for us to celebrate...

The morning we left UK I woke feeling queasy; put it down to imagination or excitement. Fond goodbyes to Gerry and Ben, taxi to Heathrow. Feeling steadily worse, with temperature, I threw up over carefully co-ordinated grey bootlegs and best black loafers. Not an auspicious start. No medical centre at Terminal Four; bought medicine from Boots, which I couldn't manage to keep down. Wasn't even sure if I'd make flight. P requested, and got, permission for use of First Class lounge so I could lie down. Sympathetic cabin crew gave us four seats in a row. Slept whole of fifteen hours to Hong Kong, waking briefly twice to throw up again, thankfully in loo. (Sorry, is that too much information?) We had an hour at HK; feeling marginally better but still very fragile, I managed to keep down dry roll and smoked chicken and started to feel slightly more human.

Stayed in wonderful hotel in Manila; staff superb and our room, with balcony, overlooked the bay. Still felt one degree under, now with streaming cold and painful cough so didn't think it advisable to swim. Shame, the pool looked lovely. Food lavish and looked delicious but no real appetite. First night there, still jet-lagged, ate mango with Pat at 3 a.m. in bed while watching 'The Jazz Singer' on the old movie channel. Next day we were out and about by taxi. Contrasts were shocking – shanty towns and slums versus expensive five-star hotels like ours. Lots of unfinished buildings around, due, Pat said, to money having run out. Visits to pharmacists – one shabby but not too bad, the other a filthy 6-foot square shack on a street corner. Peering through dirty slats I mimed hacking painful cough - not difficult in my state. Relieved to be given Robitussin, properly sealed and in date.

NY Eve. It was actually the eve of the Millennium but I was still feeling distinctly under the weather so wasn't really too interested... Sumptuous buffet with ice sculptures and serving bowls carved out of large pumpkins. Magnificent!

Walked in gardens, drinks on our private balcony overlooking bay. Fireworks and firecrackers all night; P said it would be a good time to stage a coup as no-one would have known the difference!

Jet-lagged and confused, we woke thinking it was Sunday and went to Mass Lovely church, music beautiful, led by young tenor with superb voice. Mass said by elderly Irish priest. Lots of people there but felt very isolated. Lunch in room served on table with damask cloth and single rose in vase. Luxury. Evening buffets again – everything available, both Eastern and Western cuisine, but we were just craving our own food.

Courtyard, Intra Muros, Old Manila

In at the Deep End...

Next day we drove to Batangas City. It was a holiday, so 160 km (90 miles) drive took only two hours – quicker than usual. Usually took 2 and a half hours to 3 hours, had been known to take up to 6 depending on traffic and weather. Culture shock really set in – some appalling sights, with unbelievable dirt and bad roads - depressing journey but snatches of beautiful scenery in between. Pat told me that the Americans laid rail tracks down the length of this (largest) island, Luzon, but they have never been developed. (The rail tracks, not the Americans.)

Arrived at 'our' house – nice - on private estate behind Basilica. Marble floors, chandeliers, lots of polished wood and carved furniture – traditional Spanish. Large open area on landing with lovely view of Basilica. Felt incredibly depressed by now – just wanted to leave but couldn't bear to face that awful journey again. Maid, Aida, popped in to meet me. Very sweet and she had left chicken and pasta salad and some sort of dessert in the fridge, plus vase of flowers. Met enormous cockroach en route for loo. YUK. Scream; Pat came to the rescue…

This might be a good point to explain why expats in general are usually encouraged to have maids – certainly Pat strongly advocated it, and the Company gave us an allowance to pay for same: in the Tropics it's unbelievably hot and humid, and as Europeans aren't used to working in these high temperatures they are more likely to succumb to illness.

Another reason is that the local people often desperately need the work and the income. Working for an expat family carries a certain amount of kudos, and expats normally treat their maids very well. If a maid is honest and a good worker, when an expat family leaves it's normal for that family to try to find another placement for their maid. With the best maids, there's a very special relationship with the family – much more than just 'staff'. Think it must be similar to a nanny in a good family. We were so fortunate to have Aida, and later Purita, to look after us. We thought such a lot of them and hopefully they of us.

On our first morning it was a late start for P, who left home at 7.30 instead of 6.45. Aida arrived same time to start washing with the twin-tub, outside as was the norm – it took her ages. I spent the morning unpacking, and realised I'd bought all the wrong things – not enough cotton day clothes and too many dressy clothes. Supermarket with Aida. Food basic. Fed up with meat but not much choice – in UK I wasn't actually vegetarian, but ate lots of veggie food. Wouldn't have to worry about weight: couldn't see anything I fancied. Pat came in for lunch and I wrote letters in the afternoon. I was a bit fed up but not too bad. Aida went to Saj's house (friend/colleague of Pat's who'd just moved in round the corner). We'd be sharing Aida – about three-quarter time with us, quarter with Saj who didn't need her so much.

Rang expat lady, Kathy, whose name I'd been given, sounded nice, said she'd ring soon to arrange something. Admitted that BC was more difficult than Manila. Landlord rang, sounded pleasant, to come and meet us this evening. Heard beautiful singing late afternoon from outside but couldn't force myself to go out and trace it. Cathedral bells – two, both tinny, one more than the other. Landlord and wife came round in evening – very pleasant; they invited us to meal for forthcoming Fiesta.

P was out at 6.45 the next morning, I was up and ready by 7. What for? Nothing really, but I didn't want to wait to get up after P had gone in case of encounters with cockroaches or problems with shower. In that order. Heard music again – lovely soprano voice. Forced myself to walk round estate for ten minutes, studiously ignoring neighbourhood dogs, some of whom were less than friendly-looking. Music actually came from Basilica; they seemed to put each Mass on loudspeaker. Large weeds and plants everywhere, many of which I recognised as larger versions of many pot-plants back home - even a poinsettia tree just opposite! Impressed, huh? Aida arrived with fresh veg. From market – yum! Envisaged feast of carrots, green beans, potatoes and lettuce…

Kathy collected me after lunch for a tour of Pic 'n Save, (supermarket), then to the German restaurant, where we met several other expats for coffee. Judy, owner's wife, sent two ice-creams over courtesy of the establishment and rushed off to deliver piglets. (Don't ask me why, she just did…) Pleasant hour chatting to K, source of information.

Next day there was no Aida – 'prior commitment'. Enter landlady, son and 2 painters to paint kitchen cupboards; they were here all a.m. I was fed up by lunchtime with no external stimulus, and I was missing my friends and music. Couldn't sing – still too wheezy.

Frustrated and discouraged. (I'm not normally this negative!) Forced myself to have a 20-minute walk round estate after lunch but the dogs worried me – lots of stray dogs here, and it was hard to know which were stray and which house dogs. A two-inch insect bashed for ages against netted window trying to get in: I was terrified to take my eyes off it in case it succeeded, but I finally rushed for insect spray and sprayed it through the mosquito net. It flew away leaving me in tears: I later discovered that it was a bee. Every minute seemed like an hour…

Jan 6. Aida brings daughter, Gigi, to clean empty house next door which is between tenants. Bit more energy; yesterday's black depression has lifted slightly, but still wheezy and can't sing. Cut out trousers from material I bought out from UK. Mass in Basilica at 5.30 for Epiphany, then we pop into the Shell Club, a mile or so out of town and set in beautiful grounds. Home for really ghastly meal of spaghetti and sardines, most of which gets thrown away – and rightly so. Don't try to copy it…Ever. Promise?

Next morning, still wheezy and still couldn't sing – that was the worst of all. I did some sewing and went to Kathy's in the afternoon for coffee where I met other expats. My first tropical rain – very heavy but still very warm. One of the FW drivers, Tom, took me and collected me. Journey home took one hour instead of 15 minutes, due, we found later, to there being a Mass said on the river bridge. Drinks after work with P and colleagues. Dinner on the company with Ken, P's boss, and Saj in the local Hotel. Lapu-lapu for me, the most popular fish out here. Delicious! Felt better now in general…

Saturday. P working in the morning but late start – 8 a.m. Cut out skirt. P home at 2 pm, same time as landlord, wife and son with glass-topped table for landing. Lunch and shopping. Have discovered the secret of successful car-parking - just stop wherever you feel like it. Why have we never thought of that before?? In the evening we went for meal in local Japanese restaurant. Food was good and cheap but no sense of occasion. Home feeling very tired.

On Sunday we went to Mass; the Basilica was too packed to get in but we managed to put one foot on the threshold – literally—though we managed to get in for Communion. It was quite a frightening feeling, that not only were we not in control of the situation, no-one seemed to be. After coffee at home we went swimming at the Shell Compound. Lovely pool, only P and I swimming – just ten lengths then sunbathing – nice as we had no garden and no-where to lap up a bit of sun back at the house…

Kathy turned up and introduced us to a couple more expats, but in general very few expats used it. Shame! We had lunch at home then went shopping for luxury items such as plastic food containers (much needed with ants etc.) and wine glasses. Would have loved to go to local school performance of 'Nutcracker' but P still had work to do in the evening. Dinner; Saj in for drink.

Funny story for which you have to remember the difficulty of getting anything here other than essentials: Kathy asked someone who was going home on leave to bring her HRT tablets, and her favourite hair colour, which he said he'd do. Off he went for three weeks' leave and Kathy waited impatiently for him to come back which he finally did. He handed her a parcel which she opened excitedly to find – a new telephone! His wife had bought it whilst he was home and he'd picked up the wrong parcel!! Kathy was not amused…

Next day I summoned up courage again to walk round estate; usual dogs around. Cats seemed to fare much better out here, even the stray ones. They were mostly very small and lean but looked in reasonably good condition, unlike the dogs – most of them were flea-ridden and many almost hairless with, I imagine, mange. It was awful to see them. Kathy turned up unexpectedly and stayed for coffee. Made store-cupboard soup for lunch with tinned tomatoes, onions, red peppers, Tabasco and pre-cooked rice. Surprisingly good! Afternoon K collected me and took me to Shell Club to swim – we were the only ones there again. Once home again I did a trial water-colour of the Basilica…

Amusing story from Pat: The FW managers frequently ate in the local hotel, dubbed 'Fawlty Towers' in whose compound the office was. The service was well-intentioned but appalling, though it improved somewhat later. Anyway, a number of them were in there one night and placed their orders. The orders were a long time coming but finally arrived with one exception of steak and chips for one of the managers. He waited a bit longer and in the meantime a local senator walked in, and knowing some of the group, was called over and he sat down at an empty place to join them. The waiter ambled over with his thumb in a plate of lukewarm steak and chips, and slopped it down in front of the senator, who, not having ordered it, looked a bit surprised and carried on chatting. The guy who had ordered it got quite irate seeing it cold and congealed and so the waiter strolled up again, reached across in front of the senator, took the plate and pottered round to plonk it down in front of the right guy. By this time it really looked cold and disgusting (it was usual for some reason to serve tepid food out there) and the guy stood up and stormed off. The waiter looked thoroughly confused by this time, shrugged philosophically, walked up and removed it once again and shambled back round the table, dumping it back down in front of the senator. The rest of the group were in absolute hysterics by this time...

Jan 11. Long morning of self-improvement. (Well, I can try...) Do a trial ink and wash flower painting. Thank goodness for sewing, art and reading – especially while I still can't sing. Since leaving UK I've finished 'Diary of a Nobody', 'Cold Comfort Farm', the new Clare Francis thriller, and several novels whose names escape me. I'm really into art; am experimenting with charcoal, watercolour, pencils and ink. I'd love to learn some proper technique and have been making enquiries but no luck yet, or on the voice coach, either.

Lito, a driver, and Hazel, trainee, take me to buy some more dress-making material. Find some inexpensive cotton which will do to make something pro tem just to keep busy. Later find fault across material but then it only cost just over £1 for the piece... Patricia rings in evening from Oz to confirm arrangements for her arrival on Saturday! P returns from work with mobile phone for me, for security whilst out, (I feel very grown-up), and surprise! Four letters! Save them for tomorrow to gloat over and enjoy during the long morning. Dinner in the evening with Saj at Shell Club. P and S attempt to teach me the rudiments of pool while we wait. Wanted lapu-lapu but lapu-lapu off so have pork mendue, delicious carrot soup to start and we treat ourselves to refrigerator cake to finish. Scrummy!

Next morning, P went to work; I cleaned the kitchen and discovered a huge cockroach in kitchen drawer. Screamed, slammed drawer shut and burst into tears, not necessarily in that order. Aida appeared soon after, found offending cockroach and dealt with it while I stood on the side-lines snuffling miserably...

Visited the Immigration Dept. with Pat re visas. Office had sort of shrine dedicated to the local 'Santo Nino' (Holy Child) with glass of water, plate of biscuits and dish of coins. Propitiation of the gods???

The electrical system out here is beyond our comprehension: One of Pat's colleagues was with the boss at his house, trying to get some jobs done before the boss's wife came from UK. They noticed one of his slatted windows wasn't closed properly so the guy grabbed the window handle and tried to close it but failed to see some electrical cables which had been fed between the slats. As he tried to force the window closed he severed the cable and gave himself quite a bad shock – in more ways than one!

Landlord Cesar, foreman and painters arrived next day to fix flapping roof in outside 'dirty kitchen' - where the maid traditionally did the washing and the cooking; later I tried some charcoal sketching in next door's garden, which I really enjoyed. Saw litter of seven pups through neighbour's gate – delightful! To Pic 'n Save where I found Philadelphia cream cheese – last week K found me McVities Digestives, but this latter seemed to be one off. Landlord et al came to finish roof.

The following morning Lito, one of the drivers, took me to Citimart for shopping, though it was only a very short walk. Didn't feel like going on my own – it was incredibly noisy, dusty, smelly and polluted walking up the main street. Cesar et al came back to continue with roof; no electricity outside so Aida took our washing round to Saj whence she returned later with clean, freshly-ironed washing. What a gem! Electrician arrived to investigate puddle in chiller and under fridge - in bare feet. 'Was this a good idea?' I wondered...

Saj locked himself in the shower and had to climb, all 6'4" of him, dripping wet, over the shower partition, about 18" from the ceiling... Or so I heard: I wasn't actually there... Pat arrived home smiling benignly, having just seen a religious procession in honour of the local patron saint, preceded by the town band and succeeded by a team of mini-skirted, high-stepping, baton-twirling, majorettes...

Ellen was out shopping in a local supermarket with her little boy, then aged two-and-a-half, and in the middle of potty- training. He desperately needed a wee, and Ellen, newly-arrived, assumed there'd be a customer loo and asked a male assistant. There wasn't, and he summed up the situation with a glance, held out his hand to the little boy and said 'Come with me', whereupon he took him round the back of the meat counter, lifted him up into the sink and let him wee there…

One of the expats has stopped having coffee in the office cups since he discovered the office-boy washing the cups in the loo under the flush. He now insists on paper cups and who could blame him! (The expat, not the office-boy…)

Typical house on stilts

Travelling Around

Saturday. Patricia arrives today – hooray! To Alabang, just South of Manila, in morning with Pat (Tom drives) for meeting. The following impressions of the drive remain with me:

Small carts pulled by horses, overloaded with baskets and wicker furniture – down from the mountains. The owners sell all their wares down here, sell the horse and cart, travel North again by jeepney, and start all over again. Heavily over-loaded coke delivery lorry with broken axle at side of road. Driver and mate try, unsuccessfully, to jack it up to repair. (Pat has more than once seen jeepneys, the local vehicles, overloaded with both people and bananas so they've just literally collapsed in the middle.) Push-bike, driver cycling on wrong side of road with two small children perched on crossbar. We cross bridge over steep river ravine; children swimming and jumping from rocks. Mountains beautiful, including one 'Maria Mahini' which is said to be haunted by a good fairy.

Paddy fields near Alabang, impressive. Slip-roads to and from motorway (which in any case is not yet officially open and has piles of gravel and ballast at intervals) are in fact unmade, rutted, pot-holed tracks, the access road being routed over a garage forecourt and through a gate marked 'private road' at the back where normally enterprising children marshal cars through for a small consideration. Not today though for some reason…

Down from the Mountains

I browse round real shops in a real mall nearby – what luxury – and find health shop so stock up with veggie foods and things we can't get here. Nothing like a bit of mashed potato powder to cheer a girl up. What luxury!

Shopping all day with P after meeting, mainly in a second mall – if only B.C. was like this. Delicious lunch and afternoon tea. Collect Patricia at airport. She'd arrived early in fact so was waiting for us. Good journey back here hearing all her news. Real bread and Swiss cheese for gourmet supper –good food and excellent company!

Next day was Fiesta day and Patricia came with us to Mass – joy – we got seats! Absolutely packed; Patricia found it a very moving experience. The people were incredibly devout and had great devotion to different saints – they walked round the church touching the statues with their handkerchiefs and then touching their foreheads, their babies and so on… We watched the parade - very festive atmosphere. After, we had coffee at home and waited for Aida then we all walked, (streets seething with people) taking Saj, to the landlords' for lunch: the food was delicious, cooked by Cesar.

On the way home we visited the market where Patricia and I, with Aida's help, bought dresses. There was a beautiful baby girl asleep on a market stall, but 'she hasn't got a beautiful nose'. How sad, it seems that Philippina women don't like their noses and want to be 'long-noses' like Europeans. In fact, there was an ad on Philippino TV for a device supposedly to lengthen noses. It was a weighted clip 'invisible in use'... Just for your information. Next port of call was to Biboy's, business associate of Pat's, for more food – also delicious. There was an open house tradition on this special day, Santo Nino's feast day: Biboy invited in a passing tricycle (rickshaw) driver for food… Home we trundled, tired but happy as they say, showing Patricia and Saj next door (empty house) garden en route, where we spied an enormous spider in web in garden, maybe four inches toe to toe. (If spiders have toes).

Following morning Tom took Patricia and me to Taal, a small town about an hour away, with lovely old Spanish-style houses. Wooden, many of them on sort of stilts, with capiz shells in the windows, translucent, which let in the light. Once we were out of B.C. it was a pleasant drive with exciting tropical scenery. If only B.C. had been like this… The beautiful Basilica in Taal was one of the largest in SE Asia. On then to Tagatay– views of volcano in lake were just stunning. We had lunch in a native restaurant overlooking the lake; it was possible to drive down to the lake, get a boat across, and hire a horse to ride up the volcano but we didn't have time. A short drive further we saw what was an

El Bandito

Imelda Marcos residence, then called 'Palace in the Sky', also with spectacular views. We finally arrived home late afternoon thrilled with our day out; had dinner at Caltex Club with Kathy, Ted and Saj.

18 Jan. Quiet day today. Breakfast on balcony with Patricia. Fresh mango etc… Walk to Citimart; swimming Shell Club and good dinner there later.

Patricia's last day: she leaves this am. Can't go with her to Manila as there's a shortage of drivers today, but Tom has to deliver something in Manila and pick up Ken – the boss – so he takes her. I'd have liked to go and had planned some retail therapy for us both in Alabang, but it's not to be. Instead, to Ladies' Club committee meeting then Caedo in afternoon with Kate. Find art shop but it seems mainly framing and embroidery and no luck with art lessons. Back to the drawing board, if you'll forgive the pun. Joy! Find fresh tomatoes, aubergine and onions in supermarket. Horror! Rest of veg on display are literally rotting.

Home: have second try at getting bread machine to work after unsuccessful try couple of days ago. Blade rusty so change. Spend ages measuring out water as have no proper measuring jug. Open bread mix brought from UK – shock horror! Weevilly. Very. Not in good frame of mine by this time. Missing Patricia's company. Really depressed by 5 pm. P arrives just before 7, same time as phone rings to say that computer bloke, for whom he's been waiting all day at office, has just arrived there. I am not pleased, to put it mildly. P takes me back to office with Saj; both try to cheer me up – without much success I have to add. Give me fired-up computer to 'play' on – hurray! Have waited long time for this moment so write letter. Wait in office till about 8; dinner in hotel in same complex. Marginally less fed up. Patricia rings from Hong Kong.

Sherry Shortage

Next day I still felt a bit subdued but not as bad – I went to the market with Aida and Lito. It was interesting to see unfamiliar fruit and veg, and Aida was a terrific help as usual. I bought a dress, then we went to Pic 'n Save for bread flour. There wasn't any, but I bought 'all-purpose' flour to give it a try. I made a dress – longish, bias-cut; it wasn't too bad! Later I went for swim and Kathy turned up for chat. I duly made the bread: it was ok, but had a very slight after-taste – must be the flour. P had to wait for computer guys again so collected me 6-ish and we went to the office (armed with sherry as unobtainable in BC, and it was much-needed by this time!) where I continued to type. Cooked stir-fry on arrival home; Saj ate with us.

Friday. Ben rings 7 a.m. to say he and Steve have decided on one week in KL plus two in Philippines when they come next month. Great! Can't wait. International Ladies' Club lunch at Anna's, another expat. About thirty ladies there, all very friendly. All take food – delicious spread. Afternoon finish dress which I'd started earlier. P suggests dinner at Japanese restaurant, but although food is very good and it's extremely good value, there's no sense of occasion so veggie meal at home.

P was working Saturday a.m. as were the others so I lay in till 8. Pottered happily with some art, reading, sewing and singing which I had started again a few days ago. P home 12.30. and after lunch we went shopping, stopping en route, as requested, to check contents of Ken's fridge as wife was due out the following day. Evening was a veggie meal with booty from health shop in Alabang and fresh veg brought in from market yesterday by Aida. Thank you Aida! What luxury! On Sunday we went to Mass then shopping: bought sun-dress at little stall after – sort of crinkly fabric, cost about £2 - Drove to Taal with P where I'd been with Patricia. On way home we stopped the car to photograph group of young men en route for cock-fight. It was very popular with the men; you saw guys with their cocks (naughty!) tucked under their arms, on foot, on tricycles and on jeepneys. There was big money in it out here and a big win netted them a lot of money while a loss meant at least that they got a good, albeit expensive, dinner.

24 Jan. Walk to Citimart, braving the pollution. See fire engine at what is presumably Fire-Station, hemmed in by parked vehicles, including a coconut seller who has set up his stall and who looks as if he'll be there for the day. Call me quaint and old-fashioned if you will, but I wonder what would happen if the appliance had an emergency call-out. Mind you, maybe it explains something: just before Christmas the local convent burnt down (no-one injured happily), only four minutes' walk away, but the fire engine took 25 minutes to get there...

Had a sobering experience in Citimart the other day: a little Philippina girl came up to me, smiled, took my hand and pressed it to her forehead in the ritual greeting demonstrating respect – for ELDERLY people. She was very sweet...

In the afternoon I had a nice swim - only one there, then coffee by pool. Shell Club for dinner with P and Saj. They tended not to serve hot food in the Philippines, don't know why, so I wasn't surprised to get lukewarm fish with tepid mashed potatoes and chilled veg. Politely sent it back but micro-wave not working...I woke up next morning with upset tum: could be co-incidence (P had slight tummy bug couple of days ago) or it could be the lukewarm fish. Whatever, I had griping tummy pains all morning and P called doctor who visited (seems to be the system here for expats, and I fully realised how privileged we were). Gave me medicine and by lunchtime I was starting to feel better. Supposed to be our dinner party in the evening and I'd gone to a lot of trouble getting food in. Would I make it or would I have to cancel? (I wrote this at lunchtime and even I didn't then know the answer. You'll just have to wait for the next gripping instalment... or griping...)

Later: Couldn't face preparing food, so cancelled party, gave meat to Aida for family, froze pud (Batangas version of tiramisu about which I'm not sure, 'cos all the food out here seems very salty) and hoped there wasn't a power cut as freezer wasn't very good anyway. Slept all afternoon, managed some food with Pat when he came home. Felt a bit better and managed to get a good night's sleep in spite of afternoon rest.

Wild Life

Pat told me that the boss's house was infested with termites and it would be a mega job to get rid of them. It was a new house, right on the edge of open country and the Pest Control Officer explained that, although the ground was sterilised before being built on, the top-soil which was brought in for landscaping, harboured all sorts of termites and things... Felt sorry for him and also for his wife – she arrived out here already feeling ill – what an introduction for her to BC... Saw large red ants marching along the garden wall – they looked yellow to me – which apparently could deliver a nasty nip. As long as they stayed outside they didn't bother me, and Pat saw two gekkos feasting on them later. Long live gekkos! (Small lizards – we had several in the house).

26 Jan. Should be in Manila with Kathy, at a monthly bazaar of Philippine crafts organised by the American wives there. Everyone says it's fantastic but although I feel much better I don't think I'd better risk that journey. Very disappointed! Don't want to risk walking to shops so write letters all morning.

Frustrating afternoon: make dress which is more difficult than it should be as I don't have many patterns here and don't know where to buy them. Have spent the morning typing; can't print anything as the printer is playing up and I can't find out what's wrong. Landlord brings around long-awaited video machine, but can't get it to work. Says it must be incompatible with UK videos, though he doesn't see why, and colleague of Pat has no trouble with same model. Have brought out loads of old movies and musicals, plus other films we want to see so still can't see them. It's just so difficult getting things done here and bad though it is for me, it's worse for Pat and the others – at the end of the day their brief is to get the Plant built, in spite of the corruption, ineptitude and incompetence which seem to prevail. Have brainwave later and discover that it's the printer adaptor which is faulty so can now print letters...

Later: power cut, known locally as 'brown-out'. Big FW party tonight so P rings to warn me to dig out his clothes while still natural light as it gets dark every day by 6. Have bath in torch-lit bathroom, hoping insects don't think it's night and come out of their little homes. (Thankfully, they don't, or if they do it's too dark to notice). Manage to find clothes and start make-up on landing where there is still light but can't find eyeshadow so use blusher as eyeshadow which probably makes me look as if I'm crying. Which I'm not, seriously tempted though I might be. P arrives home, power comes back on.

En route P tells of a scene on his way home: Two children, maybe ten and eight, have a barbeque going, cooking bit of meat and trying to sell to their school-mates. Guess they grow up quicker here, but I can't help thinking of the safety aspect...

Today's amusing story: P has spent the day rushing around organising this party, in addition to his usual myriad tasks. Anyway, in the middle of all this, his mobile rings – again. It's a young FW guy who is having a cyst removed as an out-patient at the local hospital. The guy is quite distressed – 'Pat, I've had the op but they won't let me come out – they're keeping me here!' Pat immediately assumes solicitous role and adopts soothing tone: 'Well it's probably for the best; they know what they're doing and they have your best interests at heart.' Young guy, almost hysterical by this time: 'No no Pat, you don't understand – they won't let me out because they want to know who's paying...'

Finally make party which is in fact good fun: P and I find ourselves doing rock and roll demo to riotous applause. No accounting for tastes! Doc who visited me yesterday is at party, very nice young guy; am a bit disconcerted when he zooms up to me and says 'How's the tum? Are the griping pains better? Hear him a bit later chatting to someone else about their ear infection. Am so glad that I don't have piles... Kathy, also at party, presents me with two avocados as a get-well pressie, out of season, as are the beefsteak toms she also has for us – both bought in Manila. What luxury!

Irrelevant note: Philippinos are extremely clean and smart people. Even poor houses have lines of washing out, often neatly arranged on hangers. Aida is an absolute expert on washing and ironing – what joy to bundle the dirty washing into the basket and have it back, often same day, latest next day, all clean, neatly starched and pressed – including Pat's socks and Y-fronts. (No not really.)

Philippinos seem to like uniforms – every school, college and university has its own, very distinctive uniform. Nurses are impeccable in their American whites,

Marine cadets, the Police, Council Office workers, Post Office clerks, all have their own uniforms. Droves of Boy Scouts and Cubs (do they call them Cubs these days?) out today for some reason, all looking extremely smart albeit in a particularly bilious shade of khaki. I suspect that if there existed a laundryman's badge in the Cubs, their mums would be extremely well-qualified...

There are armed guards everywhere including Mcdonalds, the shops, and the entrance to our estate, though I'm assured that BC is not a dangerous place. As expats we're quite cossetted really and I don't feel at all threatened. (You live and learn...)

I was amused one day to see a number of clerks in post office doing very little, except for two clerks actually serving customers and one clerk doing her daughter's hair (and very nice it looked too). Mind you, the whole of the Dispatch department was very busy. He was manually sorting and bundling envelopes into piles...

Kathy popped in for coffee, and I spent the afternoon at Kate's, FW Thai lady, who invited me over for a Thai meal. Mmmm! Really delicious!

To Caroline's next morning for coffee; she was due to leave the following day for UK. She was exhausted, had been out there for just five weeks, and hadn't been sleeping; her estate was noisier than ours. There was heavy rain whilst I was at C's, and strong winds as for the previous week, but warm as usual. Strange. I fancied a swim but part of the appeal was lounging in the sun after, and grey skies made it slightly less appealing. However, stopped being so wimpish and swam with Caroline – her last swim over here. Twenty lengths; (just dropped that in casually) and felt good for the exercise. I was surprised and pleased to find six new sun-beds to supplement the only two unbroken ones. Coffee and chat by pool after. As had become the norm, I did some Vaccai classical singing exercises between Aida leaving and P returning. Managed about 40 mins, slightly longer than usual – neighbours must be sorry my throat is better! Quiet evening, Saj for drink.

Saturday 29 Jan. P in office all morning. Hilary, boss's wife, was taken ill and admitted to hospital yesterday evening – no-one knows why – tests carried out. Ken's been up all night. P home lunchtime.

Afternoon shopping in Pic 'n Save. Seemingly random, but surprisingly good, selection of items. No sherry, sob sob, we've nearly finished the last bottle I sent out. However, settle for Peach Vodka, Baileys Cream, and gin for P. At approximately £1.50 for each bottle (yes!) we think it's a justifiable luxury... Heh heh heh... Great excitement at finding Libbys pink salmon; buy four large tins, plus Spam Lite!

Our first English Mass in the Basilica, at 6 p.m. Full, maybe thousand people, but not packed. No trouble getting seats. Music not anywhere near as good as with the Tagalog Masses, but it was lovely having Mass in English. Only saw two other Europeans in the church. Dinner at home – fresh veg (thank you Aida) and Spam Lite – surprisingly good.

On Sunday we went out in car, hopefully to find somewhere nice within a day's drive. P took me round the docks first, for interest, which I hadn't then seen. This proved to be a mistake: it was a very poor area, though as in other areas people seemed cheerful and looked reasonably fit and well-fed. It was the dogs that got to me – as already mentioned, there were so many stray dogs in a pitiful state. The lucky ones were mostly flea-ridden, the others had little or no hair to get fleas – due, we supposed, to mange. I ended up in tears to see them. They desperately needed culling and humanely destroying. There were just so many pregnant bitches around...

We headed for a peninsula an hour away and drove around, determined to find somewhere nice, but no luck. Investigated one of many so-called 'resorts' which proved to be a down-at-heel sort of coastal motel, and we agreed that we certainly wouldn't want to spend time there after P working fifty-four hour week. The scenery was spectacular, with steep cliffs and lovely views of the sea, but there was nowhere nice just to sit. Not even anywhere for coffee for which I was pretty desperate.

Drove home, quick lunch, to Shell compound for swim. Kathy, at pool, roared with laughter when she heard our story as exactly the same thing happened to her and Ted, and others. Told us that new people, either Aussie or Brits, were renovating a place in the area where we'd been - we'd even seen the sign but turned round at that point as broken-down jeepney was blocking road. We knew there were beautiful places in the Philippines – the problem was getting to them. There were several places, including some islands, suitable for a weekend, but not feasible for a day. We planned to get away the following weekend…

Weather and pool were pretty chilly - the weather felt more like England! Dinner in one of best places here. Good. I had roast aubergine with uncooked diced ginger and tomatoes, and rice.

House with capiz-shell windows

Culture and Cuisine

Well, that's one complete month out here. I have to say that time doesn't fly, tho' I know it does for P and colleagues – they're really impossibly busy. Should be in Manila today with Kathy for shopping trip but had stomach pains (thankfully nothing else) in night. (Find out later that two FW people at party had the runs all night. Could this be a co-incidence, I ask myself?) Feel fine now apart from little tenderness, but daren't risk being ill en route. Disappointed but think it's best to be sensible…

Spend morning feeling really depressed. With driver to Post Office and to put in film for developing. Would have liked to swim but can't; combination of cold water and tender tum not to be recommended. Afternoon drive around with Pat for couple of hours visiting people, and local private hospital to finalise contract with them for medical care of expats. Hospital basic but adequate; been passed both by Shell and by our own medical guy. Return late afternoon feeling more cheerful… Pat and I have dinner at home: frozen veg, (packet) mashed potato and tinned salmon, followed by packet-mix pancakes and honey. A veritable feast!

Friends ring from Reading; Mary-Anne, their daughter, is coming to the Philippines to work for three months with missionary nuns. Tells us she will be in Cebu – lucky thing! Both she and parents (when visiting her) will try to visit us… Pat and I were both shattered and in bed by 9.30p.m.

Next day we had a Cross-cultural workshop with quite a good lunch. Excellent soup, grilled fish, rice and veg, fresh fruit salad. For me it still left some very fundamental questions unanswered. (The workshop, not the lunch.) Just as we got to, for me, the most interesting part, as it impinges on my TEFL work – practical exercises – modifying way Brits/Philippinos say things directly/ indirectly, we had to call a halt to workshop, due to work demands. P and I talked bit longer with two facilitators. Once again, it was pleasant to talk to Philippino staff from FW – as at party we found it a valuable opportunity to demonstrate friendship. Driver took me home; volunteered that 'You and Mr Pat know how to talk to Philippinos Mam; you are always kind and you don't have any problems'. Was inordinately flattered…

In the evening, after a quick tinned salmon-and-cucumber butty we were back out to a concert of Philippino music, which featured a young choir from local University. Costumes and presentation were excellent, music not bad, but they gave it 110% effort and energy so they deserved full marks for that!

We woke next morning to rain, but I had a pleasant, busy day: I managed a swim in spite of the weather, which had not been good for a couple of weeks. The rain settled into a relentless tropical downpour and poured all evening and into the night. Slight earth tremor during dinner, thought it was Pat knocking the table leg, or Saj, who'd brought a veggie take-away in to join us. Not so! Another slight one apparently at 2 a.m., but we slept through...

Next day we had cloudy weather with fitful sunshine and patches of blue sky. 'This is the Tropics??' I wondered... Some rain again and 'brown-out' (power cut) for most of the morning. Aida arrived with fresh veg from the market, and lovely surprise – Kathy turned up with four porcelain casseroles, small serving dish and three serving plates. As she was leaving the next week (sob sob) she didn't need them. P brought a haul of four letters and some new repertoire from Anthony. Hurray!

After lunch went to Caedo for first of four trial singing lessons with one Lea. She was very sweet and tiny – made me feel really clumsy. I felt quite nervous as usual, working with someone new. We had another brown-out so had to troop down from the studio into the gloom of the music shop. She peered in the darkness at the music she was trying to play, the open door let in all the busy hustle of the street, someone in the shop doorway was playing a guitar so it became a bit surreal and I relaxed a bit. Tropical rainstorm when I got home – even heavier than yesterday, but P said there was no rain at the office a mile away.

Pat finished work late-ish so sent Dodong to collect me. With P and Saj to a local eating-place – thought to be the cleanest and best native restaurant in BC. Food only reasonable, but very pleasant evening anyway. Restaurant cheapish for UK but not especially cheap for this part of the world. The cost of living here, though cheaper than UK, was more expensive than Thailand, from where a lot of the managers had come, and also more expensive than Manila, due supposedly to transport costs. The same with hotels, in Manila, the islands nearby, and the resort hotels. Good hotels seemed to average £60 - £80 per room per night. Bearing in mind that this was in 2000, and that there were only three or four destinations suitable for one day out, and also bearing in mind that P and colleagues worked most Saturday mornings, it was not so easy to get out and about very far, but we kept trying.

The wall of the restaurant was half-covered with newly-painted murals; two young artists appeared during the evening to paint. We chatted to them, one was an art teacher and could give lessons - I planned to give him a call as I'd been looking unsuccessfully for an art teacher. Dodong collected us and took us home via another local restaurant, where we dropped in to have a drink with some of the Philippino staff, who were having a leaving party for one of their number.

Sat 5. P works till 4 ish. Swim in morning with Mai, Thai wife; pool cool again but bit of sunshine when we get out – maybe ten minutes. Big deal – at this rate I'll be paler than when I left UK! Coffee by pool, see single, smallish deer, with antlers, just metres away from people, near the clubhouse and pool. It stands there some minutes before disappearing in bushes.

English Mass at 6 pm, dinner with Trish and Colin, Manager of another local Plant. Had only spoken briefly to Trish, an Ozzie, on phone; FW may be able to help with her charitable work here. Enormous modern colonial-style house, makes ours look like garden shed! Maid with pink uniform and white pinny. Beautiful garden. See flying beetle on patio which must be over three inches long. (Beetle, not patio!) From safety of lounge am fascinated – T says could be coconut beetle. Delicious dinner on patio later, beetle having disappeared. Two other visitors, American managers from the Plant – all pleasant and interesting. Lovely evening!

P thinks FW may be able to help somewhere – maybe with Boy Scouts. Over 25,000 in B.C. - for many it's the only way forward and a way to combat drugs which are a serious problem among the poor here. Problem is that many families can't afford even the minimal registration fee, let alone the uniform.

Jeepney— brightly-painted public transport vehicle based on American jeep from WW II

Tropical Sunset

Local Attractions

Sunday. Wow! Whole day off to go out with P. We'd been told that Punta Baluarte, a luxurious (and fairly expensive) resort, was one-and-half hours' drive away, therefore near enough for day, so we set off. It took us two hours to drive the 60 kms (35 miles) as much of it was bad roads, though some country roads, surprisingly, were far better than in BC. Anyway, once out in country the scenery was lovely, just as I had imagined the Philippines before being introduced to BC.

It was the first nice weather we'd had for ages. After two hours, just as we decided we were lost, we found first a much smaller resort recommended by one of the expats, Laga d'Oro. It was delightful, on the edge of the South China Sea. Having a snack lunch by small swimming pool, I saw German expat wife I knew. I bought an original water-colour, in a frame, of a typical Philippine scene as a leaving present for Kathy.

On we drove to Punta Baluarte. It was beautifully-located, set in what must have been an enormous Spanish estate. Also on edge of sea, but as with the other resort it had black sand - not too inviting. It was a large resort village with two swimming pools, very well-landscaped and maintained – but it was relatively expensive to stay – the cheapest rooms, after 'discount' were £50 per night plus food – the other place was cheaper and we'd preferred it. As I said earlier, this area was far more expensive than Thailand and for most expats, away from their families, they were only out here to save money. We enjoyed coffee, a stroll and tour in the hotel jeepney.

We decided that though it was technically possible to do one of these resorts for a day trip, it had taken us two hours each way to do the equivalent of about 35 miles so - a round trip of less than eighty miles had taken us four hours. We would go back but only when we could spend a night there…

To Pic 'n Save, where we treated ourselves to a new mop (we deserved it!), cheap crockery and extra saucepans – not terribly good quality but inexpensive and they're stainless steel, not aluminium. We had enjoyed our proper day out!

7 Feb. Visiting VIP from UK Head Office – P even busier than usual. Being on the Admin side instead of his usual Training means that his job impinges on everyone else's and he has to deal with everyone's problems. The Admin Manager from the Oman Project will be available in March and is coming out here to take over from Pat. Technically P will become Assistant Admin Manager but will expand his other duties – HR, PR, Training and so on, plus local liaison, as in Oman. He'll be pleased when that happens as it will relieve him of some of the details and day-to-day problems at least.

Loudspeaker van comes round to warn that water will be off 1 – 5 this afternoon. We're fortunate in that we have our own water-tank, so it won't affect us but I phone the office to pass the word around as necessary. Remind Pat to be sure that visiting VIP hears – as I said, the powers-that-be in UK until now have just not accepted that conditions here are far more difficult than in Thailand or Manila… Later: am pleased to report that B.C. has now been declared 'a hardship posting' with extra attendant allowances and perks… The Company was kind enough to implement a number of suggestions to make life a whole lot easier…

Aida arrives, having had a good weekend with family. A few nights ago, her son -in-law arrived on his annual leave from Saudi Arabia where he works as a waiter to support his wife and son here. Very common with Philippinos – family ties are incredibly strong and it's common for family members to work overseas, often only getting back once a year, to send money home. It must be so desperately hard for them.

Aida herself worked a year in Taiwan a year or so back, to support her husband, who had lost his job, and children. Terrible and ironic – she was looking after a Taiwanese child and yet had to leave her own family. She missed them terribly, but did it to earn money to send home to them… Until recently the Taiwanese family have been trying to get her back to Taiwan to work for them again but she obviously doesn't want to go as long as she can manage to earn money here. Husband still has no job; he was previously a driver for our landlords when they had transport business but they then closed the business down. P and Company can't help as their hands are tied. Local politics dictate very strongly that only people from a certain area can be employed…

The water is off in the afternoon, but no problem for us with tank. We can't drink the tap water; we have to use bottled water even for tea, coffee and tooth-cleaning (and teeth-cleaning!) We are very fortunate in that we get enormous containers sent in from the office and it really doesn't pose a problem till there you are performing your ablutions and foaming at the mouth, only to discover that you didn't bring any bottled water into the bathroom with you...

Pick up Ellen, another nice expat who is also leaving soon and go to Shell Club for swim. Really hot today, lovely in pool. Pleasant post-swim socialising with friends over coffee and mango juice by pool. P home very late – 8 ish.

Thunder in the night woke us up about 4 am; I got up at 5 and started writing letters. P dozed till 6. Went to Citimart to collect photos. Saw a newly-born kid (baby goat variety) grazing at the entrance to our estate – cute! Discovered later that he and his mum belonged to one of the hundreds of tricycle owners, who arrived each morning in a tricycle (sort of scooter with sidecar) – Pat had seen them arrive.

Travelling in Style

A group of armed, uniformed Policemen with civvy friends outside the Police Station, were playing, on a tiny children's keyboard, presumably for one of their number, 'Happy birthday to you'. Outside the Fire Station only one vehicle was blocking in the fire engine. Said vehicle could easily be moved if necessary. If they could manage to find the driver…

Dining Out

Singing lesson this afternoon with Lea, then we had dinner with managers, wives and 'big-wigs' out from Reading. We went to a nice native restaurant—bright, clean, cheerful - with live – and loud, very loud music. Meal was an unbelievable shambles. Fawlty Towers had nothing on this: approximately twenty were at table, and we all placed our orders. We waited. No problem; we were a large group and there were other customers. We waited some more. A waiter ambled up with someone's starter and ambled off again. We waited. Waiter came back with two main courses, gave them to the right people and ambled off again. We waited. He returned with a couple more starters, by which time those already with food had finished. Ignored empty plates, returned to kitchen. We waited. He returned with two soups which he gave to Pat and me and which we hadn't ordered. We found out for whom they were intended and handed them over, while waiter shambled off again ignoring empty plates.

This went on literally for about half-an-hour by the end of which most people had something to eat. Pat and I actually received two different starters each (apart from the soups) which we shared around. Another quarter of an hour passed and I gently pointed out to waiter that there were still three of us without main courses. Waiter looked very worried and had words with waitress behind bar who was looking extremely harassed. Two of missing three main courses showed up, by which time the table was littered with dirty plates and half-eaten food. At this point I said to P that I would have a sandwich when we got home. Minute or so later my meal turned up. Hot! Wonders will never cease – Philippinos prefer lukewarm food. Only problem was that my rice didn't arrive but hey, I can live with that. Hadn't got the energy to tell them or the time to wait. Ate most of my meal (chicken for once – bit fed up with fish and no veggie dishes) had a rock 'n roll with P – our speciality – and driver took us home. Phew!

Next day there was a lunch with about thirty members of the International Ladies' Club – a very noisy lively affair. A new lady turned up, an American lady, Carol. She'd spent her first two weeks in isolation till a couple of members saw her in supermarket and tapped her on the shoulder to say 'Hi'. Similar experience to last night with long wait for food: some ladies waited two hours for their food, by which time of course most other people had finished. In fact the last lady to be served received wrong order anyway and opted go to without... In their defence I have to say that 35 ladies had turned up instead of 20 booked, but it was still no complete vindication. Individually we found Phillipinos charming and helpful, but it seemed to us that they could sometimes find it difficult to organise. ..

To Caedo later to buy keyboard – the only one in the shop – so no problem choosing. Had thought for some time it could be helpful with pitch and 'difficult corners' when learning new repertoire. Much excitement as Anthony's first audio tape arrived, the sheet music for which I had received at the end of last week. It had been sitting in post office awaiting collection but no-one had thought to tell P... Pic 'n Save, then home with Pat. Spent evening starting preparations for postponed dinner party to take place next day.

10 Feb. To Gisela's (Peruvian lady) this morning with Margret for art session. Afternoon English lesson – six ladies – as lessons go it's a shambles, as they range from fluent but unintelligible Thais to advanced. Will split levels next week. Bring delicious Thai food which we sample, leaving some for later. Much-heralded dinner party with Kathy and Ted, Ellen and Eugene, Saj and us. Dinner quite good considering it was a masterpiece of substitution and improvisation: no mascarpone for Tiramisu, so substitute Philadelphia cream cheese and condensed milk, no serving spoon for soup so use cup, not enough cutlery so nick (temporarily) from empty house next door etc. etc. Pleasant evening, breaks up soon after 11 pm.

Kathy gave me a lift next morning to Manila to her hairdresser in Peninsular Hotel – very grand. I had a badly-needed trim and colour. I expected, but didn't get, a telling-off for having chopped my hair twice with hairdressing scissors as we didn't have a proper hairdressers in B.C. Snack lunch, short visit to delicatessen for goodies including two slices of cooked ham for P, which is far superior to anything we can get here. Home in heavy traffic which takes over three hours. Both P and I very tired. Toss-up whether we can be bothered to go out or not. Think we should, so quick freshen-up and cuppa and to a club at another Plant, for Valentine's evening.

Quick aside here: Valentine's Day was celebrated in a big way - friends gave each other small presents, there were lots of Valentine's dances, dinners etc., a Valentine's Mass at the Basilica, there were heart-shaped balloons on sale, and red and white balloons, cupids and floral arches decorating the local schools. I had red roses from Pat and also from Chinese gentleman who did the computers in the office. He kept sending me presents - wanted me to do some charity work for him but I was busy typing up a long presentation for Boy Scouts. I also received a small glass ornament from one of the Thai wives. Sweet!

Dinner outside around swimming pool; décor lovely with two life-size (artificial!) swans filled with red and white roses, and bunches of red and white balloons, floating on pool. Buffet indifferent: food poor and not much of it. Promised free drinks turn out to be coke and water. Unfortunately we haven't much money on us as I've spent it all on hairdresser (!) but Eugene and Ellen come to rescue. Philippino version of Chippendales, of which we see ten minutes only and return outside. Prefer brain to brawn any time. Promised dancing after doesn't materialise. Wish we'd stayed at home…

P worked till 12 the next day, Saturday. The telephone engineer came and fixed an extension upstairs so we were one stage further to e-mail. He had actually come yesterday as favour to P while I was out and Aida had quite rightly rung Pat in office for instructions. Secretary hadn't liked to bother Pat as he was in informal meeting (!!) so guy hadn't been able to do work. Lunch then shopping trip in Caedo for fabric conditioner (we know how to pamper ourselves) and birthday pressie for friend Patrick - silk tie with Snoopy playing golf motif.

We tried two computer places to buy cartridge for printer – no luck – in one shop we were told that 'Sales Manager, who has details, manuals and prices only works Saturday morning' … P and I racked our brains for somewhere to go for the afternoon and realised – again – that there literally wasn't anywhere to go near enough for an afternoon. Both felt pretty fed up; met Ken and Hilary looking as disconsolate as we felt…

Swimming with Sharks

We had a lovely day on Sunday: Dodong took us with Saj for the day to Eagle's Point – traffic not too bad, took just over an hour, the last few kilometres on unmade roads. We arrived at EP, parked the car, and had a hair-raising short drive on steep roads in hotel jeepney. Lovely!

It was a small cliff-side 'resort', with two swimming pools, sea-water reef pool for novice divers, with ten small resident nurse sharks(!) and restaurant. It wasn't a beach resort as the beach was tiny and rocky – it was really for divers, snorkellers and 'switchers off'. We stayed there almost six hours and it was heaven. P re-introduced me to snorkelling (first time was Great Barrier Reef in very choppy weather, with ill-fitting snorkel that let in water; I'd not enjoyed the experience.) Anyway, the sea was clear and gorgeous, so I had a couple of short sessions. I was still nervous – I loved swimming but found it so strange to breathe under the water. Once I saw the coral and the fish I found it fascinating but refused to fix snorkel to mask – insisted on holding it 'just in case'.

I taught Saj to swim – only doggy-paddle but it was the first time he's swum without arm-bands, so we were both proud of our achievements! We all swam in the pools, P and I went down the slide about four hundred times, we had lunch at pool-side plus innumerable coffees and fresh-mango juices, and finally departed at 4. Good journey home then to friends' house for birthday party. Lovely Thai food…

Irrelevant aside: P and I were amused the other day when we had dinner with the 'big-wigs': the Boss, erring on the side of safety, arranged plain-clothes Police protection (armed as usual) for the dinner at the restaurant, as so many (relative!) VIPs were gathered together. Fine, no problems with that. They, the Police chiefs, plus a Philippino manager all had dinner at a table near us. Great, good idea. They obviously enjoyed their food – yes, well, that's fair enough; why not? But was drinking steadily throughout the evening such a tremendously good idea, we asked ourselves? Call us quaint and old-fashioned but we thought any danger was probably from the Police over-reacting to any real or imagined problem…

No Aida the following day; she'd warned us the evening before. It was a long day. I stayed in all morning having had a bit too much sun at Eagle's Point, then went to Ellen's in the afternoon with Carol, new American lady, and Julie, new Yorkshire lass.

Next day I ventured to the Post Office, just few minutes' walk, but the trip was not to be undertaken lightly: I counted seventeen people behind the counter, of whom only one was serving customers – there would have been eighteen, but the lady with the large circular straw tray of food on her head had disappeared outside touting for more business. Some were customers posting parcels, one was actually sorting mail into cardboard boxes in the Dispatch section, some were staff sitting, chatting, drinking juice. Some just were...

Decided to pay a long-over-due visit to local 'Library and Information Centre' next door. Gloomy, shabby building with battered wooden shelves. Books obviously old and not many of them. Dingy paintings on walls of long-dead local dignitaries, brown, curling religious pictures on shelves alongside books. Requested information on activities in Batangas – choirs etc. – anything considered. Guess what? No information, because apart from Fiesta time, there

Flower-sellers outside the Basilica

were no choirs or activities... Was given however access to chair and table and ancient dog-eared 'Historical Profile of Batangas'.

It was really depressing; everyone had an 'angle' and wanted something from us. Pat was used to this but even on social occasions like the Fiesta when we went to our landlord's, people came up with business cards and requests. That day in the Library was no exception: no sooner did I sit down than one of the Library assistants came up with a request that I pull strings for her niece, just graduated in Computer Science. I said I didn't work here so couldn't help; gave her the FW number and made my escape asap, vowing I would never go back there.

Just Desserts

The Company arranged dinner for the ladies at Benedictus (used to be run by nuns) while the men had some grown-up dinner celebrating a safety achievement. The service was reminiscent again of Fawlty Towers (though not quite as good...) Once again we had the impression that many people could only do literally one thing at a time: starters and main courses arrived one by one and over a period of time and they couldn't find the wine which was sent by the Company that morning – Kathy, normally very placid, got ratty and snapped to the waiter 'For the tenth time, could I please have a glass of red wine?' My beef – yes, I had meat, was a bit tough, but edible. Hilary's fish was stone cold; she requested re-heating which made it soggy and inedible.

Three of the group asked for ice cream, and the waiter replied, 'Yes of course mam, but could I ask you please to be patient for a few minutes? We have to collect the ice cream from the petrol station across the road.' They had to wait more than a few minutes 'cos the traffic was heavy, but the ice-cream was very nice – I tried it.

Lea arrived next day for coffee armed with donuts, sorry, doughnuts, and to riffle through my music files. What a nice lady! Afternoon to Ellen's to buy a set of embroidered tablecloths brought down from Manila – a Philippine speciality. In the evening, as P was working late, I went to the office to do photocopying for EFL lessons tomorrow. We stayed till 8 p.m. to greet Maureen, visiting from Thailand office, and took her over to the hotel.

Guy came in next morning to get us back on e-mail so I sent some test messages. Received first replies by early evening – exciting! Afternoon was EFL lesson with Kate, Anong, Tanja and Pen. Quiet evening with dinner at home.

P told me that Maureen, who had been all bright breezy and optimistic when she arrived the previous night was by lunchtime saying 'This is an awful place. There aren't any shops. There's no-where to go.' Ken and P predictably said something along the lines of 'Told you so. And you're only staying a few days...' Heard later that she's been with some other expats to the local cinema which is said to be clean and cool; must try it out.

An aside: Pat tells me that BC is particularly bad for corruption – at a high level; expats from other companies have told him at meetings that their companies would not consider doing business again in BC because of it.

18 Feb. First swim this week – Swim my usual twenty lengths or so, finishing up with length of crawl for which I get everything together for once - it felt quite stylish. (Not sure what it looked like!) Can swim for ages breast-stroke but find crawl much more tiring.

Problems with e-mail; try number of times to log on. Not engaged, seems to be a problem with provider whatever that is. Decide with Pat not to go over to islands this weekend – best two places are full and weather is terribly windy. Don't fancy an hour's journey in a tropical windstorm thank you very much. P will therefore work tomorrow and we'll go out Sunday.

Afternoon to Ellen's with Ladies' Club for her talk on Ireland. By request I sing 'In Dublin's Fair City' and we finish with food – as usual. Delicious fruit salad but I'm not tempted by anything else – it's all too fattening! Next day, Saturday, the gale has subsided but P had now arranged to work the morning.

I try again to sort out e-mail but even more problems than yesterday. Maybe caused by P fiddling about yesterday evening: when trying to log on, faced with the question 'Location?' he put 'Crap'. This comes up on screen this a.m. and now can't get connection at all. (Serves us right, I hear you say…)

P tries from office to re-arrange cancelled weekend on Oriental Mindoro but difficult finding accommodation this weekend and only decent place available needs extra, longer, outrigger (small local boat) journey. Decide not to bother as P will be working till lunchtime anyway but to go instead to Laga d'Oro, checked out couple of weekends ago. Book room as it's a fairly long way for P to drive just for the day tomorrow.

Saturday was a super day: P finished work at noon; we set off soon after. Drive took less than two hours. It was a lovely little place; there was no beach but the sea came up to the edge of the hotel garden and was very shallow. You could walk, which we did, Saturday and Sunday, along the coast. Water was warm, it was gorgeous. We swam in the small pool, ate well (too well!) and stayed overnight in a very pleasant room.

21 Feb. Aida points out large spider, thankfully in web in tiny front garden. Tells me it's poisonous but bite isn't fatal. Great! I'm pleased about that. Apparently it stays outside. Hope it's not some sort of arachnid rebel...

Lito arrives to take me to cinema. Confirms that spider 'isn't too much poisonous' but feels it's a point of honour to kill it for me. Spider is high up in tree, Lito smallish so he leaps frantically into the air several times, brandishing long-handled dust-pan. Finally manages to fell said spider and, on my request, locates him lying spread-eagled in corner by fence. Hope he's dead and not just unconscious otherwise he might come and seek revenge. (Spider, not Lito.)

To cinema in afternoon with Hilary and Julie to see 'Anna and the King' at the local cinema, which has been okayed by other expats. Surprisingly clean and cool, though the programme time has been changed to an hour later. (Hilary had gone in especially with her driver a day or so back to check time). At least the reels are shown in the correct order though: it drives Hilary crackers as they often put them on in the wrong order, and don't seem to see the problem when it's pointed out...

Hilary makes us chortle: she can't understand why her favourite bra is so uncomfortable, then realises her maid has carefully ironed it in segments culminating in two immaculately-neat peaks...

Apparently Julie's maid saw a poisonous snake disappear into her basement earlier, and then found two sloughed skins outside basement door. Thankfully there was no access directly into her house but she was nonetheless concerned, especially as she didn't have a key to the basement; the landlord used it for storage. She'd been trying to contact him without success, but she'll continue to try. Obviously...

P and I've been invited to opening of an art exhibition in a local hotel so I hurtle home, change in seven minutes flat, back to office where P is still working. Finally make said exhibition three-quarters of an hour late to find it still hasn't started. Opening ceremony, which is in Tagalog, starts almost an hour late and goes on for an hour. We haven't a clue what's happening and only catch a quick glimpse of promised art exhibits. Leave when we politely can, missing the cocktails and snacks. Shame they didn't have them first! Home for feast of fresh veggies and omelettes...

Saw an amusing notice on a house-gate: 'Never mind the dog – beware the owner' followed by picture of a gun.

I had a good swim next morning at Shell Club, plus half-an-hour reading in the sun with a coffee. Afternoon was my fourth voice lesson with Lea; booked four more but thought I might substitute piano, so I have at least a basic grounding in same. Dinner at home and early night in preparation for BIG DAY...

The Big Day arrived, and I went to Manila for American Wives monthly Philippine Craft Bazaar – my first visit – as for Hilary and Julie who travelled with us on the Company minibus, also Ellen and Liz, old-hands, who showed us the ropes. Brilliant day! It wasn't the best journey up there; traffic was bad so the driver took us on side roads, if you could call them that, through the countryside. Through villages, over rickety bridges, along unmade bumpy roads: it took us three hours to cover the 160 kms.

Finally made Manila so-called 'World Trade Centre' (pardon my mirth). First thing that met my eyes as we approached was a large crowd of people waiting round outside, which I took to be a queue. They were, however, just the drivers – maybe two hundred of them, waiting for their employers, most of whom, but not all, were expats. I was conscious once again of how fortunate we were, and when I saw the varied expressions on drivers' faces – boredom, resignation, bemusement, indulgence, I couldn't help wondering what they made of us expats... Had a wonderful two hours at Bazaar. Excellent selection of stuff, loads of it, all good quality. Cup, albeit plastic, of real coffee. Bought lots of bits and pieces including decent bread, banana bread, apple-and-walnut pie for Pat and fruit. Found lanzones, a tropical fruit I'd only heard about. Nice, taste like lychees.

Over to Alabang Town Centre Mall, where the five of us had a quick lunch in Deli France (don't laugh!) – for me smoked salmon and salad baguette with hazelnut cappuccino. Hour or so shopping. Bought three lots of really nice material –each different cotton-mix material in different colours. Approx ten yards of material, each piece 60" wide, for about ten pounds sterling in total. That would keep me quiet for a bit. Only problem was I couldn't get dress patterns, though thankfully Gilly was sending some out with Ben. Toyed with Marie-Claire magazine, but refused categorically to pay £5 for same. Stocked up with tins of veggie foods in supermarket but didn't buy frozen food as we had no cool-box.

Brief visit to deli in Festival Mall, quick drink and back on the bus. Good journey home – two hours with much comparing of loot, squeals of appreciation and munching of bagel chips. Not necessarily in that order.

Drink with Pat and colleagues then home, shattered but well-pleased with day out. Fell into bed and went out like lights.

Nearby village

Unwelcome Visitors

Well, my dears, how d'you want the news – the bad, or the really bad? Ok then, I'll start with the bad news. So, we got up one particular morning and I went into the dressing-room which linked our bedroom and bathroom. Found all doors of cupboards and drawers open. Penny didn't drop for moment or two as P was very untidy and then it dawned on me that we'd had burglars. Wallet with emergency get-out-of-the-country $300, maybe £30 or £40 in local money, my purse (from my handbag in bedroom) and P's wallet – all missing. Found balcony door unlocked, obviously lock had been slipped. A bit shocked but we were otherwise both OK – not nice to know they'd gone through bedroom as well as dressing-room…

Made cup of tea and rang UK cancelling credit cards – we had a card-replacement policy and this was done efficiently and pleasantly. P called office to tell them he would be late. Boss asked 'Is Mary alright?' P answered 'Yes' whereupon I bellowed across the room 'No she isn't – she's bloody hopping mad'.

We contacted local Police Colonel who was first port-of-call and he came round with underling. People came and went all morning, including one of Philippino managers who was sure it was a professional job, probably effected with drug spray or 'smoke gas' (Police Colonel concurred) to make sure we didn't wake during the burglary. (Common in Malaysia too apparently.) Advised changing locks, fitting grills to balcony etc. and last but not least actually locking grills over balcony doors and to side gate which we never did in case of fire. Maid founds wallet and purse just under the bed whilst cleaning – money taken but credit cards were scattered on floor. Drat, all that trouble cancelling them. Maid went to inform guard at gate, phoned Residents' Association for us, and rang Police to return for finger-printing. We were so glad to have Aida... And this was literally one of the safest estates in B.C. – The Company had taken advice on this…

And then the REALLY bad news – the fridge had completely broken down! P. touched it and got a shock. Unfortunately it was full, but not with too many perishables – we had to keep anything in there once open, and anything in paper bags or packets, because of ants etc. Put stuff in Saj's fridge as he was in UK, and informed landlord.

P and I needed to decide what to do that night, either stay in local hotel, which P said was a fate worse than death, or get our own armed guard till new security measures were finished. I favoured the latter as expat friend on another estate told me she and husband drove home last night after a company dinner to find the guard on said estate fast asleep in a chair as they drove through...

Anong (Thai) and Margret (German) turned up for informal English lesson this afternoon. P came for lunch at 4 p.m. and to see landlord, who still hadn't turned up, re extra security and new fridge (not necessarily in that order).

Five 'electricians' arrived in little go-cart-type-vehicle on tricycle chassis, with, for some reason, 'Panasonic Service Centre' painted on side. Entered with baggy shorts, screw-drivers, bare feet and embarrassed expressions. Found dead mouse behind fridge, which had bitten through electric cable and electrocuted itself. Maybe we could have patented this as a state-of-the-art mouse-trap...

P and I discussed security arrangements for keeping emergency dollars in house. Decided best measures might be to wrap money in a dirty sock of P's. Anyone going near said sock would have been overcome before they could say 'smelly feet'. Or we could have piled all money on table in full view with plastic doggie -doos atop it. Ideas please on back of postage stamp...

Our armed guard was to arrive at 6 p.m. P put table and chair in downstairs back passage (if you'll pardon the expression) for said guard. Did I need carafe of fresh water, biscuits or fresh flowers I asked? P said 'no'. Just wondered...

Electricians were still trying to fix fridge. Lito, driver, went out for new padlocks for doors. Aida gallantly stayed on late so as not to abandon us. Saj rang from UK in the middle of all the melee but just as P started to talk to him two Policemen arrived (in van bearing the legend 'Mary-Ann Christine') - Aida had asked them to come back to fingerprint the wallet and purse which had been found after they left in the morning. We were still waiting for landlord so P couldn't go back to work. He had a full in-tray which he'd hardly touched – it was a quiet restful afternoon chez Colbeck... NOT...

Meanwhile electricians pointed out date '1979' on fridge, which P relayed to landlord. Landlord insisted (in good faith) that he personally bought it three years before, to which P's reply was 'you were robbed'. Ho ho, new fridge was to arrive on Saturday!

Armed guard arrived at six; we installed him in side passage with chair and water supply, P pointed out chauffeur's(!) loo at rear of house, and at Ken's suggestion we joined other FW managers and wives for dinner on the company. We were a bit nervous about returning to house in the dark and going to bed but in fact slept well. Told P I thought we should keep the guard permanently at night – why not – the company would foot the bill and we weren't paid to take risks. Later heard that Anong was in hospital after bad stomach pains in night, and heard later still that she'd had her appendix out. Poor Anong!

25 Feb. By now Ben would be safely on his way with Steve. It would be brilliant to see them in a week's time! I had a muzzy head as yesterday - could have been the after-effects of having been drugged, but likewise could well have been due to the awful air. The locals burned rubbish morning and evening (and other times) and the air was often full of smoke – it smelt awful and hung around: it wasn't a nice place to be. P told me later that someone had volunteered that 'everyone in the upstairs office has headaches' so it could have been mild bug. Felt fine otherwise.

Pat received an e-mail purporting to be from God but I was sure it wasn't genuine as it had American spelling, and everyone knows that God isn't American.

I spent about three hours in the morning printing and sorting journal ready for dispatch the following week. It was awful without fridge as every time I wanted coffee or whatever one of us had to trot round to Saj's. Incidentally, was perturbed going round the corner to see that the house in between Saj's and our own had, as usual, the washing machine outside, but the water didn't drain into a normal drain – it just went down the drive in a long pipe and ended up in the gutter. What didn't drain away there just stayed around for hours – or longer.

Out there that can be a health hazard as water is breeding ground for mosquitoes. BC wasn't malarial, but dengue fever existed from day-time-biting mosquitos, normally in the wet season, so we needed to check this out.

Afternoon at pool with Carol and Liz. Gorgeous weather, lovely swim, coffee juice and chat after – very civilised.

P. shattered when he arrived home, so quiet evening and nice dinner – ingredients retrieved from Saj's: fried potatoes and bacon courtesy of M & S in Alabang earlier in week (they had a small – very expensive – shop there. I paid 90p for a normal-size tin of baked beans as the local ones weren't very nice).

Saturday. P works this morning, comes to lunch and goes back to office for a while. I have to stay in all day to wait for promised fridge which arrives about 2 pm. Quite impressive; what a joy not to have to walk round corner every time I want a cuppa! English Mass at 6 in the Basilica and dinner at home.

Sunday. To Eagle Point for day; P drives this time. Takes us nearly forty minutes to drive first 7 miles… Overcast day, not as warm or as pleasant as it should be, it being summer here. Still, we swim in pool, go down slide numerous times, dip in reef pool but don't snorkel – sea is too choppy. Lunch in restaurant but, though it tastes quite nice, is dripping fat so I leave most of mine. Tropical fruit salad for dessert - nice. See six people we know; that's the problem here – you can't get away from the expats 'cos there's so few places to go! We enjoy ourselves and have good drive back. Veggie mixed grill for dinner, booty from Alabang last Wednesday…

We hear that one of the Philippino FW office boys has a brother, a traffic Policeman who's won awards for his style of traffic control, which closely resembles Michael Jackson's moon-walking...

;

Health and Safety

Next morning is a quiet one at home, apart from visit to Anong, home after her appendectomy. She's doing very well, but understandably is still in a lot of pain. Last few days have been difficult for her: after her English lesson last Thursday (co-incidence, I promise!) she'd gone home and started having abdominal pains, which got steadily worse, so her German husband took her into hospital. For some reason she opted for the local Clinic, where they carried out tests and observation for maybe two days. When appendicitis was diagnosed, she had to be moved to private hospital for the op. which was scheduled for 5.30 p.m. that day.

Clinic wouldn't discharge her till her husband had paid the bill – equivalent of almost £900, but he didn't have enough money locally, so he arranged for money to be transferred from Germany, which didn't arrive for several days. Anyway, they borrowed the money from a friend so she could be discharged, she had to walk down three flights of stairs 'cos there wasn't a lift, and her husband had to drive her across B.C. at a busy time of day (although not far, the drive can take anything from 15 minutes to 50 minutes depending on traffic) to private hospital, where she finally had the op. To be fair, her appendix was not on the point of bursting, but I wouldn't like to risk it…

She said doctor was good, nurses competent but not particularly pleasant, room wasn't very nice but she managed to change to a better one. And this is a private hospital, and as expats we're in the privileged minority. Obviously, acute cases and, say, spinal injuries couldn't easily be moved to Manila because of the roads, but FW would use a helicopter where necessary; this has already been discussed.

Believe me, I do realize how incredibly privileged we are as expats, but none-the-less it's really not an easy existence – and although it's a Tropical location, it's not a holiday destination… Whilst having my jabs before coming out, the Sister in the Medical Centre had asked me to let her know about the medical situation on the Project. I sent her a letter outlining the following points:

'BC is not a healthy place to live; it's dusty and polluted, with smells, petrol and diesel fumes. Walking to the shops and crossing the road are

unpleasant and dangerous: in many places there are no proper pavements so one has to dodge in and out of the traffic. Respiratory infections and allergies are common: indoors the tiny mould spores in the air-con get circulated around, so indoors or out, the air is not healthy. Stomach upsets are common, possibly due to the Philippino habit of cooking food – meat, fish, shellfish, and leaving for an hour or so at room temperature before serving. With the humidity, dehydration is an ever-present threat.

The expat community is small, and getting smaller, with the end of one of the projects. There are very few European children here, mostly young, only one to my knowledge of secondary school age. I have to say that I would not bring children out here.

The private hospital which serves FW is apparently adequate for non-serious conditions, though ill-equipped. The staff are thought to be well-trained, and the doctor whom FW uses seems to be conscientious. One of the expat community recently had the choice of conventional gall-stone and gall-bladder removal locally, necessitating two weeks off work, or key-hole surgery in Manila. He opted for the latter, in spite of bad road and driving conditions and was back at work just a few days later!

Antibiotics are used more frequently than these days in the UK; steroids are even given to babies and young children. Medicines are on sale which in the UK are prescription-only, and a local petrol station had a sweetie jar of miscellaneous medicines the other day – probably out of date and obviously no longer needed for the persons who'd originally bought them.

There has just been the first case of dengue fever amongst the expat community – not serious, but it necessitated a week's hospitalisation in Manila, and the rainy season is not here yet, when most cases occur. There is a high incidence of rabies: with the large numbers of stray dogs and cats roaming the streets, this is hardly surprising.

Some of the FW staff literally rarely see daylight as the town-office is windowless. They leave home in the dark and return in the dark: it becomes dark soon after 6 p.m. in the Tropics. The Site offices (Porto cabins) are located on the Refinery with sulphur fumes permeating the atmosphere -

another cause of respiratory problems. Stress, depression, lack of exercise with its attendant problems, insomnia, and alcohol dependency are common here. The working hours are long and normally include part-weekends. The good news is that this area is not thought to be malarial, and local medical advice is not to take anti-malarial drugs as these are thought to do damage to liver and kidneys over a period of time...'

The afternoon was pleasant, with a nice swim at pool where I met several more expats just returned from leave; we chatted and drank coffee. Lito, (driver) usually very happy and obliging, was upset as other drivers were tied up and he was running round like the proverbial blue etc. etc. Smoothed him down, rang Pat to warn him. P dealt with situation, later all was well.

P got a video player on approval from local shop, which refused to play VHS tapes, as did the one which the landlord brought in the previous week. In both cases we'd been assured the machine was compatible with our system. Deliberately, he got it through the company so hadn't paid; hopefully we'd get an engineer out reasonably easily if they wanted their money...

Still no post; it must have been over a week since we'd had any – maybe ten days. Postal system was grim. Still no e-mail – system had been completely down, apparently as they were changing server, whatever that was, apart from mis-installation on our system which was still also waiting to be rectified.

It was very difficult getting things done, and I got very frustrated, but I realised it was far worse for Pat and colleagues. They were actually trying to build a gas plant, which was giving employment to a lot of people (though you really wouldn't have thought it from the attitude of local individuals in power). Problem was that Pat, as Admin Manager, fielded everyone else's problems, whatever they were. We were looking forward to the arrival of new Admin Manager – Pat would assist him, and could then expand his other functions.

Ben rang, very briefly and no doubt expensively, from KL to say that they'd arrived safely and 'everything was brilliant'. Couldn't wait to see him and Steve the following Friday... Popped with Pat to buy meat, yes meat, in fact, beef, Australian, for dinner the next day. Ted was coming for a meal as I'd promised Kathy before she left for UK.

29 Feb. First the bad news: e-mail system is still down – hopefully it will be up and running tomorrow in which case technician will (hopefully) come round and install properly.

Good news: Video technicians come out to see why we can't play our VHS tapes in spite of it apparently being multi-system. Bad news: Reason is that TV supplied by landlord isn't multi-system. Inform P who will go into shop.

Exotic lunch; BLT with last of the B which I got last week in Alabang. All good things etc. The L and the T were somewhat limp so I stood them in cold sugar water for a while which crisped them up a treat. (Probably removed any remaining vitamins too, but that's life – you can't have everything.) There you are, that was Auntie Mary's Little Tip for Today. No extra charge - all part of the service.

To Caedo in afternoon to finish shopping for tonight's banquet. Beef tenderloin and onions in red wine, fresh veg brought in by Aida, traditional English pud. Manage to get such luxuries as baking powder, flour and loo paper, no luck with kitchen roll, in spite of enthusiastic mime with aid of bottle of sticky orange syrup and two loo rolls balanced on top of one another. I think that I've inadvertently invented a new party game: it's called 'Mime the Shopping List'. I'll take out a patent. Am trusting you guys not to get there first and make a fortune.

Pleasant evening. Enjoyed beef with Ted, very tender and tasty. (Beef!) Steamed jam pud (microwave, 4 minutes!) went down a treat, as did two bottles of red wine, several beers, couple of cream sherries (not pale cream unfortunately, but we chilled it first to anaesthetize the taste buds) and a couple of slugs of whisky. And that was just me! (Only joking...) Later party at German restaurant for birthday of Judy, owner's wife. Free buffet and booze, plus live band, for members of Ladies' Club and husbands.

Keyboards and Committees

I'm coming on leave next month. Haven't finalised actual date yet but will have to do so soon so we can get best deal. Stay in all morning; fed up – still no e-mail. Seem only to be two companies out here which are much used - neither is apparently any good; we're working on it... Quick swim after lunch and later over to Caedo for first keyboard lesson. Difficult twisting fingers into knots - much harder than learning to drive!!

Saj arrives from UK, exhausted and fed up after noisy journey with four million kids on plane and having had his tall, lanky frame folded up like a pen-knife for sixteen hours or so. Has meal with us and in spite of that (!) is in better humour by the time he leaves.

Next day I attended a committee meeting of Ladies' Club, as requested. They were keen to get me on the committee (no accounting for tastes!) but had to be seen to go through correct procedures. I said I definitely wouldn't do treasurer, and recommended Carol as chairman. She'd be great – very American (in a nice way!) – organised, direct, forward-thinking, but with people skills too. In the afternoon I gave an English lesson to Tanja. Somewhat informal (what's new?) as three computer guys were getting us back on e-mail. Confirmed it had been wrongly installed, and after twenty minutes informed me we were back on-line. Joy! Carol and other American lady arrived for coffee and Chat with a capital 'C'. Pat came back late: he had everything to square off before our exciting weekend; after dinner we did our packing for an early start tomorrow.

We left BC just after 7 next morning; Dodong drove us to Manila. Sign seen on dirty shack: 'Best interested haircut. Days and night service. Ladies and gents.' My hair needed a trim, but I managed to resist the temptation! Large tanker up-ended in ditch, where road had collapsed. Buildings going up, many of them with builders and workmen wearing regulation flip-flops – even walking on scaffolding in said foot-wear.

We waited two or three hours in 'five-star' hotel nearest airport. D. had to get back to BC as they were short of drivers, hence the arrangement – non-passengers couldn't get into airport to await arrivals, so normally we'd have waited in the car. P had arranged for Ben and Steve to be met by Thos Cook, and put in taxi to hotel where we were waiting.

Meanwhile, back at said, I repeat, Five-Star hotel, we had a reasonable meal; I reported that the ladies loos' were very dirty (that was before I went in!) and we asked for coffee after lunch. Waited forty minutes or so, no coffee. Investigated. Found coffee in lobby on hotplate which we hadn't seen - why hadn't they pointed it out? Problem, no milk. Requested milk. 'Yes of course mam.' No milk. Waited about fifteen minutes and gave it up as a bad job in the end. This is the hotel where soap in the loos had been 'out of stock' last time we visited – a favourite Philippine expression.

Any road up, back to more interesting topics: Ben and Steve arrived tired and a bit pale and dishevelled but happy, having been drinking the night before. Taxi across Manila to New World Hotel – drive was a bit of an eye-opener for the boys after Penang. This hotel is one of the best in Manila. Not many back-packers, though! To be exact, two – Ben and Steve. Shopping in the afternoon in one of the malls near the hotel – similar to malls the world over. Wait till they get to BC! Lovely buffet dinner in evening where the boys made up for several days' under-nourishment. Trish and Col appeared at next table, en route for Korea. Like I say, there weren't so many places to go and you just couldn't get away from folks. Happily, T & C were always good company and one wouldn't have wanted to get away from them...

4 March. Our twenty-ninth wedding anniversary. We spend it chasing office furniture for FW. Snack lunch in hotel and shopping in afternoon; I feel like a child in toy-shop. Quick swim in fourth-floor swimming pool. Across from us is the high-rise commercial centre of Manila, Makati. Beautiful skyline.

To Mass in evening in chapel in tiny park opposite. White domed building, no walls. In the round. Fairy lights from centre of dome, where there's a fresco of God the Father, to the four 'corners' - if you can have corners in a round... Chapel full, lots more outside, fairy lights in trees, large bats swooping into the mini-moat. It's lovely, really meaningful: when everyone joins hands around the chapel for the 'Our Father' it's wonderful. In English, too...Buffet dinner again and we waddle up to our rooms and collapse on beds Sleep well! It's been very expensive, but a really pleasant weekend.

We bundled boys into taxi to airport at 6.45 a.m. next day for the flight to Boracay, which has one of the most beautiful beaches in the world; we would see them again the next weekend. We had a swim, and a coffee in Deli France in one of nearby malls, where we met Hilary and Ken on a shopping spree for the day. I bought some material in a sale – about 90p per yard. Saj arrived, as arranged, and we went to Alabang for lunch and a look around two of the malls; had a good journey home. Arrived about seven, laden with our booty; I typed a report for P, then snack supper and bed – we were shattered!

Aside: when shopping, we noticed that the systems were unbelievably cumbersome and bore a great deal of resemblance to what must have obtained in the heyday of the Soviet Union. P had a theory that the less bright shop assistants and managers must have been trained by Soviet ex-shop assistants. Anyway, you frequently had to have a 'manual' written receipt which you, or the assistant, took, with the item, to the cash desk.

There were usually two or maybe three people there who took over, shuffling item, pieces of paper and carrier bags backwards and forwards, often closing bag and stapling with receipt. In one shop we bought two items totalling about £4.50, which involved three assistants and six pieces of paper. In another shop we bought a box of sweets: five or six shop-assistants sorted it out and another couple looked on. It took some minutes, and just as we said 'Please don't bother' they finally succeeded.

In another shop I bought several small items, needing three people sorting into piles and writing two individual receipts before passing on to electronic till-operator and two packers. One of packers was fascinated by the magnifying-glass which P had bought for me to experiment with painting miniatures: he had a field day studying, and marvelling at, the back of his hand. It looked pretty similar to any other hand to me…

6 March. Today is a big day: There's some sort of local sanitation project being launched for poor people, and Pat has been invited to 'the Blessing of the Toilet Seats'. He has an impossible workload already, but he realizes just how important good sanitation is to health – we take so much for granted in our own society…

Am absolutely horrified to get a phone bill for one month's calls, granted many of them to UK, totalling about £280. (That's calls only – FW pay rental). Even in cheap rate, which most of them are, it costs about £1 per minute. That's far more than I paid from UK. Inform Pat who will get it checked out. He's really tired, depressed and bogged down – it's difficult to get across just how impossible it is to do business here. This Project will benefit everyone, - it's bringing money and work, at least for the next year or so, to a place where unemployment is very high and where there are no welfare benefits. Guess if you're on holiday over here, and just vegging out, or if you're a beach bum, you could have a pleasant existence, albeit not in BC, but business? Forget it.

Saj talks of a guy who wanted to open a nice little holiday resort BC with swimming pool/s, restaurant, and good accommodation, as he has on an island near here. He soon jettisoned the idea when he heard how much it would cost in sweeteners. The International Ladies' Club here, as stated before, raise money to benefit local charities but NEVER give 'em money – they actually have things done instead. Anyway, they wanted to open a little coffee shop here as there's no -where nice to go for coffee. Thought they could sell home-made cakes etc. It would be a meeting-place for expats and local ladies. That was till they realised how much it would cost in back-handers – at a very high local level.

Sorry if I sound bitter and disillusioned today – guess it's because I am. The situation is even getting Pat down, placid as he normally is. These people seem locked in inertia and fatalism. Such a shame – there are natural assets and beautiful scenery – could be a really nice place to come and visit even while keeping it unspoiled. Even Philippinos say BC is particularly difficult – corruption-ridden as it is. But this is where we have to be to build the Plant. The only thing that keeps us going is our ever-decreasing mortgage…

Later. I have lovely, solitary swim and just laze for an hour with a book. Have to admit to a short zizz too. P arrives home more cheerful. The situation doesn't change but sometimes one can cope better than others. Dinner at home – sorry, this is doubtless getting monotonous for you – imagine what it's like for us! Bit of desultory tidying up of guest bedrooms prior to boys coming. Send some e-mails. Bed; we sleep well. Funnily enough, we both seem to be sleeping better than before the burglary. Strange, that: maybe not really to be recommended as an antidote to insomnia…

Next morning started well: Aida arrived laden with fruit and veg from the market – something which never failed to delight me. Also, bless her, she had collected the photos for me which I hadn't had a chance to get yesterday. Which reminded me of a (to me) very endearing trait of Philippinos: Saj had asked Lito to collect some photos for him, which Lito duly did. When Saj arrived back in the office, not only had Lito looked at the photos himself, he was passing them round and everyone was giggling at them. It was normal behaviour – I suppose privacy is a luxury to which not many could aspire. It amused Pat and me, though…

I spent most of the morning typing, making bread rolls for lunch and having a go at flapjack, with limited ingredients and no recipe. Later: bread good, flapjack not bad. Just in case you had been wondering…

Typical country scene

Mission Unaccomplished

Pat rang me up later that morning: he had to go to Manila unexpectedly, would I like to go with him? Reason: Ken was going to Thailand on business the next day, and his passport was still with the authorities for stamping/work permit etc., which took some time. Director of Immigration who should have signed here in BC was in Manila, expected back in his office the previous day, but hadn't come. Changed his return to that day and then changed it to the next, which meant that Ken couldn't use his passport without a signature. So he asked P to meet him in a restaurant in Manila, where, it transpired, he conducted a lot of his business; it was too important for P to delegate.

I weighed up the pros and cons; trip to Manila was not to be undertaken lightly, and I really needed a swim as it was literally all the exercise I got. However, said 'yes' to P on condition we stopped off at decent food shop on way back, for several things I needed and couldn't get in BC. We agreed and off we set. Three hours there, heavy one-and-half hours in restaurant eating lurid so-called 'club sandwich' with Director of Immigration for this area. Glazed-eyes syndrome but we did our bit in small talk – thank goodness for Lito who came in with us and kept the conversational ball rolling.

Set out for home, asking Lito to stop in Alabang en route, which he did, but at a very down-market mall. Our fault, we obviously hadn't made ourselves clear, so we asked to go to one of two other malls, only short distance away. Problem: Lito either still didn't understand, or maybe didn't want to lose face by admitting he didn't know it, so he didn't take us there. When we queried it he apologised and said he'd never been there in fact. Too late now, traffic in other direction was horrendous. Drive home also took three hours and we arrived home about 9 pm, after a seven-and-a-half hour round trip - without my precious shopping. I was disappointed, but we managed to laugh about it. Quick snack and Saj came round to discuss some notes which they needed for next day. I typed them up and fell into bed exhausted after an irritating afternoon!

Impressions: Jeepney with flat tyre by side of road, ten adults sitting in it while driver and mate try to jack it up… Plastic goods pedlar on push-bike, completely hung around with brightly coloured washing baskets, buckets etc.; vendors of food, cigarettes and newspapers weaving in and out of traffic waiting at traffic lights on busy road – including man pushing small cart of hot peanuts. Brahmin calf frolicking in a field...

An open-sided jeepney/cattle truck pulled up at petrol station loos and disgorged family passengers, most of whom, including plump, elderly, grey-haired lady, were sitting on bare metal floor. They used a bamboo armchair as step, and as they pulled out of forecourt later we saw them all back on floor apart from man at rear of truck who was sitting on said armchair holding broken-latched- door closed...

Names of jeepneys: we saw 'Two Brothers' 'Three Kids' 'Gift from God' and 'Sensitive Partner'. The mind boggled.

Car on side of road, all doors open. Two people spread-eagled inside, fast asleep, third asleep on pile of dirt nearby. Bare-footed guy in shorts at top of lamp-post fixing high-tension cable with bare hands. People living in shacks thrown up along disused railway line, and along rail-track which runs round Manila. Washing hanging on fence alongside railway line and even high up in tree. I imagined portly grey-haired old lola (grandmother) heaving herself up said tree with washing basket aloft. No, maybe not – heaven only knows how they hung it up so high.

Ash Wednesday. Went to 7 am Mass, the LAST one that morning, the others having been 5.45 and 6 a.m. Church full, must have been about two thousand people or so. Ladies' Club lunch - Good swim after.

Home to beautify myself (a girl can try) before sallying forth in the evening: we'd been invited for dinner at the local home (he had several) of Immigration Director for this area, whom we'd met in Manila the day before. Was terrified but in fact, it was a pleasant evening. The Director, with bodyguard, stopped by our house so our driver could follow his vehicle. Tom was driving us in the Pajero, and the forty-kilometre drive took almost an hour as traffic was heavy. The Director, and Tom too, both used their flashers for the entire journey (so to speak!) and Pat tried out practice regal waves. Tom indicated stretch of road where he had twice seen a ghost – 'faceless white lady floating about two feet above ground.'

Assorted gathering, about twelve in all – guests, family, bodyguard, servants. I was the only woman eating – the others fluttered around dancing attendance on assembled company. The drivers waited till others were served, then ate too. All very comfortable – interesting to watch how things worked – everyone seemed to understand unwritten rules. The food was delicious – different fish, rice, sauces and vegetables. Felt a bit embarrassed – I had pre-empted a possible difficult situation and explained to the D. the day before that I didn't want him to be offended if we didn't eat meat as it would be Ash Wednesday. (It was only at a later date that we discovered the reason why, in spite of abstinence, Philippinos eat chicken on Ash Wednesday – fish is more expensive and is therefore deemed to be a luxury. In saying that we couldn't eat chicken I was effectively saying that it wasn't good enough for us – we'd rather have had an expensive meal. I was absolutely mortified when I found out, in spite of having had the best of intentions.) We left bearing gifts of mangoes and bananas...

9 March. Sad to say that it seems likely, for domestic reasons, we'll be losing Aida soon. Have known for some time that this is possibility. Ask if Aida's daughter can clean next-door house tomorrow, as the new Admin Manager and Malaysian wife will be arriving next week. Look forward to meeting them! Gigi reluctant as house has been empty for some time and she's afraid of ghosts, but Aida promises to be on hand...

Have lovely long solitary swim, and relax in sun after with good book. Not only is this, the swimming I mean, the only exercise I get, this is basically the only fresh air I get. Coffee after and home for lunch – home-made leek soup today and last of home-made bread. Tanja for English lesson in afternoon; shopping in Caedo and Tom gives her lift home while I do my shopping. Dinner at home – perfectly disgusting 'veggie choplets' which we'd bought in Alabang. Throw most of it away. Fresh veggies delicious though! P tells me there's an office party on Monday to celebrate some contract or other. Wow! What excitement!

Saw a hilarious sight the other day: drew up behind commercial vehicle at traffic lights and read on the rear of his vehicle 'How's my driving?' The lady passenger had her door open and was vomiting into the road. Guess that answered the question…

Gigi's husband Joel, home from working in Saudi Arabia, turned up with Jay-Jay, their five-year old son, to meet me. During morning, I finished typing Boy Scouts presentation; felt so good to be done with it - I'd been doing it a page or so at a time for weeks. Relief! Also made thin loose trousers – only had one pair comfortable enough to wear going to Manila so would appreciate these. Turquoise and white stripes…

Afternoon walked round to Shirley, member of Ladies' Club, who had organised talk on the Philippines. Given by old family friend, ex-Philippine Navy. Very interesting; he talked mainly about behaviour and cultural differences. Shame there were only about ten people there to listen. Delicious Philippine food for 'merienda' sort of afternoon snack. Evening Saj treated us to dinner at Japanese restaurant; not bad. Pleasant evening.

The Boys are Coming!

On Saturday P was working in the morning; he was even busier than usual, and wanted to get as up-to-date as possible before the boys came. The week promised to be even more hectic… Dodong drove me to Manila domestic airport to collect Ben and Steve from Boracay. On the journey we saw an over-turned jeepney on busy highway; passengers laughing and joking on side of road so it would appear that hopefully no-one had been injured. Also saw tanker and lorry had collided; lorry was in a very bad state. Later saw another tanker of some sort driving along with passenger sitting astride tank, and two storey open-sided cattle truck with crouching passengers sitting in bottom part, and crammed full of standing passengers up top. On a lighter note, it was a scorching hot day, maybe upper 80's or more in 'real' temperature, but saw driver of an earth-moving vehicle in jeans, long-sleeved T-shirt and blue and white knitted bobble hat. Was still working in same gear when we came back some hours later. I suppose you can't be too careful…

Domestic terminal was in a sort of shanty town, no proper signs to direct us so we were a few minutes late, Ben and Steve were a few minutes early. It was brilliant to see them again! Easy drive to Alabang for lunch and food shopping then to BC. P arrived home from work bit later after a very difficult day. P and I went to the English Mass then we all went over to the Shell Club for dinner. Only one other customer – the duty guard, but we still had to wait an hour or more for our meal. It was lovely getting up-to-date with the boys though!

Sunday we take the boys to Eagle Point. Lovely day swimming in two small swimming pools and in reef pool with small nurse sharks and turtle. Snorkelling in sea, sharing Pat's snorkel, and ok Pat, I give in – you win – I'm finally converted. Still a bit nervous as it's very rocky and we keep scratching ourselves, but snorkel for about half-an-hour and am fascinated. I'll get my own snorkel and flippers as P still has all his gear from Oman. Already have my very own (prescription) goggles. Lunch and drinks all day by pool; weather is gorgeous. See at least six people we know there. As we drive home it starts raining and has obviously been raining very heavily in BC. Aida tells me that they'd had torrential rain for two hours – we were very lucky. Quick visit to Pic 'n Save for Smartie ice-cream(!) for pud, and cold supper at home.

Noteworthy comment: postal service is abysmal here. Many of the houses don't have numbers, and we find telephone bills etc. tucked in latch of gate or inserted in gap between front door and lintel. Often they aren't for us – I'm never sure so always have to ask Aida. Apparently they don't have postmen as in UK; one of the drivers has told Pat that he has frequently been taking public transport somewhere and hears someone ask 'Is anyone going to Lipa? Do you know so-and-so? Could you take this letter to him?' FW now uses a private PO number but even so I frequently go a week without letters and then get a batch…

Next morning I took the boys on foot to Citimark to put in photos. The boys readily expressed similar opinions to ours on BC and agreed that we weren't exaggerating. Home for lunch then P dropped us off at the Shell Club, where we spent the afternoon swimming, and in the boys' case, jumping off the high board. I contented myself with a swim, coffee and a read. FW party this evening, again on Shell complex.

Party not bad, about hundred people there. Only problem was, yes, you've guessed it, cold food. Pat had specified 'very hot food, please, at eight o'clock' and instead they presented stone-cold food at half past. All food was in dishes over bains-maries, but none of burners were lit. Manageress was closeted in her office and didn't seem to understand the situation and didn't know what to do. Finally food was served, reasonably hot at 9pm. Pat was reassured to see, in the midst of the mayhem, someone with the right priorities and with a comprehensive grasp of the situation: everyone was rushing round panicking, and one little chap was just standing there, in the middle of the kitchen, oblivious to everything, just calmly folding paper napkins, as he'd obviously been instructed.

P and I had a few dances, including the obligatory rock-n-roll and we left about 10.30. Ben and Steve went on to karaoke bar with some of the younger managers and came home in tricycle about 1 a.m.

On 14th March the boys and I went, with hired driver, to see Tagaytay volcano - a lake in a volcano crater, in a lake. (I'd been there once before with Patricia when she was visiting.) We headed for the so-called 'Vista Hotel' to explore hiring a boat, but hotel was 'closed for renovation' so we had fish-burgers in McDonald's opposite – not bad. Lovely views but we couldn't find the right way down to lake for boats which was a shame, as it was then possible to ride horses up to the crater. Instead, we drove along the lake-shore; we took lots of photos, and had drinks en route home in another McD. The day wasn't as I'd planned it - we'd spent most of the time in the car. We should have taken guide-book, driver should have taken map; we'll know better next time!

Next day Dodong took the boys and me to Punta Baluarte, a coastal resort. Not too much traffic so it took about one -and-a-half hours. We paid the day rate and had a room with en-suite loo as base for the day – very civilised. Overcast all morning but sunny after lunch. We swam, vegged out, and had a very nice lunch in spite of slightly sullen waiters/waitresses. It was a lovely day out….

16 March, the boys' last day with us, we spent based at home so they could do their packing. On foot to market—it was awful. I'd only been once before with Aida and driver—ten minutes' quite dangerous walk dodging tricycles and jeepneys as there was no proper pavement most of way. It was smelly, dusty and polluted – the air was foul. Hundreds of stalls in market, thousands of people. Small dark alleys between stalls; couldn't find our way around – it was a nightmare. A superb location for a chase in a thriller film!

A group of beggar children asked for money. An incongruously sweet sight: small fluffy white dog leaning out of upstairs window, paws on sill just surveying the scene. Cute. Jeepney names spotted today: 'Jampack' (how right!), 'King Bong' and 'Spoiled'. What can I say…

New Admin Manager and Malaysian wife moved in next door; P took me round to introduce me – they seemed very nice. Afternoon swimming; Pat joined us soon after. Finally our long-promised desk was delivered, which immediately swallowed up the computer, printer and scanner and made the landing look much tidier. This was my lair, where I wrote the famous journal, wrote all my letters and did my art and my music, so it was great to see it more workmanlike…

In the evening we went out to dinner in a local restaurant. We all ordered grilled tuna – it was off. No problem, we'd have blue marlin. 'Sorry, no blue marlin'. Settled for lapu-lapu (popular fish) but it still had its head on and glared at me balefully. Ate a few mouthfuls, gave it to Pat. Ate a little of his beef. Ben's meal looked the best, chili prawns. Serenaded by local group; we clapped politely – last time that had happened was in Mexico on holiday from California years before! Home for coffee and pud prepared earlier by Aida. Spent an hour assembling journal and letters for boys to post in UK.

Dodong took Ben, Steve and me to Manila: first a quick visit to Town Centre Mall Alabang for a snack, then to airport where I saw them off. I felt very sad but would see Ben again soon when on leave. To Alabang for food shopping, home; it was a good day to be away as we'd had 'brown-out' all day – no electricity between 8 and 5. Had warning yesterday – the power came back on at 5 p.m. sharp. Luckily we didn't keep much frozen food as we didn't have our own generators. It would have been good if we could have stocked up even a little on visits to Manila or Alabang, but it wasn't worth the risk of food wastage.

Saturday 18 March. P working as usual this morning but reports that new Admin Manager has suggested they work alternate Saturday mornings, so that's got to be an improvement. Now that he's here Pat, as Training Manager, will be able to concentrate on the Training function, which is his forte, so work-wise things have got to get better for him.

Busy morning: because of brown-out yesterday there are piles of washing, including Ben and Steve's bedclothes. Can't leave it till Monday so read instruction book for twin-tub in back yard and manage to do two loads. If my public could see me now, with mi' Marigolds, and up ter mi' chin in suds, what would they say? Hang on there, wait, I don't have public at present so that's one worry less. Must be twenty years or so since I used a twin-tub (I was a child-bride) but even that had a hot water heater – this is just cold. How the mighty are fallen…

Pat comes back to lunch but has to pop back into office. We do a little shopping then I wait for him with book. English Mass at 6 p.m. then landlords come as requested to remove unwanted spare spare bed (so to speak) from landing – also carpet, which exposes beautiful polished floorboards. Much classier! P goes to collect Saj from office 7.30 but as guys are still installing computers he has to wait till they've finished. Arrives home for dinner and much needed drinks soon after 8 pm. Saj stays for meal…

Sunday based at home; P needed to get some work done collating and writing a study module that he started in Oman and had never had time to finish. We spent time re-arranging landing; now that unwanted bed had gone it was much less cluttered – it felt good. Took Des, new Admin Manager, and wife Aisha to Shell club; P and I had a swim. Tinned lentil soup for supper – surprisingly good – brought back from Alabang on Friday.

Hilarious sight which Pat had seen recently: two pigs strapped into tricycle side-car, looking bemusedly around them…

I'd been feeling a bit down for day or two, with, co-incidentally or not, slight sore throat and 'glandiness', muzzy head and excessive tiredness, Pat too, but I cheered up the following day, with good haul of e-mails from friends. Hurray! Cheering-up process continued when Lito turned up with piano-backing tape recorded and sent by Anthony. It had taken 17 days to reach me – I'd been beginning to panic as I needed it for the Ladies' Club a week on Friday. Relief!

I spent the morning on computer and afternoon swimming with Hilary, then back to Aisha's with Hilary to introduce her. We all decided to go out for day on Wednesday, problem was where to go. Hilary and I had been asking around for new places but hadn't come up with anything. Might go to monthly American craft bazaar in Alabang if nothing else turned up but would prefer not to as a) journey was usually difficult, and b) there would be our very own BC version of the bazaar on the following Saturday for charity and we wanted to support it.

P came in with automatic water heater/cooler dispenser, surplus to requirements at office. Ellen invited us to farewell drinks on Thursday and surprise surprise, she and Eugene were free to come to our party on Friday. Ditto Carol and husband. On Hilary's suggestion I had asked the ladies to bring a plate of food each, which would simplify the catering position – so everyone only had to worry about finding ingredients for one dish!! Felt much better by end of day.

Aida was to finish with us very soon – domestic problems – both she and we were very sorry but none of us could change anything. Ellen's maid Purita would be free and had expressed willingness to work for us (in spite of having met me several times). I rang her and we arranged for her to come and meet Pat and see the house on Saturday next.

Families folding the palms for Palm Sunday p.188   Typical scene below

Maggots and Machetes

Pat had to go to Alabang for day; Aida arrived with fruit and veg from market; exhorted me to try a chicco (small tropical fruit with stone) as 'They're very sweet, Mam'. Unfortunately the one I selected had an enormous maggot, almost same size as said stone. I screamed and dropped fruit, plate and all! Felt very stupid, but then what's new…

The morning was somewhat enlivened by arrival of landlady escorted by tree surgeon; we'd asked for trees directly outside house windows to be trimmed as they made house very gloomy. Guy shinned up tree one-handed, barefooted, bare-headed and wielding enormous machete, with which he proceeded to hack all around him. I was terrified he'd chop off his toes and, sort of semi-hypnotised, peered discreetly through slats of blinds so I didn't distract him…

Piano lesson in afternoon; took Aisha to show her Caedo at same time. Pat arrived home with goodies from Alabang – couldn't find rapid-action yeast but brought two organic bread mixes at equivalent of £2.50 each. What would we do without my precious bread machine? It kept me sane. (Ish). We had tinned beef stew for dinner (delicious) with fresh veg and patisserie cakes for pud. Wish he had to go to Alabang more often!

The following morning I couldn't open landing windows as enormous bee was bashing against net screens. These no longer bothered me, as long as they were not in the room, but cockroaches and giant maggots still gave me the screaming abdabs. Someone somewhere was playing 'Land of Hope and Glory' for some unaccountable reason…

Hilary and I had been trying desperately to find somewhere to take Aisha out for day, rather than Manila/Alabang, which was such a long exhausting journey: we'd heard about 'Hidden Valley' – lovely location with waterfalls. Enquiries revealed its entrance fee to be about £22 – per person; we didn't know what we'd get for that. Dollars only apparently. No way. 'Paxenham Falls' (don't know correct spelling) was where part of 'Apocalypse Now' was filmed. Thought to be a similar, beautiful area, with rapids; £16 to get in but was 'subject to extortion' (to quote guide book) unless you dealt only with the hotel there. We'd have driver but didn't feel too comfortable with that scenario, so we ruled that one out too. Someone told us there was a beautiful place south through the mountains, overlooking the sea, with, we heard, a lake - did we fancy two miles each way through mountains to unknown destination? Would save that one for Pat; would like to check it out some time. We heard of a place where they made papier-mache fancy goods. Could be interesting, but they'd probably have them at the craft bazaar that Saturday, and it was probably three hours' drive each way. Delete that one. Settled for visit to Lipa, town near BC; I'd never been but shopping was thought to be a bit better than Batangas.

It was! We started with pizza and salad in Pizza Hut – it was lovely and I was so excited! Bought lots of food, including muffins, flour tortillas, decent bread, olive margarine – there was no stopping me. Also two lovely pairs of bright baggy trousers and short-sleeved cotton shirt – the three cost a fiver (sterling) in total. Mall plus supermarket – worth visiting again; drive each way took about 40 minutes so it wasn't too far. Back to Hilary's for cuppa; home about 5pm. Quite a marathon; we'd been out since 10 this morning. Wish I'd discovered Lipa earlier, but at least two expats had told me it wasn't worth visiting. Wouldn't have wanted to go every week, but maybe once or twice a month…

'Land of Hope and Glory' rang out again the next morning; I wondered if they'd used it perhaps as a hymn setting as it was a big day – Graduation Day for local convent school. On the surface was all very American here, and key years in the educational system, including, I think 'kinder' year for 5/6 year olds, had their own Graduation celebrations. Saw girls in school uniform carrying white mortar boards and white academic robes, boys in smart white ceremonial barongs (traditional, formal, loose shirt, the best of which were made from pineapple or banana-leaf fibres) – all looking incredibly smart. Later I discovered that the older school-children used 'Land of Hope and Glory' as their Graduation song.

Busy morning with sewing. I'd planned to start rehearsing for 'Music and Fun' afternoon Friday next, but was still bit 'glandy', and 'sinus-y' and still couldn't sing. Felt fine, though, and head was ok now – day before it had felt like solid cotton wool and I'd been deaf for a time. It had been quite weird. English lesson in afternoon for Anong, now almost recovered from her appendectomy, though still sore, and to Pic 'n Save with Aisha to get goodies for the party.

Went to Ellen's drinks party in the evening. It was just a few of us there, very pleasant. Hadn't seen a lot of Ellen but would really miss her – there were fewer and fewer expats of any nationality – Liz and I had counted about fifteen left or leaving in the next week or two. Without Ellen in the expat community it would leave only four Brits – two of us FW.

I arrived home shattered but as P sat down to watch the news, the TV and all the lights went off; the air-con continued its usual racket. Strange, all houses around had lights. We found ever-ready candles and matches and P inspected fuse-box; all seemed well. Rod, the guard, came in and inspected said fuse-box too. Nothing untoward there but still no lights.

Rather than have guard sit in dark all night we rang landlady – this was 11.15, which is quite late in the Tropics. Couldn't throw any light on the situation (tee hee) but arrived in son's car swathed in exotic dressing gown, and bringing, besides the son (her husband was in the States), her maid, her daughter and her son -in-law. All peered into the offending fuse-box, and son-in-law disappeared to find an electrician. At this stage I sent P to bed as he was shattered and had his usual 5.45 alarm call. Landlady, retinue and I made polite conversation, as one does, till son-in-law arrived with electrician, who spent some time ferreting about in the fuse-box and after about twenty minutes or so found the problem in the circuit-breaker. Hey-ho! Lights came on, TV blared out, and we were home and dry. I got to bed at 12.30 pretty bushed…

Aida was off till lunchtime next day to attend her daughter's Graduation. I got up feeling really tired but spent a busy (pleasant) morning bustling round getting ready for the social event of Batangas – our party that night. Not much cooking to do as everyone would bring something. Torrential rain for a short while – maybe twenty minutes - really freshened the air up. Pat told me that the main street was flooded to a depth of 6 or 7 inches.

Rumours Abound

Heard weird story yesterday at Ellen's party, and weirder still denial today: we were told yesterday by a number of both Philippinos and Brits, that the media, both newspapers and television, had reported a number of abductions of young people in Batangas – varying between eleven and twenty persons in the last four weeks. One young woman had supposedly been abducted from a crowded supermarket and a boy from outside a local bank. We'd had gruesome details from a number of people, including discovery of bodies in local market, red car of abductors, selling to white slave trade, mutilations, Police going round all schools etc. The whole community was, understandably outraged, shocked and terrified. Coming back from the party the whole town looked like a ghost town.

This morning, Aida told me she'd heard a local priest speaking on the radio telling people that these stories were not true but had been deliberately put about by the media, maybe to distract attention from unsavoury goings-on in high places. I was sure he was telling what he believed to be the truth, but what a bizarre situation. Anything could have been possible – he could have been misinformed himself – who knows. It wasn't the first time we'd heard a local priest speaking out against wrong-doing by officialdom – incredibly brave to be so outspoken…

Later I heard from two sources that yes, the information issued by the media hadn't been true, and was supposedly to discredit a local Police chief who was tough on drugs - a big problem locally. Whatever the truth was, the fact that such sick stories had deliberately been put about was almost as twisted and bad as if the crimes had actually taken place.

Later still Pat told me that he had spoken to one of the local Police Colonels whom he knew personally: he'd imparted limited information very reluctantly. (We had the strong impression that locals were ashamed and embarrassed by this whole situation and none of them volunteered information – they had to be asked). He confirmed that the rumours were not true, but that yes, someone had gone missing in February – not necessarily suspicious circumstances – they just didn't know. Also, as we'd heard, yes, a woman had escaped from white slave traders, but was too distressed or drugged to be interviewed. Decided we'd never get to the bottom of this.

All day I'd heard strange loud wailing-type singing over loudspeakers. Many of the Masses at the Basilica were sung, usually very well, and broadcast over the tannoy, but this was different. Sounded like a muezzin singing Maori songs or African chants. (Please excuse confusion of cultures.) Aida told me that it was from the small park opposite the Basilica and was apparently the Passion of Jesus, sung in Tagalog, from a book, as it now was Lent. Later: Party and food good - everyone had brought something and Aida did lots of lovely desserts!

Next day, Saturday, Pat had his first Saturday morning off for ages but in fact he had to go into office for a meeting. Aida, by arrangement, came in for the morning to do the clearing up. What luxury! We never took her for granted.

I went to the Craft Fair for a couple of hours; not as large as the one in Manila, but it was good and deserved supporting – hopefully it would take place again, maybe on a regular basis. Prices were very reasonable but we managed to spend a fair bit of money. I bought a cotton dress for £2.50 and a lovely evening camisole and matching little jacket for £1.50, plus two limited-edition prints and masses of bits and pieces.

In the evening, with Hilary, Ken, Saj, Aisha and Des, we went to a display of Philippino dancing at a local school; apparently they'd performed in the States, France, Holland etc. We were the only expats there in a crowd of maybe two thousand, and we were ushered into the front row. It was WONDERFUL BRILLIANT SUPERB SPECTACULAR – difficult to find adjectives to describe it. Totally, completely professional, and yet also fresh and enthusiastic – it was mind-blowing and we were all gob-smacked. The costumes were amazing, the dancing incredible – similar to Thai or Indian in terms of hand-movements, but the Spanish influence clear in some dances. (The Philippines had been administered by Mexico, for Spain, for many years...)

The staging was very simple, as was the lighting, to offset the colours. Some of the dances were extremely acrobatic and my only regret is that we were asked not to take photos, but would be given an opportunity later to do so, which in fact we weren't. It was the best evening we'd had since we'd arrived!

Seen by Pat few days before: jeepney driver, with jeepney full of passengers, filling up at petrol station. Engine still running, smoking a cigarette...

Latest jeepney names – jeepney sign-spotting became a bit of a cult with Pat and me – 'Pontiac' 'God is love' 'Marshmallow' 'Peace-maker' and – don't ask me – 'Pork Chop'.

Sunday morning we went to a Tagalog Mass as we'd been out last night. As usual the car park full of people who couldn't get into church. Festive atmosphere; there were still lots of Graduation ceremonies taking place and the balloon-man vied with the flower-sellers for the most colourful display.

Balloon Seller Batana

Home for P to do some studying but he hadn't been working long when the lights went out. Aisha and Des still had light so it was obviously our fuse-box again – so much for supposed permanent repair carried out two days before. We rang our landlady; she sent an electrician within the hour who carried out what we hoped would be a permanent 'permanent repair'...

Shell Club for an hour in the afternoon; I didn't swim as I still had slight throat problem and tickly cough – didn't want to jeopardise Friday's musical afternoon, though glands had gone down and I felt fine. P and I walked round the complex – it was really gorgeous. Mainly Philippinos lived there now, not many expats.

To local Police Colonel's in the evening, duty visit to his eighteen-year-old son's Graduation party. We were sure it would just be the icing on the cake, to have present obscure business contacts of his Dad's. Not. Party was in garden, two hundred or so people there. The music blared out at about one million decibels and it was impossible to talk except in the few seconds between numbers. We were with eight other expats at 'top' table right behind band. I already knew five of them; the others, American guys, seemed very nice.

Pat spoke to one of Police Colonels yet again, who'd brought in official report relating to rumours and crimes. It appeared that there had been a couple of missing persons, reason as yet unknown, and there had been a multiple murder the previous week, for which they had arrested three men. (Whether they were the right men or not is not known!) The lady who'd escaped the white slave traders had been en route to take the Police to the place where she had been held, but had 'felt ill' en route and so the Police had taken her to hospital instead...

Some days later we heard from another reliable source that in fact Police reports had been fabricated for some reason unknown. If you've lost the will to live trying to follow this saga, join the club. One thing was clear: as expats we were told only what people wanted us to know...

Arrived home to find that lights were ok, following earlier visit by electrician, but air-con was not working. Called landlady; her son came over at 10 p.m. but couldn't fix it. They'd send electrician the next day. Again.

27 March. Phone call from Maryann, whose family I know from our church in Reading; she's been doing voluntary work out here for a month or so. Her family are coming out to visit her and she and her Mum are coming tomorrow to stay with us for a few days. Look forward to getting the latest news...

Spend the morning painting. After three weeks or so with no chance to do so while the boys were here and so on, it's lovely to settle down again and experiment. Took a bowl of fruit up to my hobby area on the landing two days ago and have been eyeing it up since then, just dying to get started on a water colour but no opportunity over weekend. Must do it today before the fruit goes rotten! Best thing about painting fruit is that you can eat the models after...

Many people here have absolutely no sense of safety whatsoever – accidents are deemed to be meant to have happened; there's no sense of personal responsibility or of cause and effect. Which is leading up to the fact that we saw a jeepney yesterday full of passengers, lots of them also sitting on the roof – nothing new about that – but right on the front there is, up top is, with its parents, a baby... Ken and Hilary had day over on Mindoro yesterday. Apparently they travelled on the FastCat hydrofoil, and were horrified to see that once the passengers were seated inside, the captain put out plastic chairs in aisles, and crammed the passengers in like sardines. There were lifejackets under each 'proper' seat, but the others not. He proceeded to fill the fuel tanks with jerry cans from a parked jeepney, the driver of which was, yes, you've guessed, smoking a cigarette...

We have TORRENTIAL rain this morning and the yard is flooded; I go out there to find Aida still doing the washing and put my foot down. Washing machine is under small corrugated roof, and on sort of pallet, but yard is couple of inches deep in water and I just don't think it's safe. Ask her to wait till later.

Bowling this afternoon; Ladies' Club has been quiet since we arrived; Hilary and I are both trying to get people doing things, and now that so many expats are leaving and are not being replaced, it becomes even more important to mix. Eleven people in all, at least seven different nationalities and everyone chats happily. Am not keen on bowling but don't mind supporting it from time to time.

Sunny smiles

Oh, Doctor I'm in Trouble...

Ring Pat in office; tentatively say maybe I should see doc tomorrow as still have this tickly cough and wheeziness after over a week; wonder if it's an allergy. Within half an hour doc appears! Confirms my glands are still up, probably allergy – maybe to moulds in air-con system - which get circulated every time it goes on. Gives me prescription for medicine – thankfully not for antibiotics...

They seem a bit free with antibiotics here, and you can buy them, and lots of other things which are on prescription in UK, in the pharmacy. In fact, even worse, at a local petrol station, Pat saw a jar, like a sweetie jar, full of assorted bits and pieces of medication. It was obvious that people had taken in their left-over medicines... 'Bad cough, sir? No problem, I'm sure I have something here – yes look, and it's only a week or so out-of-date', or, 'Piles, missus? Well, we're out-of-stock at the moment but you could try this calamine lotion. There's probably enough if you just scrape the dried out bits with a sharp knife'...

With Pat, do food shopping for expected visitors and for Ladies' Club on Friday. Can't find proper cake tins. To pharmacist for medicine – 'All gone'. Try another, successful this time. Doctor has prescribed 'a tablespoon' three times per day and there are no instructions for dosage with bottle; I realise he means dessertspoon, as he said 15 ml.

Nothing exciting in cupboard or fridge so make fish-cakes with instant mash, tin of sardines, seasoning and chili sauce. We eat it with tinned mushrooms and my last jar of cherry peppers and it's surprisingly good...

Reluctantly I had to tell Aida she must finish with us soon. Not our choice, and we'd waited for weeks to see what would happen. If I'd waited any longer I'd miss my opportunity to have Purita as our maid, who'd been Ellen's maid and who is also fantastic. We were really sorry to lose Aida, and have told her so. Spent the morning baking for our visitors...

Afternoon had third of four piano lessons – I found it so difficult – far more so than when I'd learnt to drive – there was so much more to remember. Suppose the only thing is that you can't kill anyone with a piano – not unless you throw it at them anyway. Why is it that I practised at home, and yes, I did practise, then I got to a lesson and I was all over the place. There was one particular exercise that I always ended up with one finger left over…

Later Lito took me to meet Melly and MaryAnn who'd be staying for a few days; they were church friends from Reading. No problems collecting them – in fact they arrived a few minutes before us. Pleasant evening at home chatting, drinking and eating – joy! – English choccies which they'd brought with them.

Melly, MaryAnn and I went out next day; Pat had managed to lay on extra driver, bless him. Not much choice; we went to Eagle's Point. Reef pool was drained for cleaning, and no-one seemed to know where resident sharks had gone. Lots of rubbish – mainly paper, some plastic, in sea – certainly wouldn't have wanted to go in sea while it was like that. Complained; suggested Management should take the boat out with net and clear – it was all close to the shore, and the shingle beach was totally littered. Later we noticed some of it had disappeared. We swam, ate, drank, went down the slide, and MaryAnn snorkelled. Pleasant, relaxing day in spite of torrential rain for an hour in the evening.

Melly suffered from slight dehydration and sunstroke; Maryann and I dosed her with re-hydration salts, water, and banana – very good as it replaces lost potassium. Saj came in for drink after dinner.

Melly and I braved the dust and heat and walked to Citimart next morning. Melly was well-travelled, and had been all over the world but this was her first time in the Philippines. She was amazed to find just how 'third world' it was.

Tanja came in after lunch for English lesson and we explored the delights of past simple, then MaryAnn and I went to the Shell Club for a swim. It was school holidays now, the schools had April and May off and went back in June so there were some children in the pool. No problem; we had a good swim and relaxed for a bit before returning home. I had a run-through of my songs for the next day and moved furniture round in preparation. Hoped it would go well…

The Lounge in the Villa

31 March. The Big Day! Busy morning preparing food; Aida does her special mango layer pud, her daughter Gigi bring plates of beautiful, tiny, pastel-coloured cakes and they prepare here (so Melly can watch) masses of coconut pud. Only problem is they make such vast quantities of everything and we give a lot of it away – Aida takes some home for the family, we give some to the drivers. Coconut pud, for example, takes three pounds of grated coconut, one and a half pounds of corn-flour etc. etc…

Anyway, there are sixteen of us, of eight nationalities, so it's very cosmopolitan. I do three numbers; MaryAnn does a solo and a last-minute duet with Lea, my piano teacher. We have a round, a quiz with silly prizes, and finish the musical part of the afternoon with six-part rendition of Schumann's (not the famous one) 'Orchestra Song' which I've done before with audiences, and which is great fun.

Aida's last official day; so nice that she can join in. She's coming in tomorrow for a few hours to get everything up-to-date for new maid. Food really good; instead of going out for Melly and MaryAnn's last evening, we bring pizza in, Saj joins us, and we consume the left-overs.

Safety, Spiders and Soft Porn

Pat was MC for a prize-winning ceremony for a local school art competition on the theme 'Road Safety' at a local hotel. Melly, MaryAnn and I all went along and it was quite enjoyable. About three hundred people there; it went off very well. Excellent prizes, lots of excitement, super choir to entertain us and a very praise-worthy theme. Hoped all concerned would spread the word, as safety standards in all areas were very lax. Speaking of prizes, the first prize was a complete computer package, and just before the event one of the FW managers had just logged on to make sure everything was operational. He'd found he was in a soft porn programme, which needless to say he immediately removed...

Next day I took Melly and MaryAnn to catch coach to Manila where they would meet husband Jack and son John at the airport. We'd enjoyed having them here; I'd miss them. Quiet afternoon, English Mass at 6.

Sunday began with the appearance of a BIG spider on window of bedroom, which played hide and seek with Pat for half an hour, jumping behind blinds when he went near. Don't normally kill spiders but thought it may be politic, and two insect sprays and a rolled-up newspaper later, Pat succeeded. I felt quite guilty but was glad Pat was here to deal with it. Morning in with odd jobs and tidying, so new maid had an easy start next day. I experimented with bread-making using ordinary yeast, which had Melly had found in one of the shops.

Afternoon Pat and I went to the Shell Club for swim and sunbathe. It was the first fresh air and sunshine we'd had for several days – it was lovely to be out-side. FW office had no windows so Pat only saw daylight when he was out and about; my only fresh air and exercise was when I went to the Shell Club during the week. Otherwise I was indoors almost all of the time – walking was not pleasant as the streets were far too hot, dusty, dangerous - in places with no pavements - and too polluted to walk far.

3 April. Purita's first day as our new maid. Pat and I are really sorry to lose Ai-da but Purita is lovely too. She's been looking after Ellen, Eugene and their two little boys, all of whom absolutely loved her. Also she's a very good cook; her spring rolls just melt in the mouth...

Finish making a pair of shorts which I cut out yesterday; we're going over to Mindoro, nearby island, this coming Friday for long weekend and I realise I'm desperately short of shorts. So to speak. The idea is that it will give Pat much-needed break before I go to UK on leave. The trip, that is, not the shorts. Very little food in house so for dinner we have Spam Lite (again!) with sort of stir-fry made from diced potatoes, two left-over onions, chunk of ginger coarsely chopped, two sliced green peppers and a sliced sayote, which I don't think exists in UK. Guess what? It's delicious! The food situation is challenging but I enjoy making meals out of what little food is in the house. (Most of the time!)

Next day I helped Saj to interview Ruth, new maid who is friend of Aida's and who worked for Ken and Hilary for short time. (Good maids got circulated round the expat community, like English newspapers and magazines – neither of which we could get in BC.)

To Shell Club for swim; read in sunshine for short while. For dinner we ate the most delicious spring rolls which Purita had prepared that morning. She'd also dug the tin of rambutans (like lychees) out of the cupboard and had added them to a fresh fruit salad which she made without being asked...

Next day was pleasant: morning meeting of those willing to get actively involved in Ladies' Club. I volunteered to take over activities programme when Liz left. Quick lunch at home, then art lesson. Only me there for water-colour and we did a still-life with pots. Sketch no problem but painting was more difficult – absolutely no technique. Could only get better! Just me and a young lad for charcoal class; then just as we moved on to our first portrait, tutor had to leave – someone had driven into his car just outside the hotel where lessons were taking place. Both parties had to go down to Police Station to sort out insurance report. One lesson to go, the next Wednesday, before my UK leave.

Evening Pat and I went round to dinner with Carol and Hobby. We felt ashamed when we saw how nicely they, or maybe Carol, had decorated and furnished their home. It was modern and light; Carol had painted everywhere white, with lots of ethnic touches, and gorgeous rattan furniture, which we already planned to buy too. Our house was traditional and rather gloomy – for coolness – but I found it very depressing. Only exception was my lovely landing, though, which was light and spacious, with beautiful view of the basilica. My den...

View of the Basilica from the Landing Window

Tropical Island

Very pleasant evening. Another couple there we didn't know – American too. Lovely meal; fresh tuna steaks, green beans and wild rice served in pumpkin wedges, followed by American cheesecake with sour cream topping. YUM YUM. Dodong drove us so Pat could have a couple of drinks. We still couldn't get used to having a maid, and a security guard who opened car doors, ferried shopping, and swept path, all unasked, plus use of driver when we wanted.

On the way to Carol's we'd seen a jeepney which took the record for overcrowding: the inside was full, and there were about fifteen people hanging on round the top. Dodong said it was probably off to one of the mountain villages and as not many jeepneys go there, people don't have much choice. It turned off the main road and headed up the hill, the outside passengers hanging on for dear life, and its one working rear light disappearing into the night... Hope they take roll-call fore and aft but I doubt it...

Felt a bit fed up next morning; not sure why. I enjoyed my mornings – 'my' space, but whole days were very long while P was at work. Felt too down to sing. I imagined the neighbours were jumping up and down with pleasure though... Experimented a bit with charcoal which I enjoyed.

Pat popped in as usual for quick lunch, which broke up the day for us both. He'd seen a guy on a bike with his dog sitting astride the crossbar, paws on handlebars, looking happily around him...

Anong and Tanja came round for English lesson, then I went for a solitary swim at Shell Club. Did thirty lengths just in time; we had an absolute downpour. It would have been difficult to swim in such heavy rain but the real problem could have been with lightning; thunder had been hanging around. Felt better for swim and fresh air, but what about the next day - our long-awaited trip to Mindoro; hoped the weather would be ok – there'd be no point in going if the weather was like this, as there was nothing to do but beachy things. Watch this space...

Saj came round, and we finished Purita's lovely spring rolls. Pat and I packed for our long week-end away, fingers crossed... Torrential rain continued all evening. We slept like logs.

The Island

Friday 7 April to Monday. Mindoro! Go on earlier ferry as one we'd originally intended to use is out of service. Travel out, and three days later back, on overloaded ferries, as Ken and Hilary did the other week. Extra passengers on small plastic stools in aisles below decks, and in space on small enclosed deck. Refuelling of ferry takes place, what's new, with operator smoking cigarette...

Stay in one of most up-market places on island, having exchanged dark room downstairs overlooking wall, to an upstairs suite overlooking the sea. More expensive, but worth it. Island bit seedy, but charming, and we switch off for three days. Dinner two nights in hotel, one meal good, one uneatable so switch to sort of Australian transport-type beach café further along beach. Excellent food here, piping hot and inexpensive. Only hitch is one evening when I just fancy a roast. No problem, choice of four different meat roasts on menu. Ask if I can have roast, but substitute, instead of meat, vegetarian burger which is also on menu. 'Sorry, too difficult.'

Sunday Mass in small chapel, walls open to fresh air. Singing nearly lifts roof off. European missionary priest says Mass. See fierce-looking, mean-eyed black German shepherd dog swimming around looking worried, trying to mind his flock of small children who are messing about in water.

Take banca, local outrigger, to other lovely, isolated beaches. Buy my own snorkel, and snorkel from said boat out in 'Coral Garden'. Not successful as I have problems with mask, get into real difficulties and can't snorkel back to boat - can't swim either as reef sandals make swimming proper very difficult and we've drifted with the current away from the boat. I need Pat's help to get back to boat – he drags me, he and boatman haul me aboard. Scary. Very. Feel quite shocked. Snorkel off beach to restore confidence. Scenery gorgeous.

Philippinos seems to spend a lot of time sweeping – Aida used to; it took ages as often they just use a bunch of twigs. We wonder if it's some sort of mindless soothing ritual, but that's just surmise. We see a hotel waiter raking the strip of sand near hotel gate (there's no litter) and another waiter sweeping seaweed from rocky area on beach…

Arrive back in BC mid-afternoon Monday, feeling different people compared to when we left on Friday. Break has done us good…

Pat was now on leave for a few days, but had to go into work for an hour or so next morning, then spent rest of morning working at home. Afternoon we had a lovely swim at Shell Club and relaxed in the sun after with a coffee. On way back, we saw a bushman obviously down from the mountains; jet-black, bare-footed, and stark naked apart from tiny loin-cloth and bushman's knife hanging from his belt.

Back home, where Pat continued to work. I reminded him he was on leave, but he pointed out that if he was in the office he would get continual interruptions; this way, he got far more done, and would take time off in lieu. Fair enough.

Tinned ham for dinner with instant mash, processed peas, jar of red cabbage and can of asparagus. Not worth Purita bringing in loads of fresh veg that day or next, but she'd be shopping and cooking just for Pat as I was going on UK leave. Although I loved cooking – and improvising – it made more sense for Purita to do more cooking anyway; she loved it and could bring fresh ingredients in with her in the morning. She and the other maids obviously got better prices than the expats. She'd also learned how to use the bread machine!

12 April. Pat still on leave but has to go into office. I fine-tune packing for UK. Am looking forward to it – obviously – but wish he could come with me. It's too expensive, though, and will take up too much of his leave.

Third and last art lesson in afternoon – for time being. Traffic appalling; the ten -minute journey takes about forty minutes. Learn to use charcoal, and start another still-life with potted plant, and small painting of rice-fields from a photo. Remo tells me my 'anatomy is very good.' Think he meant my art…

Finish preparations for UK. Thos Cook, with whom FW work a lot, have said they'll try to get me an up-grade. No promises. Never managed one yet, but it would be so nice… Suddenly realise I have no sterling to get from Heathrow, and no-one will accept pesos. Difficult to get dollars tomorrow but Saj comes to the rescue with loan. Phew! Panic over. And that, dear readers, is where I leave you, for the time being at least.

TO BE CONTINUED. Possibly…

Oh, ok then: you've talked me into it...

I had an awful journey to UK starting with chaos at Manila airport, but an interesting situation occurred: Philippinos, although gentle, charming and pleasant for most of the time, have a great capacity for violence. Perhaps in recognition of this, there is a very strong moral obligation on each Philippino to act as peacemaker if necessary. I'd read about this, but saw it for myself in action in the airport.

Queues meandered around to the Check-In desks in a somewhat haphazard fashion. An argument broke out between a European and a Philippino passenger. The European insisted that he was there first, and called the Philippino a liar, whereupon the Philippino jabbed the other in the legs with his baggage trolley and down went the European. It looked pretty unpleasant for a few seconds, when suddenly, out of the queue, and from two totally different directions, a Philippino gentleman and lady suddenly materialised and started to calm down the irate Philippino. One patted him soothingly on the shoulder, and the other murmured calming words, so that together, within a very short time they had totally defused the situation and then they disappeared back to their places. I was fascinated --and very impressed.

On the journey, the only other thing of note was that, having paid exit taxes as instructed beforehand, and having queued for some time to get out through Immigration, I was told that for some unexplained reason I had to pay another 1010 pesos, which I had not been told about (Thomas Cook do all our ticketing and documentation) and which I did not physically have on me. It was already take-off time, and I was the only passenger for the flight who had not been allowed through. Total panic (on my part). The authorities kept referring me backwards and forwards to each other, not caring, not helping, not hurrying up. I was desperate for a wee and gagging for a drink of water. Finally, a little runner, one of two who was trying to help, grabbed my credit card and rushed to the bank to get pesos, while I rushed to the Ladies and begged a drink of water from someone as 'I feel so faint'. (Not true but I was desperate.)

Finally helpful runner grabbed my bag and hurtled through the airport with me following close behind. I was last on the plane – they were waiting for me – and we took off - half -an-hour late. I was mortified!

Great leave in UK. Lovely to see family and friends again, and catch up with all the news. Met our new lodger for the first time, and visited tenants in the flat which we'd recently bought from Gerry and which we rented out. Hectically busy, both socially and with lots of jobs and paperwork to attend to, much of which had been building up for almost four months. Quite run-down and low when I arrived in UK, for whatever reason, still with intermittent swollen glands and with infected gum which necessitated removal of wisdom tooth. Improved throughout the leave and managed to fit in lunches, meals with friends and couple of parties, breakfast birthday party with friends, visit to London, loads of shopping, and singing in couple of concerts for elderly folk. High spots of leave were – of course – seeing family and Linda, my longest-standing friend, with visit to see renovated Covent Garden opera house. I thought that Floral Hall was magnificent.

Plumbing problems whilst home: two radiators jammed. Twice. Called the Gas Board to fix. Twice. 'It's them thermostat rads, see, love, they always do that.' Suffice to say that the third time, when I was rushing round on the last morning of my leave, they jammed again but I fixed `em myself with the hinged end of a stapler. Also gave son Ben a tutorial on the subject; hoped that would be the end of the matter. If not thank goodness for Gold Star insurance cover with the Gas Board. It's peace of mind yer see love. End of commercial...

Singing lessons again – I had at least two private lessons each week, plus several repertoire lessons with small group of friends. Delighted to hear from Anthony that my vocal efforts on my own had paid off – he saw distinct improvement. Worked on upper B flats throughout leave but great excitement during final lesson, when, en passant during vocal exercises, I managed a top C sharp!! Impressed, huh? I knew you would be...

In Performing Mode

Karaoke Carry-on

Long, tiring, but reasonable journey back to Manila, where Pat met me and where we stayed for weekend. Was very relieved, as was Pat, that Lufthansa hadn't charged me for my excess baggage, which should have amounted to £150. Went and bought some paperbacks to celebrate!

It was lovely to see Pat again and to enjoy the luxury of the New World hotel. Tracked down a multi-system TV and video, which we bought, and couldn't resist another purchase – a Karaoke machine!! No, don't laugh; I hadn't taken leave of my senses – it was exactly what I'd been looking for over two years. Panasonic, tower-type about four feet tall. Good quality sound with large speakers. Meant I could practice/record my music and use for proper backing ...

We returned to B.C. Sunday afternoon. Supposed to take other FW guy down with us, but thankfully he opted to stay in Manila and come down later. I say 'thankfully' as when Dodong arrived to take us back, we had the utmost difficulty fitting everything in the car. There was Pat, me, Dodong, and four shop assistants trying to shove everything into a medium-sized saloon car. The boot was already almost full with large, rigid suitcase, large holdall, bulging music briefcase (me) and briefcase (Pat). At this stage I broke down in hysterics and giggled manically, pausing briefly only to take photo before collapsing in giggles again. In the end we had to take TV and karaoke machines out of their boxes. TV was wedged sideways on front passenger seat, video was inserted into boot, and karaoke machine tower was wedged between Pat and me on back seat for duration of journey. We literally couldn't see each other and I spent the entire journey (record timing thankfully – marginally under two hours) unable to move, with it leaning heavily against my shoulder..

Pat set up all our new toys during the evening and we watched video of small concert in which I'd taken part during my leave. Although we rarely watched TV it would be great to see all the videos which we'd brought out with us.

12 May. Our en-suite loo and guest loo not flushing; one of double sinks leaking badly. Landlady advised, who contacts plumber. First meeting of the new Ladies' Club committee. I'm to help with charity co-ordination with two other ladies, and possibly to arrange the events calendar. Meeting productive;

lots of ideas bandying backwards and forwards. New brooms etc.

Afternoon catching up with journal, letters, and painting. Ring Remo re lessons, but he's too busy to start again this month; will do so next month. Arrange with Aisha to go to Alabang tomorrow for food – we'd planned to bring some down from Manila but just couldn't fit anything else in car! Had planned to do some music this afternoon but landlady, maid and plumber were all here for couple of hours – latter doing necessary plumbing, others just 'supervising'.

Next day I had lovely time in Alabang with Aisha, getting luxuries like decent bread (!) also wholemeal bread-flour which we couldn't get in downtown BC, and then some essentials like karaoke tapes(!!). Real coffee in one of several delis, and lunch in another. What bliss! Good journeys both ways, only two hours in spite of flooded roads in places –we'd had absolutely torrential rain on and off for days. And the rainy season hadn't even started yet.

Purita told me that the sink was leaking again so had summoned plumber who arrived at what would be singing time. Here we go again. Purita, bless her, had been cooking for me all day as we'd invited friends for meal – her famous spring rolls for starters, fish curry with rice and side salad, and an enormous fruit salad for afters. There'd apparently been a brown-out for most of the day so we turned fridge up to maximum and shoved everything in till later.

Successful dinner party in the evening. Food delicious – what a treat and a privilege – to have a pleasant day out and come back to a dinner party prepared by someone else! Des and Aisha came, Saj, Nigel, who was with Pat in Oman and who'd arrived here a few weeks ago, and Steve, visiting from Thailand, who'd very kindly shepherded Gerry and friend around, and wined and dined them when they were over there during their travels.

Raining again next day – nay absolutely pouring. It had been tipping it down for most of the previous few days. Some of the locals seemed to wear summer clothes with wellies but I drew the line at that. One had one's standards to maintain… Anyway, it was a shame about the weather as it was the Ladies' Club lunch, about an hour's drive away at 'Mermaid's Hideaway' which belonged to a Philippina married to a Brit. They'd just opened a new resort there – small hotel with swimming pool built onto terraces in the cliff. It would have been lovely on a nice day but I guessed it'd be pleasant anyway.

Yes, it was. Weather mixed but we had a good old natter; I was now in charge of coercing people into organising things, non-specified, to try and maintain our sanity. Those of us who'd had it in the first place! Speaking of which: during the proceedings I'd been to the Ladies'. Couldn't find the light switch, and there was no window so it was very dark. I'd held the door open while I oriented myself, then locked it (obviously) and in the dark managed successfully to locate loo and basin. Emerging I'd realised that I still had my sunglasses on…

Got promises from different people to do one-day Mah Jong workshop, calligraphy session, pizza-making session, and book circle, besides the usual weekly play-group. I was planning a decoupage, 3-d greetings cards/pictures, session which I loved doing, plus, surprise surprise, at least one more music afternoon. There was to be weekly bowling for them wot liked it and I had to agree with someone who commented that there seemed to be a more friendly and positive atmosphere in the group generally than when I'd first arrived.

Had planned to use up Purita's delicious spring rolls for dinner, but changed my mind and kept them for tomorrow, when I realised that the lovely Brussels sprouts I'd bought in a deli in Alabang had cost £3 per pound!! So we had sprouts for dinner, with fresh potatoes (courtesy of Pic 'n Save) and proper bacon – also from the deli! Yum… With our new video player Pat and I were watching half-an-hour or so of 'Dance to the Music of Time' each night. At that rate it would take us weeks, but it was excellent; Pat had already seen it twice…

Torrential, incessant rain again – it appeared we were on edge of typhoon – wouldn't have liked to be in the centre. Some local roads flooded, bad flooding in Manila. Afternoon with Aisha checking prices in local supermarket so the Company could hopefully, review package and situation in BC. Some things were cheaper than Manila, some unavailable. Watch this space…

Next day started well with call from Gerry. Lovely surprise! It was pouring with rain again – chucking it down. I had a hectic morning with frequent phone calls – many of them re Ladies' Club. Cuppa with Aisha in the afternoon and we decided to check out the Avon shop, same company as in UK, as it looked quite good from outside. Didn't normally use their products in UK but they must have been better than the very basic supermarket brands here which seemed to consist mainly of 'whitening lotion' or 'whitening cream'. So, what first? The good news or the bad? Ok then, the good news first. Well, we found a stationery shop which was quite well-stocked – certainly the best, if not the only stationery shop here. Looked for but couldn't find, sticky bits for decoupage session, but joy! Found thick double-sided adhesive tape which would do nicely thank you.

Right, the bad news: the Avon shop was really down-market. Shabby, with half-empty shelves, cheap and nasty packaging and limited goods. Like I imagined a provincial Soviet Russian shop in the fifties – no, probably not quite as good as that! Ok, well at least we'd tried. Come back Alabang, all is forgiven.

Des and Aisha suggested meal out that evening with us and Saj at a local eating-place. I agreed reluctantly as we'd had so many poor meals in BC and we'd actually stopped eating out because of this. (Manila was different – good international hotels with European standards – and prices.) Pat and Des were very specific – ordered in advance to make it easier for staff – and specified sizzling-hot. Well, the fried rice was hottish but tasteless, salad croutons were literally stale cubes of toast which had gone soft, the fish was hottish but greasy, the chicken was sizzling-hot but a lurid bright red and tasteless, and the steak was also sizzling hot but like leather. I just ate a few mouthfuls, the others not much more, and – this has a happy end – we put the rest in a doggy bag – Pat's idea – and gave them to two stray dogs.

Saturday. P works till 1 p.m. I sleep in till 9 – latest ever down here. Reason, awake ages in night, as was Pat – and later we hear, Saj. Put it down to MSG in food – it's happened more than once when we've eaten out. That or upset tums – take your pick! Keep busy with journal, beaver away with some art. Am hooked again! Another singing session; have managed several this week. After lunch P and I go to Shell Club; don't swim but walk briskly round perimeter, not far, maybe 1 kilometre. Sunbathe and coffee. English Mass, dinner, then to newish bar to meet some of the others, expats. Walk home, early night.

Purchases and Pizzas

Sunday was an exciting day! To Lipa – about 40 minutes' drive, to check out small family place which made high-quality rattan furniture. P thought it would make the villa more homely – it was quite formal, and we didn't have anywhere really comfortable to sit – we could take it back to UK when we finished. Saw some nice stuff; decided to go back in the near future to do a spot of bargaining. Pizza, real pizza, really nice, in Pizza Hut,. Height of luxury for us after BC - Pat bought two nice pairs of shoes in sale for £20 (total) and I bought two good quality tee-shirts and sun-dress for about £1.60 each.

Sign outside a local cemetery: 'OPEN DAY TODAY'. Don't ask me…

Art afternoon. Working on some pen-and-ink/wash sketches, which I was really enjoying – I was looking forward to starting my art lessons again when Remo had time.

Weather was incredibly hot – seems hottest I'd known it. 31 degrees in Manila, whatever that was in 'real' temperature. Suffice to say it was really dripping hot and humid – the humidity was the worst thing. Aisha and Anong came round for a chat; Anong didn't stay long as her three-year was somewhat lively, shall we say?

Quiet evening with P. – almost finished 'Dance to the Music of Time'. I must say that, though I never watched TV or videos in UK, it really was a godsend, and if we were not going out, we had dinner upstairs where we had a small dining table, and watched a video. Dinner was yummy – fresh broccoli and potatoes which Purita had brought in earlier, with last of bacon from Alabang. Cooked all dry and crispy. Just wanted to share that with you!

Tanja came round next morning for English lesson, but we just had a long chat as we hadn't seen each other for about five weeks. P. came home for snack lunch as usual, bringing with him FW visitor down from Manila for meeting. Afternoon I'd planned a swim but in fact transport was a problem today and instead I spent a pleasant afternoon doing art and singing, plus preparing for 'Music and Fun' afternoon on Friday. (Fat chance of any fun chez Colbeck…)

Evening was a party with contractors, at Shell Club. Chance to meet some of the new people out here on the Project. Good party, hot food – not very tasty, but hot, for which we praised the staff lavishly. Good music, albeit loud, and it was interesting to meet some new people.

24 May. Aisha, Carol and I meet lady who has asked for help from the Ladies' Club for her son, John-Larry, who at eight years old is thought to have had a stroke. Discharged from the local hospital; nothing more they can do for him until and unless he has an MRI scan in Manila. Father unemployed, so they hope we can help. Three of us go to Hospital on spec and three paediatricians give us almost half an hour talking about John-Larry's case. We'll talk to Ladies' Club and hopefully get their agreement to release some money.

Trip to Hospital was an eye-opener. Very basic equipment, very shabby, counted at least five stray cats strolling around in the corridors. Food hawkers, lots of people hanging around. See tiny baby, born one month ago, two months premature. So sweet – hope he'll make it. Afternoon just sun-bathing at Shell Club. Have to confess I nodded off as it was really hot and I was tired…

Spend the next morning preparing for music afternoon. That is, Purita does all the hard work with cooking whilst I do the fun stuff like wrapping parcel for pass the parcel, test the backing tape for the umpteenth time etc. etc.

Twelve of us in all, which is a reasonable number, especially as two ladies are in hospital, one is sick-visiting, and one is leaving so is up to her eyes. As before, I did a short entertainment – 'Old-fashioned Girl', Music Hall medley, and 'Why do I love you". In spite of that (heh heh heh!) I think it went well – people said all the right things, but then they would, wouldn't they? Superb food – besides Purita's delights, other people brought things too and I ended up sending food home with everyone. Evening is party at Anong's. Des and Aisha have drinks with us first then we walk round. Food delicious – thank goodness for Thais!

On Saturday Pat was working: Hilary and I drove over to Lipa to visit Mandy in hospital; she'd just had the most enormous ovarian cyst – and an ovary – removed. Was cheerful but obviously not feeling so hot after such major surgery. Lipa Hospital magnificent after BC; Hilary and I decided to make strong representations to FW to use this one or Manila. Local private hospital was really only suitable to be a first-aid station. Coffee in a fast-food joint – even this was luxury after BC. Pat finally arrived home about 3 p.m. and after lunch worked on his studies. English Mass at 6 p.m. then we drove to the Japanese restaurant from which we'd planned to collect steamed veg and rice to supplement green curry left over from party at Anong's. Only problem was that restaurant wouldn't steam meal (they had done last time) and as I didn't want fried meal we came out empty-handed. Back home for dinner out of tins...

On Sunday we went to Lipa in morning as Pat and I were still not sure if we wanted rattan furniture, or if so, what. Had chat again to couple whose business it was, collected quotation, and came away to consider till next weekend. Swam at Shell Club after lunch; coffee and sunbathing by pool. Lovely to be in the fresh air. My first swim for about seven weeks. On our return we saw a religious procession leaving our estate with majorettes, band, beauty queens, and statue of Our Lady on dais... Fiesta later; Pat and I popped down to see part of disco dancing competition and musical chairs ...

Flower Sellers

Aisha and I went to Alabang the next day, for coffee, lunch, and shopping, plus more comparing of prices for Company comparison list. Total panic in supermarket when I lost trolley: searched everywhere, couldn't find it so started shopping again from scratch. Only problem was that list was in first trolley. Did as much as I could but realised I couldn't take any perishable or frozen food back as we'd been warned of 24-hour brown-out 10 p.m. that day till 10 p.m. the next day...

Pat and I, plus Des and Aisha, opted to go to hotel for night. We could – perhaps – have managed without lighting, but I personally couldn't have managed without the electric fan. We rarely used the air-con as it was so noisy, but at temperatures of about 31 degrees and more, and high humidity to boot, the fan was, to my mind, an essential. Was surprised that not many of the others followed suit. Dinner first at home – meal at the hotel was not to be undertaken lightly. Drink in bar with other expats, then early night.

Brown-out continued all the next day. Cancelled Tanja's English lesson and my French conversation with Nicole – it was too hot for comfort. Saw from TV that Manila temperatures had been 31 – 35 this week. Most days only New Delhi had been hotter. Spent quiet day at home pottering and trying to keep cool. Dinner at Caltex Club in evening. Stopped en route to deliver something to Trish, who persuaded us to have pre-dinner drinks. Power finally came back on 11 ish in evening.

Inside the Basilica

Nature Notes...

...for you nature lovers out there: I loved the vegetation in the Philippines – coconut and banana palms everywhere – so tropical! That month, there had been really gorgeous trees in bloom, all covered with scarlet blossoms. Also a few trees covered with bright purple flowers – Hilary had one just outside her door.

Hadn't seen many interesting birds, but had seen what looked like a kingfisher one day, also small bird with long beak which looked like a humming bird. The crickets made an incredible amount of noise; all started and finished together on some secret, pre-arranged signal. Really! It was strange. Also the previous week or so there'd been an incredible racket from frogs (or toads maybe – read on). The other night P and I had seen a huge toad hopping along the road into Aisha's garden which was about nine inches long. The toad, that is, not the garden. Aisha saw it too, the next morning – splattered on the road. Shame...

P had told me several times about the office mouse (or mice – how do you tell them apart?) We'd been sitting quietly in the office the other night, and I'd been doing my e-mails, when this little mouse appeared on one of the desks. Disappeared and re-appeared on top of some files, then popped up under a filing tray. We were fascinated – watched it for about twenty minutes, but the piece de resistance was when he – twice – climbed up a polystyrene coffee cup, hung inside by his back legs, and sipped the cold coffee dregs. He was so sweet!

The other Wednesday should have been in Manila at monthly craft bazaar, but American Embassy cancelled it for security reasons following recent bombs in Manila. Tanja, incidentally, was actually in Mega Mall when that bomb went off. She and husband were in a shop – there was an explosion followed by panic. People were injured in the stampede —some with broken arms and legs. Tanja and co locked themselves into the shop and waited to be rescued, some twenty minutes later, by the Police. They supposedly have picked up the instigators, about thirty people, many from the military and the Police. Incidentally, to give you some idea of the enormity of the problems out here, 60% of Manila Police live in squatter camps, and are paid less than our security guards, which is very little. (Not our choice – read on.)

The Company got down an independent security consultant from Manila the other day; he thought that the political and economic situation was deteriorating, and that although he felt there was little specific danger to expats, nonetheless we should all be taking extra precautions. Hence, we had extra locks and bolts, and remaining un-grilled windows had grills fitted. Also now one security guard daytime and two at night, to look after us and Aisha and Saj on either side of us. He felt that our major danger was actually just from petty crime, so, as we were already doing, we shouldn't wear jewellery out, shouldn't stick to a routine when going places, and it would be best to avoid the local markets. Most of it was just common-sense stuff but in fact many expats didn't respect these guidelines and some of the expat companies there just didn't seem particularly interested in security. FW, happily, was very security-conscious.

Which brings me to my earlier comment: our security guards came from the agency which does security on the Site. They did twelve hours on, twelve off every day, for peanuts, and NEVER had a day/night off unless they requested it, when, we suspected, they were not paid. P and the Company had looked at ways of improving the situation but the problem was that they knew full well, if they insisted that a guard had day/night off and paid them for it, they would just work somewhere else for that session anyway.

Some interesting occurrences from expat community: Philippino Office Manager went to investigate non-delivery of concrete and found that the problem was no sand. Reason; the supplier's lorry was being prevented at gun-point, from delivering... A local crane company was very put out when an expat company got in a crane from a Manila firm. The Manila crane was found with its tyres all shot through, but luckily the local firm were able to step in and do the job. Surprise! We heard from the Philippino Manager that a domestic flight was high-jacked in mid-air. The pilot was told to fly elsewhere but didn't have enough fuel, so was told to go down to 5,000 feet. The hijacker divested everyone of their valuables and stepped out of the plane, parachuting to the ground, but unfortunately not to safety, as the parachute was home-made and didn't work.

We got lots of wrong numbers on the phone – and some suspect ones - so weren't surprised when the phone rang at 3 a.m. the other day. P answered it, paused, then picked up a whistle which he kept right near the phone and blew it with all his might down the phone. Yup, it sure was an obscene call but I'm not going tell you what the guy had said. Suffice to say that we were both sniggering so much we couldn't go back to sleep...

Security guy came down again from Manila. Confirmed that overall situation – economic and political - was worsening. Hostage crisis continued in Mindanao but he said that economically it just wasn't sustainable to maintain attacks against the Abu Sayyaf (Islamist separatists) – it would have taken twice the Philippine GDP... In fact, I'd recently heard on the TV that at least one island in the Philippines, Coron Island, had been granted independence. Maybe this would have implications for the future...

Special Delivery

Mah Jong and Mamba

Mah Jong workshop at Hilary's with lunch in Caltex Club. Twelve people there, most of us new to the game. Several games through the day, by the end of which the basics were starting to become clearer. Very cosmopolitan as usual – about ten nationalities there today.

We had an invite to one Nestor's house for 'fiesta' – fiestas going on all the time just now in different barangays (small sections of town – like electoral wards). Turned out to be just Nestor, P, me, Des and Aisha. Very elaborate meal – ladies of the house (and nephew!) had obviously been slaving over a hot stove all day – but none of them joined us – it wasn't the custom. Nestor produced whisky for everyone and urged us to 'help yourselves to wine'. Des was driving and Aisha and I didn't like same so we made polite noises and opted for water all night.

Next day we organised a last-minute session with DI (dance instructor) at Aisha's next door – she had even more room than we had. Ten ladies attended; DI, Benji, friend of Lea's, was very good. We all warmed up then did cha-cha, swing, and started the mamba. Really good afternoon – I ended up translating into both French and German for different ladies (obviously!) which added to the fun. Everyone wanted to do it again – soon – so we fixed a date.

Tripping the Light Fantastic

Pat and I went to Alabang next day, (Saturday) in afternoon, where we failed to get a suitable exercise machine, which we'd been chasing for a week or so. Had a look around and bought food and goodies for street children's party on Monday. Grabbed a sandwich which we munched in car on way back – it was really much too late to have set off for Alabang – you needed a whole day, but we couldn't manage that.

Sunday. We'd been invited to a wedding - one of FW Philippina office girls marrying an Ozzie, in the Basilica. Interesting – 36 people in bridal party. Arrived at reception a little late, with Des and Aisha, Genelle and Mark, after a pre-reception drink chez Des. All seats seemed to be taken, so we discreetly left. Home for snack and over to Shell Club. Walked round grounds and sunbathe – didn't swim as number of children in pool. Pleasant afternoon.

Quiet, pleasant morning next day chez moi. Prepared games for children's party this p.m. Trish collected me with a sack of goodies and off we trundled to Mcdonalds. It was actually Shirley's little girl's second birthday party but a number of ladies (me included) and children had been invited, plus the fourteen children who were in an orphanage locally. Great party, lovely children, loads of fun. Arrived home somewhat exhausted!

6 June. Tanya comes over for coffee: she will be leaving sometime in July. Most of the Siemens guys have already left – quite a lot to Mexico, which I imagine must have marked similarities to the Philippines!

Afternoon is pizza-making demo at Carol's. Just eight of us there. Carol is what I think of as a typically traditional American 'home-maker'. Makes her own yoghurt from starter which she brings down from Manila and then uses to make muffins etc. etc. Anyway, back to demo. I've often made pizza, but Carol's is better. We eat said pizza with glass of red wine – very civilised.

Evening: landlady comes round to discuss various jobs we want done. Din-dins with fresh veggies from Alabang, video, bed.

Next afternoon there was a Ladies' Club committee meeting at Carol's. Lots to discuss, including 4th July party (we'd be on leave – Murphy's Law), helping John-Larry, the little boy who was ill (Trish had taken him up to Manila to the Children's Hospital the previous week, and to a local specialist the day before, who recommended an ?echogram? so we were proceeding on that) and the barbeque that Friday to raise money for John-Larry. Busy morning, home for lunch and small group of us did decoupage in afternoon. Just five of us, Peruvian, NZ, French, Portuguese and me – I relished the cosmopolitan atmosphere, more about that in a second. We pooled ideas and materials, spent pleasant afternoon making greetings cards and chatting.

To digress: when I arrived the majority group was German: though the ladies were very pleasant, they didn't mix much outside their own group, and there was little happening socially. Now English-speakers were in the majority and were extremely friendly: there was now a lot going on. Hilary had commented the other day, how things had changed for the better – in that respect at least!

Latest jeepney name worthy of note is 'Unexpected Edition' – imagine they meant addition…

Mireille came next day for first English lesson – not many more as she and husband were leaving soon – she was here unofficially as her company didn't send accompanied men. After lunch to Hilary's for Mah Jong. Twelve of us. Game was starting to make sense and I would continue when I could. Not my first choice of activity but better than, say, bowling, which I refused to do.

I was a bit fed up all evening; didn't know really why but guessed I was tired of filling my time with things just for the sake of doing something. Didn't feel I was moving forward with art – teacher too busy with his company – and although I worked most days at my singing it was difficult to see an objective. Missed my e-mail too! I felt virtually incommunicado. Still, things were better than during my first stint – people were friendlier, and more ready to join in.

June 9. Meeting here re 'Quebala' which is a meeting of various expat Ladies' Clubs from all over the area – takes place every few months. Our turn to host this time; we need to decide location, catering, and format - hence the meeting. Only three of us have remembered said meeting, so we discuss possibilities but can't make decisions as we have insufficient information.

Calligraphy session this afternoon at Janet's – she's not an expert but did a short course whilst on another posting; it's fun to pool what knowledge, talent or skills that we have. She tells us that she and husband have to move out of their rented house here at three days' notice as agent says 'FW wants to rent house'. Hilary and I are outraged and I phone P to sort it out, which he does. It appears to be sharp practice on the part of the agent – it happened also to the house next door to Janet – what a co-incidence – the two landlords are related. Anyway, on hearing this, FW pull out of the deal. Quite right too. A very pleasant afternoon, just six of us, and we finish with martinis and nibbles. Quite civilized!

Evening is the barbie for John-Larry; takes place at Trish and Colin's who have the most enormous house you ever saw, on the Caltex compound where he is Manager. Good party, about 50 expats from different companies, which is a refreshing change – the Ladies' Club used to organize these 'do's' in the past but this is first time since we've been here. P and I've organized just a couple of games – passing oranges under the chin (chins in my case) which has everyone is hysterics, and then handball with balloons, predictably filled with water. Everyone mixes well and has a good time. As usual out here, it breaks up early – most people gone by 10 pm as most of the husbands are working tomorrow.

View of Distant Basilica

Saturday. P had to work longer as they were all moving to the new office on Site, instead of present location which was a mile or so away. The building contract had had to be given to a local company: gap under door couldn't be rectified as when door opened it jammed on sloping floor, just to quote one instance...

Hilary, Aisha and I had all had the Batangas Blues at some time during the previous week or so. Arranged to go to Lipa, had coffee in Pizza Hut, looked round the shops for an hour-and-a-half, bought a few bits and pieces, pizza in PH, visited supermarket. Better than B.C. P worked all day on the office move, as did most of the others.

Cats – the Musical...

We had absolutely torrential rain for an hour or so, with thunder and lightning seemingly right overhead. Pat finally came home tea-time and told me that there was a foot of water down the main street and even the car park at Batangas Plaza Hotel was flooded – in spite of the flood ramp at top of slope. (Colleague told us later that he saw rats in life-jackets rowing furiously across the car-park!)

Trip to see Boy Scouts Variety Show in the evening, a very short walk away but took the car in case the rains started again. As usual, we arrived on time and as usual the proceedings started 40 minutes late. Well, the show. There was a lot of talent there, and obviously everyone involved had worked their socks off. We particularly loved all the dancers – traditional and modern – and especially six little kids, three boys and three girls doing Latin American. You should have seen those hips! The kids were absolutely delightful.

But – two big buts. The last item, which should have been the climax was an interminable play about the environment and it lasted about half-an-hour - far too long – about twenty minutes too long to get across the message about respecting the environment. It was in Tagalog, but even the locals looked bored and we practically had bed-sores.

The other but – an enormous one – was that there was no concept of noise pollution. The louder the music supposedly the better and sometimes it literally hurt your ears. (In shopping malls and shops it could be appalling). That night, true to form, it was painfully loud throughout, much of the time accompanied by whistling and screeching from feedback. Everyone seemed oblivious to it, except the expats, but it ruined the show for me, and in fact two young children with lovely voices who did solos, just didn't come across well. Shame.

One thing that kept P and me amused was watching the stray cats chasing around throughout the show. One stage-struck feline went twice up the steps onto the stage but got stage-fright and then changed his mind...

Sunday 11 June. Mass this morning in Tagalog as we couldn't get there last night. Pat studies all morning and I prepare lessons for seven-year-old Roy, a

Dutch boy, whose parents are out here with Shell. The Shell school here is closing as the teacher is posted to Nigeria and the six or so children are leaving, but not Roy. Can't do it on a regular basis but don't mind doing a one-off lesson or so though as they are stuck at present.

We go to Shell Club after lunch. Walk round grounds; it's roasting hot and there are children in the pool so we just sunbathe after and read. See several birds we've never seen before – black and white with long beaks – interesting – must try to find out what they are. Home to make pizza, inspired by Carol's demo last week. Used to make it in UK but this is first time out here. Yummy! See 'Wag the Dog' on video which we enjoy. Only a quiet day but it's been good...

12 June. Philippine Independence Day so few locals working. Needless to say, expats are working and are incredibly busy – the office move, started Saturday, continues. Mega problems on the Site – there has been a strike for several days of one particular (local) firm, who haven't paid their workforce. Reason, no money. Can't easily change contractors as all steel is locked up in yard of said company. As I say, this creates mega problems and no-one knows what will happen – high level meetings yesterday and this morning. Watch this space...

Surprised on this public holiday to see landlady turn up with engineers to overhaul air-con which is incredibly noisy. Each room at moment has large gaping hole in wall. They carry each large unit out into the open actually to clean and service. That has to be an improvement – you should just see the dust and filth on each one and left behind in their housings!

Give Roy an English lesson; he's bright and it goes well. He departs happily with smile, packet of crackling candy and plastic dinosaur. Must remember that with my adult students... Torrential rain again this afternoon. I have afternoon in sewing and try my hand at pastry – first time over here, but although not bad, not good either. Flour seems different – sort of silky-ish and slightly damp feeling – like corn-flour, which they use a lot. Maybe it is. Must experiment...

P arrives home just after six, which is great, to tell me the main street is flooded – again - and small children are wading almost up to their waists. No doubt they think it's great fun, but I think I'll pass on that one, thank you very much!

We hear that Genelle, newly-arrived FW wife (Australian, husband Brit) has had her purse stolen in Manila. It was pouring with rain and a lady offered a 'lift' under her umbrella to cross the road, which G. gratefully accepted. Half-way over she felt jostling but didn't think anything of it till she reached the other side, found her bag open and a newly-bought t-shirt was missing, plus the purse in which she keeps her small change. It's common for pick-pockets to work together and create a distraction. Makes you cynical…

Next morning Tanya and Bianca came for English lesson. Bianca, sitting in on Roy's lesson yesterday, had decided that she'd like English lessons too. Afternoon should have been dance session with DI at Anna's, but DI didn't show up so we played 'Taboo' instead which was hilarious. Six of us, two Brits, two Philippinas, Mina, Portuguese and Gisela, Peruvian. Good afternoon!

Pat had to go to Manila next day for several appointments, so I opted to go with him. Good journey thanks to new road which was now officially open; piles of ballast had been removed but verges and central reservation were still unmade, and there were no service stations, emergency phones or lighting, so nothing else had changed. I did some shopping while P was busy; we snatched a quick sandwich in between his appointments and I joined him for his last appointment, with the British Council. No time to do hoped-for food shopping; we had much-needed Italian meal in shopping mall and headed for home with Dodong. Fantastic electric storm kept us entertained for much of return journey – magnificent lightning – both sheet and forked – around the mountains and behind the palms. Watched it for ages. What a show!

Spend the first part of next morning getting music and quiz ready for next day's 'Music and Fun' which was to be preceded by Gisela's farewell Peruvian lunch. We had an unwelcome visitor – an enormous, but ENORMOUS – spider, on the inside window in the lounge. Purita hadn't arrived, security guard was next door so I photographed it(!) and waited till he came back. He confirmed that it wasn't poisonous, as did Purita when she arrived soon after, so I left it where it was and just kept a weather eye open… Aisha came round for chat and cuppa; she was off on several weeks' leave the coming weekend so I'd miss her, but then fortunately I would follow soon.

Just a Wee Anecdote...

Something amusing happened to Pat a few days before: Remember that bit about, quote, doctors and nurses have seen everything before, so never feel embarrassed when going for medical treatment? Yes? Right:

Pat went for a routine medical check-up, which included a urine test. British nurse in charge sent him to Philippina nurses to get specimen bottle and thence to loo to produce said specimen. When he explained to said Philippina nurses why he was there they immediately went into paroxysms of giggling. British nurse in charge came in and said to Pat – 'Where is it then?' and he had to say that they didn't believe him and couldn't stop laughing. When P finally obliged (in privacy!) they clustered round to see litmus test like it was something good on the telly... These were professionals! It was seriously weird...

I had a swim at Shell pool then short sunbathe (had lost my tan almost completely as I didn't get up to the pool very often during the week). Joined P in office where we waited for delivery of office table. I collected my e-mails during this time and sent some brief replies. Home, to start packing for Manila and for forthcoming holiday, as it would be a busy week.

An irrelevant aside here: the land there was extremely fertile and just about anything grew – frequently more than one crop per year. The place could have been the garden of Asia, except that few people had the organizational skills to set up an export system – and to be fair, too, they were greatly hampered by the appalling corruption. If I'm repeating myself I apologise...

Anyway, to continue: it was a tragic indictment of the economic situation that the greatest source of revenue for these islands was the money sent back to support their families, by Philippinos who had gone to work abroad – so-called Overseas Contract Workers. These OCW's – like Aida, our last maid – worked abroad, where they could earn more money, as waiters, maids, cruise attendants, nannies and in other domestic posts – and frequently had to leave their own children to the care of other members of their (extended) family. It was an iniquitous system, and funnily enough just a few weeks before I'd met a Philippina, a head teacher of an elementary school, who was then writing a book on the educational problems faced by the children of these OCWs. Not surprisingly, they achieved less educationally than the children whose parents had not had to leave them to work abroad.

Tanja and Mireille came next day for English conversation. We were invited to a dinner at the Shell Club that night and my heart plummeted. In UK – or anywhere else, I loved eating out, but there, we'd been disappointed so many times. Anyway, there were only the Managers and wives going to the dinner, to talk with visiting FW VIPs, and we had very little food in, so I would go along.

Pat arrived for lunch soon after 2 pm – he was making sure arrangements were in place for Sponsors who were arriving in Manila next day from all over the place – arranging hotel, meeting, travel and so on. I taught Roy again in the afternoon; P rushed in for quick shower and over to Shell Club to check arrangements for the evening; I followed with driver about 7 p.m.

It transpired that arrangements for next day's Sponsors' meeting had fallen through. The ship from which operations were directed, and which they were to visit overnight, had broken down so they couldn't go over there. The Sponsors were flying in from overseas, many at least from Europe, so those who could be caught before they left, were requested not to come. For some, however, it was too late, including one of the biggest big-wigs, so we still had to go to Manila to meet him and entertain him overnight. I didn't want to be done out of my shopping trip – had also planned visit to hairdresser…

Well, at the dinner it was like being back in the army, when regimental dinner nights were an occasion for a three-line whip, and when you spent the evening making animated small talk to people you didn't know, with every appearance of enthusiasm. In fact, the people concerned were all pleasant but it was difficult when you didn't know who fitted in where – this being my first Project in the field, so to speak, I felt at a bit of a loss.

The food – well, the food. The staff really had tried their best; it was obvious they really had made an effort. The food was well-presented – it looked good, and it was hot, so that message had got across. But what I had – a tiny bit (my choice) of grilled salmon, was greasy and flabby (how could you get grilled salmon to be flabby? Must have been a trick of the trade.) And my veggies were suitably al dente but with a film of grease and little taste. Pat and I agreed that, with Philippino food, everything tended to taste the same. Bianca, a very sweet Dutch lady, volunteered to me yesterday that the Philippinos seemed to have the knack of taking good food and getting the worst out of it... I filled up with two helpings of fresh fruit salad – delicious and for which I complimented the staff - and came home to toast and honey.

Pat left for work next morning soon after 6 a.m. – he had a busy morning looking after the VIPs before we left for Manila at midday. Midday – one o'clock, two o'clock, three o'clock passed and finally Pat managed to get home. We left the house at 4 p.m. and estimated that, with the new road now accessible, though not officially open, from Lipa to Manila, two hours should be fine to check into our hotel and give Pat time then to get to airport to collect very VIP.

Problem: we had a tropical, really torrential, rainstorm. Local roads were badly flooded and it took us four hours to hotel. Saw people paddling up to their ankles in water and we knew one particular local road would be impassable, so we took the other route. Saw hilarious sight: we'd stopped in the middle of a traffic jam on flooded road, and a tricycle chugged by through the water. The tricycle was named 'Sea-farer' and the driver was wearing a Titanic T-shirt...

P had arranged limo to collect VIP so we arrived at hotel just ten minutes before VIP arrived from airport. Phew! Cutting it fine but luckily everyone understood the transport problems. We had drinks with Ian, the visitor, and then P and I had a meal in a French restaurant – one of several different restaurants in the hotel. This hotel was one of several really top-class hotels we'd stayed in Manila – possibly the most stylish. You can tell I was getting a bit blasé, though, 'cos I no longer grabbed all the freebies; I'd got quite selective with 'em. Grown-up or what?

21 June. Nice breakfast in hotel, then P has appointment with Ian at the Embassy so I disappear downstairs and have my hair done by Mr Edwin. Luxury – how nice to be pampered after you-know-where. P and I nip to supermarket for a few fresh veggies to last us till we go away. Buffet lunch then back to BC, bringing Ian with us. Good journey this time – two hours – exactly half the time of yesterday. We hear that FW guys took two hours to get home through the floods last night, instead of half-an-hour...

Every time we go to Manila or Lipa, we pass a particular poster hoarding which I always think deserves mention in this epistle; it must have taken hours – nay, days, of brainstorming to come up with this. Bet some-one got promotion out of it. The advertisement is for National refrigerators, and the slogan is as follows: 'National refrigerator. Always with you.' Wow! Pithy or what? What can I say?

Spend afternoon doing bit of hand-washing for hol (if my public could see me now!) and working on new repertoire. Absolutely love one particular Mozart piece, 'Widmung' (loose translation 'Dedication') - have been working on it for about a week. The neighbours must know it off by heart!

Pat comes in and it's over to Caedo where FW are bowling - one of the young FW guys has couple of teams on the go to enter local bowling competition soon; it's been well supported apparently but we're not interested. Tonight we go to chat and show solidarity. Nice to see people; we stay an hour and go home for supper.

The following morning I went over to Mireille's, with Tanja, for coffee. Both would have left by the time we got back from leave – both of them were desperate to go. Mireille told us that twice in a few days, her basement had been flooded – with dirty water – to a depth of about 30 inches. Yuk.

Should have been at Mah Jong this afternoon but decided to stay in and make denim wrap-over skirt from material from Alabang. Skirt has cost less than two pounds sterling to make.

We had THE most spectacular electrical storm that either of us had ever seen. Once again we had torrential rain – heavier than ever, but it was the thunder and lightning which were so magnificent. For maybe half-an-hour, the sky was lit by vivid mauve light, and time after time we saw forked lightning split the sky from top to bottom. We sat on the landing and watched the show for about twenty minutes – it was incredibly exhilarating. Suppose it was pretty commonplace in this part of the world, but we saw lightning - and thunderbolt – strike dome of Basilica, which, very surprisingly to us, remained unscathed.

It had been standing since the 1600's so I guess it had been built for this sort of weather.. We heard later that part of a local refinery had been struck by lightning and had caught fire. Saj came round to dinner – really delicious, spicy fish curry, made by Purita, and followed by fresh fruit salad – ditto. Delicious!

I'd kept the next day free, knowing we were going away the following day. It turned out to be very pleasant: I finished my wrap skirt, and was very pleased with it, then Trish turned up unexpectedly to collect promised Airwaves chewing gum which I'd brought back from UK and which she loved. Hedi, Hungarian, fluent English, phoned to say she'd just finished a proof-reading course in English, which she also did in her native Hungarian. Could I please go over her finished exam with her that afternoon? No problem; it would be a pleasure.

Later in the day we had a visitor! Small, furry, tabby and white, and so cute! Obviously abandoned; we'd heard him crying for several days now on and off, and twice the guards had taken him food for me. This morning I dispatched Rod to look for him and take him food, as I could still hear him crying, and he turned up holding this tiny bundle of feline fluff by the scruff of the neck. His eyes were open and he was pretty lively (the kitten, that is, not Rod) so I was sure he'd be ok, although normally he'd still have been with his mum.

Purita and the guards were lovely with him; Purita made him a bed in a washing-up bowl lined with an old towel, but he preferred to explore and to sit under the air-con outlet. I warned them all to be careful with bites and scratches, as rabies was always a possibility, and tempted though I was, I hadn't handled him yet. Call me wimp but I preferred to err on the side of caution…

Phoned Pat at work to tell him and he was less than enamoured; he hardly had time to blow his nose let alone worry about a cat. (That's a very loose translation of what he said.) Anyway, he arrived home, took one look and was captivated. Outside, near guards' table we found a small box with aperture torn out of side, filled with some sort of fibrous material. In answer to our question Rod replied that it was a 'comfort room' (Philippine term for loo). All mod cons etc. What a load of scribble – almost a page written on the little visitor. Couldn't decide whether to call him 'Willow' (as in Pussy), Catkin, or Feisty, 'cos he was…

Post holiday

First, Bangkok – it was busy, bustling, sprawling, shabby, exciting – what I thought of as a typical Asian city, if there is such a thing. There were more signs of developing prosperity than in the Philippines – even looking at the vehicles told you that. In the Philippines many of the vehicles on the road were decrepit and not roadworthy – including public transport. In Thailand most of the vehicles looked well-maintained, and the Government there was trying there to bring in crash helmets for motor-cyclists. Many of the riders were wearing helmets – though not all with the straps fastened, and in Ko Samui it was another story again, but it was a step in the right direction... Pat saw a general improvement since he'd been there a year ago, and Hilary and Ken, whom we met during dinner the next night, (they were co-incidentally there too for a few days), saw very obvious signs of improved prosperity since November.

A highlight was a river trip lasting three hours - out in fast boat, return in converted rice-barge. Spectacular temples and buildings, but we loved seeing the daily life of the people who lived on and along the river - people washing-up (yuk), fishing, buying and selling veggies from the narrow boats – brilliant - our favourite memory of Bangkok. Sunday Mass was in English, in a beautiful white-painted church, constructed and decorated in style of a Buddhist temple – all gold-leaf, filigree, twirls and Oriental motifs. So unusual to see a church built to blend with the local style of architecture; we were most impressed.

Candles before the Buddha

Evening buffet at the Oriental, one of top Hotels in Bangkok, on the river-side, watching lights and boats. Lovely. One small problem: I developed gastro-enteritis during the night and had to see doctor next day as we were moving on and I couldn't dash between bed and loo on a plane. Happily the medicine worked and tho' I felt fragile the next day, we made it to Ko Samui.

Ko Samui is lovely – it's a small island in the South of Thailand. We arrived at a diddy little airport, which is a tiny airstrip surrounded by lush vegetation and bougainvillea. The airport buildings consisted of several thatched huts and we were ferried the couple of hundred metres over there in a Disney-style blue and white open train. The luggage was brought over manually and everything was welcoming, charming and efficient.

Hotel was lovely—largest swimming pool we'd ever seen in a hotel, specially one on the sea as this is. Some of the accommodation was in rice barges – not ours – but people told us later that in fact they were quite dark inside. Our room was very colonial, with balcony, and overlooked beautiful gardens, where, a few days later, we saw a snake! Oo-er! We were very excited...

The beach was lovely; we were in a small, very pretty bay. We found a tiny beach which we had to ourselves most days. In fact, it was so hot we limited our actual sun-bathing to sensible limits but we both loved the sun and we felt so good and so relaxed in such beautiful surroundings. Lying on the beach one day we were thrilled to see four eagles circling overhead. They obviously thought we were possible prey and we kept still as long as we could to watch them. When we moved their hopes of an early lunch disappeared; so did they.

Lots of tropical butterflies fluttered around, and tiny birds with long beaks and bright green throats. It was also very sad to see a large raccoon-type creature in a cage not much bigger than itself. It appeared to be some indigenous animal, maybe aggressive and almost certainly very sharp-toothed, but I remonstrated gently with owner's friend (owner not around) and suggested that he should point out to the owner that living creatures need space to exercise. Maybe he let it out at night – even on a chain that would be better. I hoped so: it was awful to see animals of any sort in small cages.

Several semi-domesticated dogs lived on and near the beach. We were extremely careful about them as rabies was rife, but in fact they were quite sociable and delightful and one particular one loved to go in the sea with any reasonably friendly holiday-maker – he just seemed to like the company. Sweet!

One day we did a half-day tour of the island, and although it was interesting, it was a bit touristy for us and we preferred to do our own thing. Gerry had been there years before, when it was totally off the beaten track; we were disappointed to find there was quite a lot of building in progress and it seemed at risk of over-development in the reasonably near future.

Island Shopping...

We saw two adults, two small children, and puppy, on one motor bike. Not a crash helmet between them, not even the pup…

Most evenings we had dinner in a beach-side restaurant – often watching electrical storms and lightning flash around the bay, though in fact the day-time weather was gorgeous for duration of holiday. Lights all around the bay; it was so pretty. One evening we saw a Polynesian(!) dancing show, which was enjoyable, though slightly marred by a very American commentary.

Pat and I treated ourselves to some personally-tailored clothes: Pat had a tropical suit in cream linen mix, I had two pairs of silk trousers, long skirt, short-sleeved jacket and tunic – in navy and mid-blue, so it was mix and match. We had several fittings and finally took delivery 15 minutes before we left for the airport. What with that, and with me locking us both out of room in the middle of packing, things were bit fraught, but we gained access again just in time.

Back to the Toy-town airport. Checked in then through Immigration to 'Departure Lounge' – other half of thatched building. Just time to pour complimentary coffee – but not to drink it – and the Disney train whisked us over to waiting plane. The runway was too small for jets, with very pronounced dog's-leg – so it was propeller plane again. We took off half-hour early and flew lower than in a jet – all down the coast of Malaysia. Stunning views.

Singapore – wow! Sophisticated, cosmopolitan, well-ordered, spectacular buildings, loads of shopping malls, good night-life, clean streets, organized traffic, not a Policeman in sight, and no armed guards anywhere! Not a typical Asian city, and I knew that some people found it too sterile and clinical, but we loved it. Singapore didn't have as many resources as our friends in the Philippines, and had then had only forty years of independence – that in a dictatorship, whereas the Philippines had had a hundred years of democracy and independence and had achieved very little. We all knew the reason – corruption.

So, back to base: We visited Raffles twice for drinks, once in the famous Billiard Room Bar where legendary tiger was shot, and once in the Long Bar. Met Aisha, who came from Singapore, and who was home on leave, for Indian meal on river. Saw Indian dancer/singers; interesting, but we didn't come out humming any of the tunes. Lovely to see her, then P and I did a river-trip. Beautiful city anyway, but at night, with all the lights and the skyscrapers, and dozens of brightly-lit restaurants, it was just magical.

No time for day-time visit to zoo as both P and I had one day's illness each – in my case it was the buffet again. But, BUT, we did the night-time safari there, which was then unique in the world and which was great. You walked, or rode in silent electric trams, along tracks from which you could see the animals, seemingly in the wild, in simulated moonlight. Lions, tigers, cheetah, giraffes, elephants, buffalo, etc. – all confined in their spacious jungle enclosures by judicious use of unobtrusive moats, electric fences and so on. It was brilliant.

Fine Dining

Back to BC.

All good things come to an end and we had a good flight back to Manila. Arrived to find that there had been two typhoons raging during our absence – one from the East, one from the West. They'd had incessant rain for a week, and Manila was flooded: we drove through floods, though the driver chose his route carefully, and at one stage it was between two and three feet deep. One poor guy on the pavement was almost up to his knees…

Lovely weekend in Manila. Favourite church, in the round, situated in park, for Mass. Did lots of shopping including food for return to BC. We had two suitcases, two rucksacks, two cameras, two bottles of water, new lap-top bought in Singapore, box of groceries, and about eight bags of shopping. We never believed in travelling light…

9 July. Good journey back to BC to find our lovely little kitten got run over about a week ago – we're very sad, but not surprised – he loved to play in the road. Purita has house spotless as usual, and big bowl of fruit for us. Rod, our guard, is waiting for us. We hit the ground running – cook dinner for Des, as he's on his own while Aisha is away, and Saj joins us for drink so we can catch up with all the news. Saj brings bundle of mail for us – joy oh joy!!!

Apparently, the Client offices in Alabang were ransacked last week in protest against fuel prices. Forgot to tell you earlier in this journal that same offices suffered attack from rockets and machine guns at the end of last year. Ah me! How tedious life is out here…

Stayed in the house all next day; literally didn't set foot outside, but for once it was no problem. Pat was catching up at work – everything has a price - didn't get in to lunch till 2.45 ish, but at least he could normally get in, which we both appreciated.. Kept really busy with this journal (I needed it more than the recipients!), letters, last bits of unpacking, altering skirt and trousers bought on hol (not the tailored ones), piano, and of course my singing. Normally have a good bellow 7.30 – 8.30 in the morning, before Purita comes and while there's only one guard on duty.

Dinner at 'ome: smoked salmon bought from Alabang on Sunday, good bread ditto, and salad, followed by Purita's excellent fruit salad. Why does food feature so much in this journal I ask myself, and answer almost immediately, well I guess it's that a. nothing much happens, and b. we can't take it for granted as much as we might do in UK. Pat and I discuss arrangements for Murder Mystery Party we're having this weekend – should be a laugh, and to my knowledge no-one has done it yet out here. Watch this space…

Morning chez moi which wasn't a problem as I knew I'd be going out later – that's the way I liked it -singing, journal, and letters. Rod, one of the guards, turned up with badly swollen eye; someone had apparently elbowed him when he was playing basketball yesterday evening. He insisted it was ok.

In the afternoon I went out with Trish, Hedi, Jo, and visiting lady Shirley. We had an appointment at the local Government Hospital, where a tour had been arranged for us so we could ascertain how/if the expat ladies could help. The doctors we met seemed extremely nice and probably very competent, but it was an awful place, shabby, depressing, and in parts at least downright filthy – the delivery room in the Maternity Department was worst of all. Had been to the paediatric ward once before, when I'd counted five stray cats in the neo-natal area but today I saw only one kitten.

We were horrified to learn that there was approximately 100% tax on medical equipment… Trish and Jo, both trained nurses, said that there was a noticeable improvement since the last time they'd visited the place, but the other three of us, laymen, were horrified by the lack of hygiene. Relatives or friends had to stay with each patient to look after them, as basic nursing care was non-existent – there was one nurse to about twenty-five patients. Equipment was less than adequate. Back to our place to talk things over about how we might help....

Spent the evening, or rather P did, almost installing e-mail, but we had problems so he opted to take it into work the following day, where someone would help. One step further anyway… Home-made thick lentil soup, home-made bread, and fruit salad for supper. We must have been bustin' with vitamins!

Next morning I had my usual vocal warm-up and bellowed even more assiduously than usual, as I thought I might have found a useful music contact;

Was going to see him later. Spent an entertaining half-hour making silly notices for the Murder Mystery party on Sat, which was to take place in an Italian restaurant. . Hence, 'Pleesa, no speeting' 'Donta aska for credeet' 'Signor, pleesa lifta da lid' etc etc. Small things amuse small minds etc. – too late - I said it first!

Well, it was an interesting contact I made – but the voice coach he suggested was in fact the one I'd heard about when I first arrived. He came down from Manila once a week to teach, but on Sundays, which was my only full day with Pat. So, back to square one, but he promised to try and think of someone else.

Anyway, through the Ladies' Club I got to hear of a prominent local family who were very musical. Their ancestral home, as it was termed, was extremely well-preserved and Pat and I had really wanted to see inside it. I rang up one of the family, an elderly gentleman called Tony, who was friendly with some of the expat ladies, and explained I was looking for a Bel Canto voice coach; did he have any suggestions. He invited me over and that's where I went yesterday.

First, the house – it was gorgeous - traditional Spanish style, built about 1883 in grey stone, covered in thick ivy, with capiz-shell screen windows. The style was called 'Bahay na Batu' – house of stone. President Tate, the American president, had slept on the enormous four-poster bed: there was still a bullet embedded in a door jamb from a gun wielded by a disgruntled Philippino who took a shot at the President and missed. When the Japanese had invaded Luzon the family had fled to the mountains, living in very hard conditions until the war was over. They returned eventually to find their father's house burnt to the ground, but this, their mother's house, still untouched.

I waited downstairs in a sort of baronial hall, stone-flagged, with white plaster walls, huge peeling wooden doors, carved oak banisters and a number of parlour palms, about seven foot high, in stone pots. The wide, wooden-stairs were completely dovetailed - no nails - and there was a black-and-white-tiled area just off the landing. Upstairs, it was a huge open area, sort of L-shaped, all polished wooden floors, traditional wooden furniture, capiz-shell windows open to the street, and photos of the ancestors around the walls. Tony showed me his late mother's bedroom with carved oak four-poster bed, chipped enamel wash-basin, and hand-painted oil lamp. I was bowled over.

Ancestral Home

Back to Tony, a delightful, charming gentleman, who'd given me an hour in a very busy day, and who, like the rest of the family, was very proud of his house. He was a semi-retired lawyer, had studied music at University of the Philippines, piano at Julliard in NY and voice with Pavarotti's teacher, no less. He was a concert pianist and he proceeded to play me some Chopin and some Mozart – all from memory. It was just wonderful, and I had tears in my eyes at one stage!

He sang me a couple of show numbers which he enjoyed for fun, and then I sang for him. Thought I'd be petrified in such illustrious company, and sure, I was a bit nervous just at first for the start of 'Widmung' but I settled down and he was so nice that I really enjoyed myself. Even did a Music Hall medley for him with taped accompaniment, just for a giggle! He organized concerts once a year – and invited singers, including Charlotte de Rothschild, from overseas. The last one had had 160 in the audience – told you his house was large! The British Ambassador was a personal friend, and the Duke of Gloucester had visited his home. I felt so privileged.

Shopping trip next morning getting food for the MM party – Purita was doing the fruit and veg part of it at the market for me. The trip was complicated by heavy traffic caused by damage to roads during the heavy rains the previous week – in places the road was just disintegrating, and there were holes along the side of road. Pat had seen a tricycle driver drive into a hole in the road the previous day, who had to be towed out.

Afternoon Maj Jong at Hilary's. Very pleasant, nice crowd. Forgot to say that Pat, Tanya and Carol had each seen four-foot lizards crossing the road recently – Carol at least three times – I was very envious!

14 July. Spend the afternoon at Trish's; sixteen of us there. Trish, with help from ladies on the Caltex compound, makes the most incredibly beautiful quilts which she then sells/auctions for charity. They're a cross between collage and patchwork and anyone lucky enough to get one has an heirloom on their hands. Anyway she's suggested that the Ladies' Club should do one for the same reason, and we start it this afternoon. It's to be ten-inch squares, background unbleached calico, and each square has a bear, colourfully dressed, and doing bear-like things – cooking, shopping, gardening and so on. Mine, predictably enough, is a diva-bear…

Couscous and roasted veggies for supper – Pic 'n Save have more expat goodies each time I go in – with Purita's delicious banana cake for pud. Am I making you jealous?

Murder Mystery

Saturday. P at work for most of day. I spend a very busy, but very pleasant morning getting ready for Murder Mystery party this evening. Purita has made the lasagne – not your common or garden one; this is a new recipe I want to try, with bacon and just a tinge of orange zest! - and I continue with Tiramisu a la Batanganean, white bean and garlic dip, minestrone salad, red onion and rosemary Boboti, olive focaccia, roast Med. vegetables. Humorous signs to go up around the 'Italian restaurant' which is the setting for the party. Costume ready – I play the widowed Mama. P will be the spiv-type son.

Party is great fun; there are eight of us, most in costume, all entering into the spirit of the thing. An absolute shambles as far as the Murder Mystery goes – one couple arrive twenty minutes early, before we're changed, one couple arrive twenty minutes late which normally wouldn't matter but in this case it holds up the proceedings. One couple forget their glasses and have to borrow magnifying glass and reading glasses from P to read their clues and instructions, and one lady, Malaysian, speaks very quiet accented English which we can neither hear nor understand. But apart from that everything goes with a swing and is hilarious…

The next day, Sunday, we lay in till almost 9 a.m.(!) then cleared up from the party; we ate the leftovers for lunch and dinner. Quick visit to Pic 'n Save in the afternoon and a stroll round the estate to get some fresh air as our hoped-for swim hadn't materialized.

Walking round the estate we heard loud twittering, cackling and rustling in the trees, looked up and saw a cockerel and hens up there near the top of a twenty-foot tree where they were obviously roosting. I was sure they couldn't fly but we saw them lurching from branch to branch…

Shopping next morning with Lito and made skirt; afternoon Carol, just back from leave, came over. After, I just had time to make sleeveless top to match skirt - touch-and-go with the material and also with time - had promised to meet Trish, Hedi and co in the evening to discuss our latest charity project – to buy some specific equipment for the local hospital.

A couple of asides: The polite form of address which Philippinos use when speaking to expats is 'Sir' and 'Mam': we were amused recently to get a letter from Aida, our ex-maid in Taiwan, which began: 'Dear Sir Pat and Mam Mary'...

A newly-arrived FW wife who had travelled extensively with her husband on FW projects commented recently to Hilary that, of all the places she'd visited, this was not the worst. That accolade went to Bangladesh, but BC came second. Super slogan for the tourist board 'Come to BC for your holiday; it's better than Bangladesh!!!' Hilary had told me some time ago that it reminded her of when they were on a project in Poland twenty-six years before. Carol volunteered today that she'd been told that BC is one of the worst places for corruption...

By this time I was enjoying life here; I had friends and interesting things to do, BUT, of the 45 Ladies' Club members, several were nominal members only and never joined in anything, and of the remainder, there were only about nine or ten ladies with whom I'd chose to spend time. Another big BUT, of those eight several were either leaving permanently, or going on long leave in the next few weeks which meant things would go very quiet again. One or two more FW wives would be coming out but not many others, as projects were finishing, so things could change again very rapidly...

Anyway, seven of us met up at Europoint for a drink and discussion on how best to buy the, quote, oxi-pulsometer, or maybe the pulse-oximeter, which the local hospital needed. Trish was to approach companies, both expat and local, and we were having a birthday party BBQ for Hedi; people were to be asked to make a donation instead of taking her a pressie.

18 July. Follow up a lead for voice lessons which turns out to be fruitless – 'I mainly teach kids pop; for Bel Canto you'll have to go to Manila' - but lady sounds really nice and we have good chat. We plan to have coffee soon...

Hedi and Clary, new FW wife, come round to help me plan next week's music afternoon. Will be fun to have more input; Hedi plays the guitar and Clary, who's done a lot of choral singing, is happy to join in. Watch this space. We have a pleasant couple of hours deciding on a programme and arranging a quiz – nice to have other people on board!

Afternoon is dancing session with DI – warm-up, cha-cha and swing – I love the latter, prefer it to rock and roll; the difficulty (for me) is that you dance it to the same music, but the beat is different. There are thirteen of us at Anna's, plus DI, and we have a very lively, but exhausting afternoon. Fresh lapu-lapu for dinner (fish) but I overcook it and it's like leather. Still, perhaps some people would enjoy baked leather with chillies and pine-nuts. The roast potatoes and red cabbage courtesy of Europoint are the best thing about this meal.

Quebala day at T's house, about whom, and which, I'd written quite recently. A lovely day. Over forty different ladies from different clubs, of many different nationalities. First we socialized over tea, coffee, and snacks. Then the serious part which was the allocation of club funds to deserving causes – the only case we were asked to help was an eleven-year-old boy suffering from leukaemia. We opted to give him everything in the kitty, which would be a great help to his parents. Lunch at midday, then an impromptu concert with T, brothers and two friends from Manila – a professional pianist and singer – and a lady from one of the clubs, who is a brilliant pianist. Yours truly also did a duet with T, which he'd asked me to do last week; he'd suggested 'All I want of you' from 'Phantom'. In such illustrious company I was a bit nervous, but it seemed to go well and I was so glad I didn't opt out because of nerves!

Next day Pat was to start work at 6 a.m. instead of 7 a.m., but would supposedly finish at 5 p.m. – he was out by 5.30; I stayed in bed till 7 as usual. Quiet couple of hours writing up yesterday's Quebala for the newsletter, letters, e-mails and so on, then lunch with Hedi, Carol and Trish to discuss Hedi's forthcoming birthday bash. Eight of us played Mah Jong at Hilary's after which it was home via Pic 'n Save. Traffic was appalling – again. P finally arrived home at 6.30, having been out of the house for thirteen hours. He was in good spirits – said that the early start had given him time to get things done while not many people were around. Supper and bed; another exciting evening!

I spent a pleasant morning the following day then to Trish's to continue our quilt. At least, that was the idea, but it didn't quite happen that way: some weeks ago, at the Scouts show here, we'd heard a young boy pop singer who'd been absolutely fantastic in spite of the dreadful PA system, and Trish had decided that she'd like him to come along and sing at our big charity 'do' the following Saturday – Hedi's charity birthday BBQ. Trish had made an arrangement to go and see Romil, who was twelve, with his family, to ask him, and she took Genelle and me along for company. Junior, her wonderful driver/ general factotum took us to a very poor area near the docks.

The grandmother was waiting for us and took us through narrow, muddy alleyways between the dilapidated houses: we arrived in a very poor, shabby dwelling, where Romil, mother and family were expecting us. The little boy, who was at school, was also basically the bread-winner as the father didn't work – we didn't know the details. There was a karaoke machine in the corner which I suspect had probably been given to them, or maybe they'd bought it instead of the usual TV, which wasn't in evidence.

Trish asked Romil if he'd like to sing us a song, as Genelle hadn't heard him. One of his sisters helped him to select a backing tape from a small selection, he picked up mic, and totally unselfconsciously, sang 'You light up my life'. It brought tears to our eyes. He sang some religious song. By now Trish and Genelle were crying and I had tears in my eyes. Passers-by heard the music and appeared at the window where they stayed throughout the mini-concert.

Dad appeared with a guitar and says 'Would you like him to sing Jerusalem? Whereupon the little four-year-old girl piped up 'Jerusalem, Jerusalem' in perfect pitch. So the father played and Romil and sisters sang for us. The four-year-old, and the eighteen-month-old, who were not supposed to be singing, couldn't resist joining in from time to time, the little girl in harmony, can you believe. I'd left my camera in the car as I thought it wouldn't have been appropriate to take photos but in fact they were flattered, so I took loads of shots. They all had so much music in their blood and we were so moved to see that materially they had nothing, yet the father had been able to give them so much music. Trish made the arrangements for next Saturday. We said our goodbyes amidst laughter as it started to rain again and the roof started leaking on the people sitting below. I made it to the car and then burst into tears – it was such a magical experience…

To Nigel and Halima's for drink after dinner but we didn't stay late – we were both tired after the very long day.

Saturday Pat went out early; Mrs L phoned and came round for chat bringing mangoes; I invited her to the Music and Fun on Friday as I knew she loved music. Lito came to collect me for FW culture workshop; he was 45 minutes late as the bridge had been closed for some sort of procession to do with Batangas Day. No warning, no advance notice. Lito happily knew a short cut and although we arrived very late the workshop was only just beginning. Nothing new for us, as we'd read up a lot before we arrived, and we'd done a similar workshop when we first arrived. Lunch followed; it was very good and also hot, so of course I complimented them. Home via Citimart where I purchased goodies like mosquito spray and drain-cleaner – well, a girl has to treat herself from time to time! Pat arrived home just before 5 p.m. English Mass at 6 p.m.

Sunday. P goes in to work briefly at 7 a.m. to let in cleaners. It's Batangas Day today and there's a big parade and celebration in the town so we potter down with cameras and take loads of photos. The parade is just assembling and the colours, the outfits, the people, it's just phenomenal. None of the participants we speak to seem to know when the parade will start so we don't wait for it – think we've got some good photos anyway.

Home for coffee and P does some studying, then to Janet and Don's for Don's birthday lunch. Evening Hedi and Tim, Nigel and Halima come over so P and I can brief Hedi Tim and Nigel on short, funny sketch we'd like them to do on Saturday next at Hedi's charity birthday 'do'.

24 July. Busy day; new contact, one Jinky, a Philippina (lady) comes over. Possibility of learning piano with her/her husband. Also, she's a voice coach, but not Bel Canto. We talk about the possibility of doing some duets for fun; am going to see them next week. Paulien (sic) arrives unexpectedly bearing masses of photos from last week's Quebala so we plan to arrange them as a montage in a frame as a small 'thank you' to T. Janet spends several hours here arranging said montage; I help but it's mostly down to her and we end up with two really excellent montages – think everyone will be pleased. Vernon turns up with Pat to finish installing printer on new lap-top – we'd hit problems but he soon sorts it out for us.

Next day Hedi and Clary came over to sort out the music for Friday afternoon. We had a fun-packed afternoon arranged, but that was nothing to what was planned for the charity BBQ on Saturday night. Watch this space…

We had lunch in tiny new restaurant, run by Philippino couple for expats, which I'd been meaning to try for ages - lasagne. Quite good. Then dance session with Benji, dance instructor and Andre. Great fun; we did swing, boogie (my favourite) cha-cha (different from the steps which we all knew) and dabbled in one or two others. We were all Ginger Rogers when we danced with DI, but left to our own devices it was another story...

We were all exhausted at end of session and as we staggered on to the coach Val said 'Our husbands think we have it easy – they don't know half of it.' This raised a chortle, as did an overheard remark when we stopped at Pic n' Save en route for home. Val, Clary and I, all ladies of a certain age, got out of the mini-bus and walked up the steps into the shop. Young chap outside chatting to his mates was heard to say 'Ooh look, the Spice Girls'

Typical House

Party, Party, Party…

I spent the next day in Manila and Alabang – first to the monthly American Ladies Craft Bazaar, which I'd only been to once before. On the way there we  saw a farmer crossing the two-way 'motorway' (happily not as busy as motorways in Europe) riding his carabao. (Sort of ox).

We bought lots of nice things at the Bazaar, where by chance we met most of the Batangas Ladies' Club for coffee, and then it was lunch and food shopping in Alabang. One of them Carol, American friend, had nasty red weals from wrist to elbow on her left arm. Apparently, swimming off Mindoro, she'd been unlucky enough to get a stray jelly-fish tentacle wrapped round her arm – it wasn't even attached to the jelly-fish. The poison from them can bring on a very nasty reaction. After several days of suffering when she got home, she'd remembered that she had aloe plants in her garden, and had wrapped the leaves round her arm, which had taken a lot of the pain. It was a good day out, if a long – and expensive one.

The next morning was really nice: Jo and Paulien came round to see the two montages which Janet had done for Tony and we took them round to him. He was delighted to have such a good memento of the Quebala, and, what an honour, took us on a tour of his penthouse. Even Paulien, who was a personal friend, had never seen it before. It was right in the centre of BC, near his old family home, and it was the third floor of a modern, vaguely 30s, office block. Inside, however, it was beautiful – marble floors, wood ceiling, paintings of the old family house and other old local houses, muted green blinds, copy of La Pieta (sorry purists, no accent on this keyboard!) and busts of Mozart, Beethoven and some other musical 'friends'. Old cabinet full of antique china and porcelain – it was impeccable taste, very simple and stylish and beautiful. But the piece de resistance (still no accents!) was his white grand piano, which he played for us – sadly not for long – but he insisted that we sang again the duet 'All I ask of you' from Phantom. Such fun!

In the afternoon Trish and I introduced Romil to Tony, as the latter wanted to hear him sing. We used my place as Romil could sing to his backing tapes on my wonderful karaoke machine. We decided on four songs for Saturday, two secular, two religious, one of which was 'Jerusalem'. This Romil sang unaccompanied and in good pitch. Tony was impressed, said he had undoubted talent but needed lessons and guidance. Romil had had some lessons before paid for out of the Mayor's Fund, but the money had run out and the lessons had stopped, so we decided to see what we could do between us.

Tony took us to see site of new hospital which he was having built. The family owned a lot of land and property in/around BC. They were said to be one of the richest families locally, and one of the most generous. Neither surprised me – he's such a lovely, delightful, approachable man. Asked me to do my Music-Hall number on Saturday…

Spent the next morning getting ready for Music and Fun in the afternoon, plus journal, letters and some time on water-colours, which, until day before, I hadn't done for ages. Meeting before music afternoon to go over details for next day, when I was informed that Pat and I had been volunteered to do the charity auction as it had to be people who were entertaining and theatrical. So why choose us, I asked myself? Twelve of us at music session which was not as good as usual – didn't know material so well and I had a slightly croaky throat. Still, it was all good-humoured; everyone joined in and it was nice to have Hedi and Clary on board. Nice tea after; lots of the ladies had brought stuff with them. Aisha turned up, back from hol – nice to see her again.

Come Saturday Pat was working as usual in the morning; I had preparations to make for the evening. By 9 a.m. I'd made a mountain of potato salad, had an hour's sing, and by ten I'd done a small watercolour that, modest as always, I was quite pleased with. Pat finally got home at 2.30 and the pace hotted up. It was like old times; we both had costumes to prepare (he was in a sketch with Hedi, Tim and Nigel which we were directing) I had my backing tape to check for the 'I'll Make a Man of you' number, promised bunches of flowers to put ready, plus potato salad to prepare and stuff for the BBQ which latter in fact we forgot. No probs – there was loads of wonderful food.

Well, the party. Wow! Trish and Colin, whose brainchild it was, had given use of their enormous house and garden where the festivities took place. Lovely warm evening, tropical plants, fairy lights – I felt I was in a glossy magazine. About hundred and twenty people there. Tony and brother performed first, with, in Tony's case, Mozart, Chopin and Beethoven, and brother, who also had a magnificent voice, entertained with two classical songs: I don't know what they were as I was inside changing.

Anyway I did my 'I'll Make a Man of You' number, clad in a suitably appropriate cabaret-type outfit which had 'happened' from bits and pieces and was, though I says it as shouldn't, rather good. It consisted of fishnet tights, high heels, black sequined mini-skirt and royal blue satin fitted jacket with black velvet reveres. Or should it be revers? Also had Pat's officer's hat and swagger stick.. Had already briefed sound technician, explained when I was to perform. Tape was in correct place, we'd decided on volume. Had also explained that there was a bit of spiel and barracking first then I would nod to start the backing tape. With me so far?

I made a suitably theatrical entrance, played the crowd a bit, and nodded to the technician to start the tape. Problem, he hadn't recognized me in my get-up, was totally flummoxed and put tape on wrong side which was blank. We turned it over but he had now of course lost the place. He found the number but had been playing it so softly that we'd gone too far and were way into the song. He continued to try for several minutes while I panicked inside but entertained the audience with banter, and just as I decided to do it unaccompanied, he found the place and we were away. Think in spite of everything that went wrong (or maybe because of it!) it had gone well, and several people complimented me on my ad-libbing. Pretty nerve-wracking though… Later did Phantom duet with Tony which people told me also went well.

Hedi, Tim, Nigel and Pat did their two-minute mime which was always amusing, but today they all hammed it up like crazy; it was hilarious and lasted about five minutes. It ended with Pat and Hedi playing it for all they were worth and they just brought the house down – it was superb.

Our little discovery, Romil, sang several numbers but hadn't been very well that day, and wasn't quite up to scratch, which was a shame for him; he did well, but not as well as usual. Dinner followed, then Pat, Hedi and I did the auction which was fun and raised quite a lot of money. Colin took pledges of money from the expat companies and that made a lot more. I didn't know the exact amount, but we'd reached our target, and the Hospital would soon have its pulse-oximeter.

Hedi and I chatted with the doctors, as Hedi had what seemed to be a good idea. Each patient always had to have a 'watcher' with them, to do basic nursing which the hard-pressed nurses didn't have time for. When the watchers weren't needed they just sprawled on the bed or in the chair and did nothing. Her idea was that perhaps they could help with hospital cleaning and specifically gathering dirty plates up so that the stray cats would be less tempted to wander indoors. They, (the doctors, not the stray cats), thought it would be a good idea and had themselves considered a similar scheme in the past but had never implemented it. They were to have a staff meeting on the Monday and would suggest a trial in one of the wards. Watch this space…

Sunday. Mass this morning then Pat does some studying. To Shell Club after lunch and we almost have a swim but are too lazy, also there are a number of children in the pool. We walk round the compound and relax in the sun with a cup of tea. See a large black bird with red-edged fan-tail – never seen one before – must try to find out what it is. Nice, quiet, relaxing day!

Next day we had a Ladies' Club committee meeting in morning at Shell Club. We were all delighted with our combined efforts from the Ladies 'do' Saturday night last – good party, and what was more important, we'd raised all that money for the Hospital. We heard, too, that John Larry, the little boy who'd had a stroke and whom we'd helped, was much better, was walking well, and was back at school – how wonderful! Apparently the condition had been caused by rheumatic fever earlier in the year. He would need medication for a bit longer but not permanently.

In the afternoon Janet rang to tell me she was leaving for Taiwan at the end of the week, so she came over for a chat and to say she was organizing lunch at Europoint on Wednesday…

Re-cycling and Tricycles

Had a trial piano lesson arranged with Jinky one morning but she turned up in a tricycle to tell me she had a PTA meeting and couldn't make it. Our phone had been out of order for nearly a week, hence the fact she hadn't been able to phone us. Rest of day would be busy, so quiet morning didn't come amiss.

Afternoon we had dancing at Ana's with DI: fun and energetic. Just five of us plus two DI's. Evening to FW party at a local restaurant to say 'Thank you' and 'Bye' to subcontractors who had finished their part of the job. Buffet unbelievably bad, but the dancing, with different DI's, was excellent. Planned to organize session soon with some of husbands and DI's so husbands could become Fred Astaires to our Ginger Rogers.

Next day Mrs L took Carol and me to Social Welfare Office to hear about a scheme under which newspapers, phone directories and drinks sachets were re-cycled and made into handicrafts by underprivileged children and women. We were taken to the Environmental Waste Office to see full range of these craft products – baskets, ornaments, photo frames etc. made from narrow spills of rolled-up newspaper. Lovely products; we arranged for a selection to be brought to the Ladies' Club luncheon next week and we hoped we could get something going for them… Lunch at Europoint with about ten of the ladies to say 'Bye' to several who were leaving/going on leave in the next few days.

3 August. Computer session with Nicole and Jo at Shirley's computer school. Afternoon Mah Jong at Shell Club as Hilary has gone away; there are nine of us there so we play three tables of three. Evening to Trish's for girls' informal dinner to say goodbye (again!) to Janet. Lovely evening, thirteen of us; typical girlie talk. Four inch bright green grasshopper lands on Jo next to me, who commendably doesn't panic. Neither do I, but I'm not much help either; I gently and ineffectually waft an impeccable linen napkin over it but that doesn't dislodge it. Finally it moves on with a bit of help from Janet, who is from NZ and is made of sterner stuff.

We had a brown-out all next day but luckily we had a gas cooker so Purita could make some delicious cakes for the afternoon's Bring and Buy. In fact quite a lot of people came—twenty or more, and we all had a good time and raised 6,000 pesos which was nearly £100! We were all pleased and planned to do it again in a month or so; it was a pleasant way of raising a bit of money for a good cause. Would contact hospital doctors and discuss what we should buy for them.

Jo told us that, returning home from Trish's the previous night, she had found a snake on the doorstep...

Pat saw an amusing sight earlier: a particularly grubby shack bearing the legend 'We sell good clean meat' – and three cows were standing there peering in the window...

Hedi rang to say that she'd just heard she'd passed her proof-reading exam. She was Hungarian and was fluent in English; she deserved to be proud of herself. We were having dinner with her and Tim next day so would have good cause to celebrate! Absolutely torrential rain in the evening, which was unfortunate because door-lock was playing up; P had to call landlord out at 8.15 p.m.

Saturday. Trish and Junior, her driver, took me, Gisela and Mina to the infamous Divisoria Market for the day, in Manila. Good drive up there, en route we saw my first water buffalo - huge - being loaded with fruit.

Trish, a regular at the market, briefed us first – no jewellery, no handbags, and no wandering off. We had a brilliant day – Trish and I bought loads of fabrics of superb quality for which the maximum price I paid was 35 pesos per yard – about 60 pence, and 60 inches wide. Bought lots of other bits and pieces, all at unbelievably low prices, had lunch in Mcdonalds, and finally hit the road again at 2.30. The drive back was enlivened by an electric storm and torrential rains, which caused flash floods – more than once we drove through flood waters up to the axles of ordinary cars – thankfully we were in a people-carrier...

Floods delayed us on way back so there was no time for me to go and change before going back to Heidi and Tim's on Trish's compound, where we were due for dinner. Instead I went back with Trish, where I had a shower and called Pat who brought clean clothes up for me. He, I, Trish and Colin, went round to Hedi's for a lovely barbeque. Just as well, as I would have been much too tired to cook...

Sunday. Mass at 11 a.m. I'm very upset by the sight of two tiny abandoned puppies in Basilica car park. We buy them cooked meat from street vendor – they've obviously been weaned, and P will take food later. Toy with idea of having them humanely destroyed – a kinder fate than usual for most of the dogs out here, but P thinks we should give them a chance. Quiet day; P has almost finished his studying. We do a bit of shopping but that's about all the excitement for today! P goes back later with food for pups but they've gone; we hope someone has taken them home.

The following day I went with Hedi, Jo and Purita to visit the so-called 'street children' – think they lived in and around the market area, and were certainly extremely underprivileged. They were coming back from their showers and had all just washed their hair. The staff combed the little ones' hair, and they - the little ones, not the staff (!) giggled when they saw the photos from our last visit. It was their 'milk day' – on Mondays they had a mug of fresh milk each before their story. An older, teenage, boy, took a sack of shredded paper to sell to the egg vendors in the market for packing, to make himself a few pesos. We took a few bits and pieces and we all agreed that it would be good to get something going to help them, though not sure what or how at this moment ...

To Jinky's next morning for a trial piano lesson. I reluctantly did the ten-minute journey each way on foot – it was thoroughly unpleasant and polluted. The pavement, where it existed, was narrow and studded with loose slabs. There was a dead rat in the road at one point, but this was less unpleasant than the dead dog in the market yesterday... I found it impossibly difficult playing the piano in front of someone else – it was bad enough on my own! But she was very patient and gave me manageable exercises to do; we talked music after. We were keen to do some duets together just for fun – although she was soprano, she wanted to try doing the lower part; we hoped it would come off...

Afternoon was a dance session with DI, combined with Mina's leaving 'do'. Five of us dancing, two DI's and several observers. Swing, cha-cha, boogie – my favourite – and we started the tango. Mina was leaving at the weekend and was in tears – there was such a great group of people there. Gisela gave me a leaving present (her leaving, not me) of a stretched prepared canvas, as she knew I wanted to experiment with oil-painting but hadn't been able to find the canvas in BC.

I was really tired by the evening as I usually woke up with P soon after 5 a.m., so we had a quiet evening watching TV. Saw a CNN ecological report on the Philippines which stated that the Philippines were 'on the edge of an ecological disaster'. It was possibly already too late to save from extinction the Philippine eagle, which was the national emblem and of which species only five hundred remained.

The monthly Ladies' Club lunch next day was at a tiny restaurant run mainly for expats by Philippino couple who'd spent a lot of time in the States. We managed to sell 2688 pesos worth of handicrafts which was quite a lot out there – about 50 pounds sterling, all of which went to our newly-discovered charitable project. Lunch was a disappointment; most of us had lasagne, which was tasty, but which in my case at least was barely lukewarm – that was the second time in this place. Was not prepared to eat tepid minced beef however tasty, and as there was no microwave in the place, I left most of it. And that was after Hedi had asked specially for everything to be piping hot... Carol told me later that, having visited the market a number of times, she absolutely never bought minced meat there for hygiene reasons; she didn't eat her lasagne either...

We heard that the new road, which had considerably shortened the journey to Manila, was not safe to use at night: figures from the Governor of the Province informed us that 14 people had died on the road since June for different reasons. Locals had put boulders on the road to stop vehicles or threw rocks through windscreens in order to rob the occupants; animals wandering on the road created an extra hazard. In our case FW discouraged staff and families from driving at night, and generously paid for us to spend a night in Manila when necessary.

We also heard that our fund-raising party the previous Friday had raised, not enough for one pulse-oximeter, but two, which was brilliant. One would go as planned to the regional hospital, the second to another local state hospital.

10 August. Carol, Mayette (Philippina friend of Trish) and I go down to the Regional Hospital and talk to the Chief Medical Officer there and another doctor about Hedi's idea for involving the 'watchers' at the Hospital in cleaning. We bounce ideas around and decide that we'll provide some suitable tabards with Hospital logo and/or slogan for a trial in one of the wards. The doctors will decided how to implement the scheme, and Mayette will talk to her husband about posters introducing the scheme and encouraging pride in the Hospital and involvement; we'll meet up again next week to discuss progress.

On to visit children in welfare home, where Trish has taken over English teaching from Janet. I've got Ronnie interested in helping/organizing English for the street children; we're going to see them again next week. (We're talking about two different establishments here). To my place for coffee and Trish promises us bright red hard-wearing cotton for trial tabards.

Afternoon is Mah Jong at Aisha's next door, as Hilary is away. Ten of us. Aisha has just acquired a lovely little Siamese cat from Willy Fong. Gorgeous little thing, really pretty, and guess what? She just matches the marble floor! Colour co-ordination or what?

Hey, and guess what happened again the next day? We also acquired a cat – kitten rather, slightly older than the one which had got run over. The new one was sweet too, seemed very clean, healthy and inquisitive. Gave him several lots of sardines through the day; every time the door opened he came in, and twice, even though he was so tiny, he followed us up the stairs.

We had another Music and Fun session that afternoon, our fifth one; it went very well; Hedi, Clary and Jean all did some songs and I was particularly pleased that Jinky and her husband turned up. Jinky sang an English and a Tagalog song – she had a very nice voice – and her husband played for her. I did a selection of songs.

Tripping the Light Fantastic

Saturday. Pat worked till 2.30. During the morning I went to Gisela's, who did a lot of oil-painting, and who had promised to help me get started in oils. Spent a pleasant morning there painting and we finished with lunch – Gisela's husband was to be working all day.

Bad news: disappointment when I got home; had picked up some bread-flour in City-market, new brand, properly sealed in sturdy bag, and relatively expensive for BC. Opened same to make some herby bread sticks to take to Aisha's tonight, but – catastrophe! The flour was full of weevils, so no bread to take with us (we had DI session booked to teach the husbands some fancy footwork!). Took instead some of Purita's orange and cinnamon cake as my contribution. Planned to stock up in Alabang or Lipa asap... Good news: I used what little bread flour I had left, added some all-purpose flour and some dried herbs, and – hey presto! Had some delicious little light herby rolls. Well I never...

Evening was great fun; it was Des and Aisha, Nigel and Halima, Pat and me plus Benjy and Andre, our two Tuesday DI's. Dinner first then we danced for about an-hour-and-a-half. Worked on so-called company dance, cha-cha and swing, all of which I'd done already but the object of the exercise was to get the husbands up-to-speed too.

Sunday. Morning in; Purita brought her little girl over – she was very pretty, so we finished a film taking photos of her. Which reminded me of a humorous thing that had happened the day before:

Remember our new ginger kitten? Well, through the window I'd seen one of the guards, sitting opposite the house as they often did, with a wriggling ginger-coloured bundle in his lap. Thought – how sweet; would take photo before they moved. Rushed upstairs to find camera to take photo from upstairs window. No film. Rushed downstairs again to where I'd seen new film on dining table. Rushed back upstairs, loaded film. Set film on sports setting in case they moved, crept to window, gently parted blinds, focussed camera, and realized what Gerry was doing – he was cradling a foot in his lap and was cutting his toenails...

Afternoon we had a shopping spree in Caedo and later we had a walk round Shell Club – it was very hot – and our first swim for ages. Over to see Wulf and Clary to discuss a problem on Site, and a quick drink with Des and Aisha. Tinned soup for supper, as by now it was late and P had an early start tomorrow – he'd have to leave at 5.45 a.m. Yuk.

Visited the 'street children' with Aisha and Ronnie, daughter of one of the expats. Ronnie, a TEFL teacher like me, was happy to help get some English activities organized for the children; we planned to start next Monday. Not many children in there, so we asked the staff to spread the word during the week that there would be 'special' activities the next Monday morning. The children were supposed to be rehearsing a dance for Family Week but with the exception of one small boy, Rolly, were too embarrassed to dance in front of us, so Aisha and I showed them the 'company dance' which we learned on Tuesdays, instead!

In the afternoon P took me to a local school of architecture and art, where FW were setting up a technological library for them. It was Pat's major responsibility in terms of Sustainability, and one he cared deeply about. I had appointment with two ladies in the Design Department, whose students would, we hoped, produce some posters for our hospital project. We discussed slogans and designs and they hoped to have some initial designs ready for the following Monday. Great – fingers crossed!

The building itself was appalling. It was new, but unfinished, and was not much better than a glorified building site. It was bare unfinished concrete and the fire escape had no guard-rail so you could literally step out into space. It definitely would have been classed as not safe for use in Europe, but as P said, what's the alternative? Probably the money had run out (we'd been told that 50% of the educational budget 'disappeared') and heaven only knew when it might be finished. This way at least the students were following their course of studies.

Saj came round to dinner – first time for ages. We had couscous and loads of veggies which I made into a sort of North African tagine with prunes, cinnamon and mint – it was actually quite nice! Would keep this one in my repertoire. Purita's famous fruit salad to follow, and Saj had brought proper cheese – cheddar and blue, as opposed to the local processed version which was obtainable from two shops in BC.

I chalked up a 'first' next day – my first ride in a tricycle. Just up to Jinky's, only a few minutes. Spent some time with her on piano, then we looked out some suitable duets and tried out a Mendelssohn song. Stayed for a chat. Afternoon to Ana's for dance session - about ten of us. Besides our usual dances we started the mambo. Oo-er! Pat was working late-ish to prepare a presentation for following day, when THE big-wig – Chief Executive, was coming from UK.

P had to go to Manila to collect said VIP. Carol, Linda and I spent the morning starting to make the tabards for the hospital. We got quite a production line going – one cutting out and pinning, one (me) on the sewing machine, one neatening and ironing. Managed to cut out fifteen from the bright tomato (yuk, yes I know!) material which Trish gave us, of which we finished one as a sample and half-made five more. Carol took these home to finish; the remaining nine we would do next week. Afternoon should have been doing our charity quilt but in fact it was the same three of us, and as we didn't have the special backing fabric we couldn't do much. Just chatted and drank tea – no hardship!

P finally arrived home at 7 and we had a quick supper and went out again: FW had organized a bowling evening (!) which was very popular with most of the staff. Specific idea was that it gave the visiting VIP a chance to meet, and chat with the staff. We didn't bowl and didn't stay long as we were both very tired.

Received an SOS from the Ladies' Club: the little boy with leukaemia to whom we gave the money from the Quebala, had had a blood transfusion of 30 units, but he couldn't be discharged from hospital until the equivalent amount of blood had been donated on his behalf. Yes, really. All the expats passed the word round, and those who could donate went down to the Red Cross and did so – they refused mine – I think because I was too small. Had to confess I was relieved as it was the only thing I was phobic about…

Mah Jong in the afternoon at Aisha's but I was very tired and not in the mood so I just had one game and sat it out with a cup of tea. Karen, who was the only expat in Lipa, told me that she had joined Rotary there and was involved with their charitable work in Lipa. They had a project whereby they were trying to put computers into schools and train teachers, who in their turn would train their students, in the use of the Net. She told me of one teacher who hadn't been paid for eight months – 'That's the way it is here.' 50% of the educational budget just 'disappears'. An ex-headmaster had donated land and had a school built, but it had never been used because the authorities hadn't appointed a teacher. Karen told me that, over the past year, Bill Gates had donated at least one hundred computers for universities in the country; although they had arrived in the country, not one had then found its way into any university…

One of the ladies told me that the President's newest idea was to stop corruption. Dearie me, that was a novel idea; what would they think of next? Yea, well, what's been stopping him so far? Could it be the idea of elections next year that had prompted his statement? Cynical old me.

Here is the result of the 'Most People on a Tricycle' contest. The winning entry is ELEVEN people – all adults. Spotted by Karen…

Carol came in briefly on her way home again and brought me up to date: apparently the Government Hospitals Inspector had gone into the hospital a few days ago, and had found that it wasn't up to scratch (surprise surprise!). The Chief Hospital Inspector would be coming down to see them in October by which time, of course, they would need to demonstrate major improvements. So, they were desperate to implement our scheme and were falling over themselves to take action. They agreed that we needed maximum publicity – local radio and maybe TV. The more publicity, the less likely they were to backslide but of course now they also have pressure right from the top. Didn't know if we'd be ready to roll before my leave but it obviously had to happen soon.

Speaking of the local radio reminded me that at least three times recently Pat and I had heard them giving the wrong time – ten or fifteen minutes out…

Saturday. We've had a visitor during the night – another kitten, smaller than Orlando (we'd finally named him after Orlando the Marmalade Cat—from one of my favourite books as a child.) New kitten has an eye infection but otherwise is seemingly healthy and such a pretty little thing – white and tortoiseshell mix. Pat found her snuggled up to Orlando.

Mah Jong and Markets...

Next day Junior, Trish's driver, took Carol, Aisha, Gisela and me to Divisoria Market. (This was a notorious place and it was later closed down). Trish was away on leave but kindly set this up before she went. We took also another escort, one Willy, who, like Junior, carried shopping and generally kept a very close eye on us to see we were all safe. With two escorts we split into two and Carol and I spent a pleasant couple of hours looking for fabrics (nothing stupendous today) before we met the others in Mcdonalds.

Quick visit to handicrafts section of market then it was back to the car park. While waiting for the others Carol and I made the mistake of looking out of the window of the car-park; the filth and the squalor was unbelievable – and people were living here in large numbers. And the river – I'd never seen such a polluted river – it was foul. We were so privileged, and so insulated, as expats...

Over to Alabang for a quick visit. Almost jettisoned visit as traffic was nose-to-tail – never seen it so bad – the journey should have taken one hour maximum – took us almost two. Anyway, we were very low on food so brief visit to Santis deli for smoked salmon, pastrami and cheese, and popped into health-food shop for wholemeal bread flour, as we could only get white in BC, then it was back on the road again. Back in BC just before seven, tired, as they say, but happy. Home-made soup and bread, ditto, for supper.

Willy F, a Chinese business associate of Pat's turned up next day with rack of lamb and salmon steaks; he had quick coffee and he and P disappeared to Site for short time. Started to rain; when P returned it was too late for hoped-for swim so we walked round Shell Club instead. Des and Aisha came over for roast lamb with all the trimmings plus P's favourite, jam sponge pud and custard. Not bad for a last-minute meal...

Next morning was busy: I went to see the street children with Carol and Ronnie; we did lots of activities in English. Some of the children went to school, some didn't – if we could get them speaking some English at least it might help them later on hopefully to get a job. (The educated people, and those working with expats, spoke English, but the local language was Tagalog.)

Not an easy morning, as the children's ages ranged from 5 to 17. We did 'The wheels on the jeepney go round and round' which is the Philippine version of, yes, you've guessed it, 'The wheels on the bus etc.' We all sat behind each other on the floor, and it culminated in 'the brakes on the jeepney go EEEEEEEEEKK!! Ronnie was brilliant, with some really good activities; I was so glad to see her!

Back for lunch and finished the tabards for the hospital, then Pat and I went to the local University for my appointment with the Art Department. The students, first-years, had done an excellent job on the posters and the samples were ready – apparently the students had been really keen and did them in two days. The staff were very enthusiastic about the scheme and the publicity for the University. I arranged to go back on Friday with Carol to discuss the posters proper and also to meet the students.

Went to a cocktail party and preview of (very expensive) art and antique sale at a local hotel, run by a sister-in-law of T. Several expats had turned up, and what seemed to be the local socialite fraternity. Nice to see Tony again, but otherwise nothing of interest. A lot of the furniture, though beautiful, was too heavy and large to fit into Hamilton Road.

To Jinky's for piano lesson and singing session on one of our duets, but things didn't turn out as I expected: I arrived to find Jinky somewhat distraught and very relieved to see me. Her six-year old, AJ, had been at her sister-in-law's on Sunday, two days before, and lay on the floor to have a rest after lunch whereupon the family dog bit him – on his head.

Panic all round, I gather: AJ was rushed in a tricycle to the local private hospital just a few blocks away. Doctors there did all the right things including of course starting rabies shots – just in case. They now had to wait a week, have the dog put down and have the brain tested for rabies. It was a serious threat out there but nonetheless I was able to reassure Jinky that, no, not all dogs had rabies; although the dog's rabies jabs had run out they had only just done so; the dog had not, so far as Jinky knew, been bitten by another dog; AJ had already started his course of shots at the hospital immediately following the incident, and so on.

What a dreadful worry though for them all – to say nothing of the hospital bills.

Very few people there were able to put anything by for such an emergency. Apart from wealthy people, most people had no option but to live very much hand-to-mouth. I offered to leave but Jinky wanted me to stay so I stayed and practised alone most of the time – it was so nice to play on a real piano and I enjoyed the morning. Jinky helped me with a couple of exercises. She didn't feel up to singing, understandably, but was much more cheerful when I left.

The afternoon should have been a dance session with DI but Ana had cancelled; we were on the edge of a tropical storm and it was fairly windy with resulting intermittent brown-outs. If there was no electricity there was no air-con – an absolute must for a dancing session. Spent the afternoon instead putting pockets on the hospital tabards. Not as much fun but it was so nice to finish them!

Purita and the guards told me that they were worried about Orlando, who was, they thought, getting fed up of sardines and who wasn't eating. Tough, was my immediate reaction. Willow, his little friend, had no such qualms and was losing her nervousness. We were having Willy's salmon steaks for dinner but as I prefer fillet I was happy to donate my salmon steak to the Be-Nice-to-Orlando campaign. Decided we couldn't feed cat best salmon with guards looking on, so cooked salmon and rice for guards too; it was normal out here to give food to maids, guards, drivers etc. when there was surplus food for whatever reason. After every party we made sure we took lots of goodies out to the guards…

Speaking of the cats, we'd seen them several times comfortably installed on the guards' table near the front door; their favourite bed was on the guard's hat…

And speaking of the guards, we'd had to have one of them moved; Purita told me that he kept coming to the door when we were out, asking her for coffee – Saj's maid said the same. He also did his hand-washing here, to which we'd been turning a blind eye, but apparently he'd been using Saj's washing machine… Purita and Rod knew how completely we trusted them and had been extremely embarrassed and uncomfortable at his behaviour. One of the expat ladies had just had to get rid of her maid for persistent pilfering; we knew that we were extremely fortunate.

Today is the American wives' Philippino craft bazaar in Manila. Aisha, Gisela and I have luxury mini-bus to ourselves as other FW wives prefer to go together – all six of them. Horrendous traffic going up there – takes three-and-a-quarter hours instead of about two-and-a-half, about an hour of which is spent crawling five lanes abreast on a three-lane highway. So far as we can make out, reason for hold-up seems to be jeepney severely overloaded with aubergines so that the chassis has just given out. (Pat has seen this happen several times before, but usually it's bananas for some reason.) Meet a number of the other BC ladies at bazaar as usual. Buy lots of bits and pieces but nothing of any import. Over to Alabang for lunch, look around and food shopping.

Over-crowded Jeepney

Better journey home to find that Willow, our new little adopted cat has gone missing. Hope she's met with either her Mum, or a new owner, but am not optimistic. P comes in with bundle of mail, some dating way back – one or two things were urgent, including long-awaited repertoire tape from the Maestro.

The following morning Carol, Nathalie and I visited the local hospital to discuss progress of the new project. Met a Doctor Nato who'd been doing his homework, and was very enthusiastic. Bearing in mind that the patients attending this hospital were mainly poor and ill-educated, his idea for implementation of the scheme was so simple it was brilliant: Local government was based on the barangay system: towns/cities were divided into so-called barangays (about the size of an electoral ward but with administrative powers).

These barangays were divided into 'puroks' which were basically a group of houses. Anyway, the hospital project was based on this system: The hospital was already divided into five 'stations' , number five of which was the paediatrics ward, which was where they planned to carry out a month's trial. If this was successful they would extend the scheme. The scheme would re-name each station 'barangay' and thus the paediatrics ward would become 'Barangay Five'. Each bed-space would become a 'purok' and the patient's 'home' for the duration of their stay. Each watcher would be responsible for the cleanliness of their 'home' and a selected watcher would be the barangay Captain with overall responsibility for the barangay as in real life.

Nato was bowled over by the tabards but even more so by the sample posters submitted by the students – he was just so excited. 'I'm speechless' were his words... He was keen to launch the scheme on 1 September, which was just eight days away. Carol went through his check-list of action to be taken – including contacting the media and sending out invitations. It was going to be a big ceremony with mega implications – we just hoped they'd see things through. We were keen to be supportive but not to do it all, and had made it clear that we'd be pulling out once the scheme was launched – it was up to them, then – we had other commitments. Our check-list included seeing the students again to talk through some amendments, where necessary, to the posters, having a suggestions box made for patients' own ideas, physically helping to put up the posters, and buying buckets, mops, garbage bins and liners etc. etc. to give them a good start. Watch this space...

Popped briefly into local museum to see beautiful water-colours loaned to them by Tony P. Planned, as did Carol, to commission paintings by the same artist of Tony's ancestral home.

Afternoon was Mah Jong at Aisha's – eight of us there. Carol and I visited the local University whose first-year art students were doing the project posters for us. We met the students – 30 or 40 of them, and discussed their art-work.. Everyone was very enthusiastic. Arranged to collect finished posters next Thursday, day before the launch. Here were some of the suggestions: not all were suitable and not all were used: *Hit that shit! : Zap that crap!* (Those two were our ideas!); *We share – we care – OUR hospital ; Cleanliness saves lives; No germs in OUR hospital; Bug-buster; Say no to dirt!; We hate bugs!; Bugs go home; Grime-buster; no flies on us; We're tough on dirt...etc.*

On to Pic 'n Save where we cajoled the Manager into giving us long-handled dustpans and a discount on other pieces of cleaning equipment. Managed to fit in our own shopping and home for lunch. Val, Clary and Jean came in afternoon to continue embroidering our teddy-bear quilt which one day would, we hoped, be sold/raffled/auctioned for charity.

Saturday. P was working as usual most of the day. It was a long week for him and the others too. I spent a quiet morning at home pottering apart from a brief trip to Caedo looking for suitable rubbish bins for the hospital. Still couldn't find what we wanted – we were looking for standard, kitchen-size swing bins which would take liners, but so far hadn't found them. They were obviously deemed to be unnecessary luxury items in BC, but we managed to get Scotchbrite cleaning pads for the project…

Afternoon I made pizza and a delicious so-called Indonesian salad for the evening which was dancing with DI, then dinner with Aisha, Des, Halima and Nigel. Pat too of course! It was a good evening; dance session first - cha-cha, swing and boogie. We all enjoyed the session and had the most incredible dinner after. Apart from my pizza, which wasn't brilliant, it was all prepared by Halima, from Borneo and a brilliant cook. Yum! was all I had to say…

Sunday Mass next morning; the huge Basilica was packed, and there were a couple of hundred in the car-park. We found chairs in the 'Prayer Room' across the car-park. Not only was it in the shade (it must have been upper nineties in the sun) but we also had the benefit of a fan overhead. We were amused to see a young boy proudly sporting a new t-shirt bearing the legend 'ANSTERPAN – Holland'… Freshly-brewed coffee after on the balcony and P worked. Shell Club for quick swim and home for lunch. Late afternoon we went to Des and Aisha's (again!) to christen their new barbeque.

Next morning was visit to the drop-in day-care centre in the market. Twelve children were there today as the schools were on holiday for some reason. Ronnie once again was superb; her activities were brilliant, and we had also Val, Clary, Jean and Linda to help. We had enough to do a rota system if people didn't want to go every week. It was exhausting; my carefully-planned and prepared game turned to mayhem and we resolved to change the rules somewhat if we used it again… Great fun though and the new volunteers enjoyed it too!

Customer Service.

Afternoon Carol and I went to Lipa to finish getting cleaning equipment for hospital. No luck with large rubbish bins but found two Winnie-the-Pooh medium-sized ones which were better than nothing – especially as it was for the children's ward.

Only snag was that the youth serving us had problems: the two bins we decided to buy were displayed snugly stacked one inside the other with one top inverted and the second top in its normal position for use. With me so far? Took up less space that way. Ok? So the youth proceeded to separate the two bins and two tops just to check there were four pieces. Good thinking. But then tried to carry them over to pay-point as four pieces. Carol said 'No, stop!' and re-assembled them into original stacking format to carry. He looked puzzled but acquiesced. Arrived at check-point. Paid. Said youth tried to pack each rubbish bin into separate bag. Carol was just about to explode. I leapt in at this point. 'No, stop! Too much to carry!' (I already had carrier bag.) Youth looked puzzled again; our fault - it was obviously too much for him to take in at once.

On a happier note, we had the most beautiful view of the mountains around Lipa; it was really quite spectacular.

Rang Tony to ask about commissioning a water-colour of his house by the artist, Fernandez, whose pictures Carol and I'd seen in the museum – they were wonderful. Tony gave me details of Christina who was pianist/accompanist and who might be able to help me as a repetiteur with my music. Rang her and fixed to start after my hols – for out here she was fairly expensive. Would give it a try anyway – she sounded nice, and I believed she was good. Watch this space…

29 August. Morning in for a change; should have been having piano lesson at Jinky's, but she has to take her little boy back to the hospital for stitches out after his dog-bite. We re-schedule.

Dancing session in the afternoon at Ana's. Only four of us with DI which is great. Start with boogie, and continue with cha-cha and swing. Great fun, but this is the last one before October as so many of us are leaving/going on leave.

Evening P and I manage to track down Christine, about whom Tony told me; she's been away in Europe for several months. She's a singing teacher of, I think, show songs, and pianist/accompanist – Tony thought she could help me with repertoire. We manage to find her studio and there's a copy of Vaccai (musical exercises) open on the piano; it transpires that yes, she does teach Bel Canto! She seems very nice and is obviously very popular. Her schedule is absolutely full apart from a Friday late afternoon, half-hour slot, which is fine. Neither of us is free this Friday so it will have to wait till after my leave but it will be something really to look forward to...

When we come back we see the most enormous moth (or butterfly but suspect the former) which fell out of a tree. The guards rescued it and popped in on shelf in the car-port out of Orlando's clutches. Pat measured it against his outstretched hand and must have been over eight inches wing tip to wing tip. Incredible – sort of browns and beiges in a beautiful pattern.

Purita away today ill. Visit to see Dr Nato at Regional Hospital to tie up ends for Friday. He's still bristling with excitement and enthusiasm and has done really well with invitations and media arrangements. Roll on Friday!

The following day I have to go to the hospital, the private one this time, for routine tests – we're supposed to have regular check-ups. Too late for my piano lesson, which is a disappointment. The doctor apologises for keeping us waiting; he's been attending to someone in Casualty who's almost lost his hand in a fight. Needless to say, the patient wouldn't talk...

Today is a really busy, exciting day: Carol and I go to the University to collect the hospital posters, which are excellent and all of which will be displayed. On to Pic'n Save for cleaning materials to go with new equipment, stop by hospital to tell Nato that all is on course for the big ceremony, and finish the morning going to see the ladies in the office which deals with the handicrafts made by disadvantaged women and by prisoners. They're delighted to see us; Carol is keen to get samples of their best work to show to the lady in charge of craft stalls at the monthly bazaar, to see if they can have a stall in the New Year – it's booked up till then.

In the same building are several other departments, including the Agricultural

Department, where we meet a vet who answers our queries about rabies injections for animals. P and I want to get Orlando vaccinated and Carol is concerned about her maid, who has acquired two stray dogs, one of whom is very aggressive, and quite rightly she's worried about her children. The dog has obviously been very badly-treated in the past, and will probably have to be put down. Vet agrees to vaccinate Orlando for us and both Carol and I have confidence in him. It's difficult to find a good vet out here; I hear of one vet locally who bent three needles giving jabs to a nervous cat and some vets seem to be attached to pet shops which are pretty dire, so this is a very good contact. Orlando is probably too young to be neutered but we plan to have that done when it's appropriate.

Home for supper with Pat; we pack for the weekend as we're going away tomorrow afternoon to Laga d'Oro. Also collate everything to be taken tomorrow – posters, buckets, mops, brooms, dustpans and brushes, scouring powder, pads, cleaning cloths, disinfectant etc., plus suggestions box made by FW carpenter for patients' own suggestions on possible improvements. Willy, a contact of Pat's, is trying to get my article on the scheme into one of the national newspapers where a friend of his is on the staff. Fingers crossed…

Rush-Hour

142

Malacapao

Well, we were back again in downtown BC, having had a good holiday in Palawan. We almost hadn't got there though: the airline, Soriano, couldn't confirm our flight until just two days before, as the big resorts took most of the flight seats, and anyone going to the smaller resorts as we did had the unclaimed seats. (If they were lucky, as we were.) We'd arrived at the domestic airport to be told variously that a. the 9 a.m. and only flight had already left, and b. that the airline was no longer operating. Happily Dodong was driving us and ferreted about till he found the right place.

It transpired that there was a long-running court case involving Soriano and it was probable that the competition wanted to put a fly in the proverbial ointment. Anyway, Soriano were brilliant and we waited in a spotlessly clean lounge with complimentary refreshments. The flight itself in a small 19-seater plane, was very good and comfortable, and flying low as we did, we had superb views.

Palawan consisted (and probably still does!) of hundreds of islands, many of them sheer, bleak forbidding cliffs dropping vertically to the sea, others with beautiful beaches and lush tropical vegetation. It was very reminiscent of photos we'd seen of China, and also of Vietnam, and was still almost unspoilt.

We stayed in a sort of back-to-nature retreat run by a sort of English/Ozzie/Philippina hippy lady, (her philosophy, not her dimensions) on a small island, Malapacao. The retreat could cater for up to twenty-five guests but throughout our stay maximum number there was ten. We stayed in small native-built cottages, all on the beach, which were charming; the bathrooms were basic but spotlessly clean. The food, veggie with some fish, was fantastic…

The view from our window was of the majestic Princess Rock, which was then featured on the cover of Lonely Planet Philippines., with two small huts on the

Rock which were inhabited, and two primitive cave-dwellings up in the cliffs where the people lived who gathered the birds' nests for soup. One night, looking across the bay in the darkness, we saw a tiny pinprick of light about two-thirds of the way up the Rock which were apparently said people gathering the nests. You should have seen the vertical, jagged, Gothic cliffs – what an uncomfortable, downright dangerous way to earn a living…

We spent the week swimming, snorkelling, reading and painting (me), and island-hopping. One favourite trip was to another island with a huge cave which we entered by climbing through a small opening, then it just sort of opened out – amazing! Most of the islands were deserted and we loved our boat trips and island visits. The food was vegetarian and truly gourmet; everyone ate together at tables on the beach where, in the evenings, we watched the sunset.

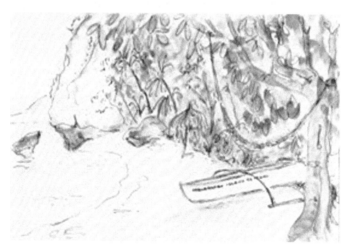

One evening we went by boat round the other side of the island to wait for dusk, when literally thousands of bats poured out of a cave and streamed away to the mainland like a huge swarm of bees. A magical experience!

Ladies Who Launch

It was the launch of the hospital 'Watchers' Brigade' scheme. Carol and I spent an hour or so at the hospital, supposedly helping to put up the posters from PBMIT. (State University). In fact, four girl students arrived with their tutor, and with Carol's and my driver they put up all the posters. Carol and I were delighted to see everyone with the bit between their teeth, so stood back and watched...

Only ironic note was when we followed a trail of sticky-bit paper backing to find my driver, putting up all the notices saying 'Keep this hospital clean' and 'OUR hospital be proud' etc. – and dropping the bits of paper on the floor! Carol and I made a point of picking them up and encouraging him to help... Thanks to Willy F, our report was published in one of the national newspapers.

Back home for couple of hours then back to the hospital. About forty students from PBMIT plus tutor and Dean, local radio and TV, and others turned up to support us. Everything went off well. Planted idea with PBMIT tutor that maybe students could paint murals in children's ward during their long holiday starting in April. Playgroup mums were actively talking about painting the said walls in bright colours so that might fit in well in providing good surfaces for the murals. This one was outside my province but I hoped it would go well...

Returned home very briefly to collect suitcase and off we went to Laga d'Oro. Drive took us almost two hours, much longer than it should but there was a lot of Friday evening traffic, and the road through Batangas was, in parts, no better than an unmade, rutted, country road, which slowed us up somewhat. The other side of Bauan the roads improved dramatically and in a number of places there were road-works where children directed the traffic and waved money-tins hopefully at us as we drove through. In one place a dog was standing watching our car from the side of the road, and as we drew level with him he bunched up his shoulders and launched himself at our car – thankfully Pat missed him. Talk about one kamikaze canine... We saw a tricycle, bearing, as usual, a name, but in this case the sign-writer had obviously run out of space as it bore the legend 'Till death us do P'. Arrived in time to switch off and had drink before very pleasant dinner. (The place was German-run – I rest my case!)

Saturday/Sunday. This weekend we're in the throes of a typhoon. Saturday we have strong winds all day; spend most of the time sitting on the patio reading. Have several games of table-tennis – first time for years. Mass Saturday evening in nearest village. Music is lovely – congregation sing beautifully and priest harmonises. Wonderful! Saturday night – all night and Sunday – all day – we have torrential, but torrential, tropical rain-storms. Get very wet just walking across the car-park to Reception. Spend the morning as Saturday; leave after lunch. Good journey home.

Monday morning we visited the day-care centre for the street children. Eight of them. Ronnie, as usual, had lots of activities arranged and Val, Clary, Linda and I helped. Particularly good today; the children were getting used to us and everyone had a good time. After lunch I took three boxes of unused prescription drugs down to Regional Hospital; Willy F's contact had donated them. Unfortunately, those that were (even just) out of date couldn't be used by the hospital. These would be passed to a free clinic for poor people where most of the patients couldn't afford medicine. The other drugs they could and would use. To Shell Club for an hour's lie in the sun. It started to get overcast and by the time I got home it was torrential rain again – on the edge of another typhoon.

Mandi, the current chairman of the Ladies' Club rang me, and told me that, because of the rain, schools all over had been closed that day. I asked what difference the rain made – was it the possibility of brown-outs? Mandi said no, the school had explained on being asked that it was because they didn't want the children struggling in and getting stuck in the traffic. Only trouble was, they hadn't told anyone until the children had actually arrived at the school. There had apparently been jeepneys full of children having to turn away… And these were supposedly professionals applying such twisted logic.

5 September. Jinky comes round, supposedly to give me a keyboard lesson but I haven't seen her for a couple of weeks so we spend a lot of the time just getting up-to-date. We do some piano, though, and then Mario comes and we all have a good warm-up with Vaccai and then Jinky and I potter about with the Letter Duet. (Mozart, Marriage of Figaro, if you'll pardon the name-dropping.) A bit hit and miss, and Mario is limited with his five-and-a-half octaves on my keyboard, but it's fun. Mario's niece collects AJ after school and brings him over; I've promised to do some informal English activities with him and accordingly we all play games for half-an-hour or so. A really nice morning!

See a sign on a shop: 'We sell ice-cream 25 hours per day…

Afternoon I go to do some shopping as Nigel, Halima and Des (Aisha is away) are coming round to dinner. Chilli, very nice, and blueberry and apple crumble and custard. Good! Brown-out just as we finish dinner so we rummage round for candles and matches. Orlando, who is allowed in the house sometimes, but not always so he doesn't get too used to it – and us – has a wonderful time. Somehow, in the dark he's found a biro on the marble floor and is tapping it backwards and forwards. When he tires of that he kills the carpet fringe – again. And again. Electricity comes back on about thirty minutes later so that's not too bad. It's not so much the lighting as the electric fans and the air-con; it's normally too hot to use even a sheet in bed…

Next day was a whole free day! Couldn't remember the last time I'd had even half a day free. Wouldn't have liked it very often, mind you, but from time to time it was good. Went to Shell Club for an hour in the morning; I was very tempted to swim but I hadn't got shampoo and everything so just had a coffee and a lovely long read in the sun.

Purita informed me that one of the guards told her Aisha's maid (Aisha is in UK) wasn't happy alone in Des and Aisha's large house – she was convinced that there was a 'body spirit' there. I remembered that Gigi, our ex-maid's daughter, who came to clean that house a couple of times also thought the same thing. I think basically, Philippinos didn't like empty houses and I'd heard before of other 'haunted' houses. I sent Purita round to chat to her and see if she was ok. Purita returned soon having reassured her; suggested she put the radio on for company…

Pat was interviewing new staff all morning. The maid of the Manager with whom he, Pat, was interviewing, suddenly turned up in a tricycle, panicking, telling him his electricity had been cut off as his landlord hadn't paid the bill…

Copied an old T-shirt dress this afternoon. Had had the original nearly twenty years and it was still going strong; it was getting shabby but was just so comfortable! Was pleased with the new one; it would be very useful. Evening we finished remains of yesterday's chilli and rice –and fine-tuned packing for UK.

Pat had applied for permission actually to come into airport with me when I left on the Saturday. Normally, only passengers were allowed into the airport; there was a possibility he would be allowed to come in too as far as Check-In but they would only let him know the day before if his request was granted. It was such a boring airport – worst I'd ever known – facilities were extremely limited, so I hoped he would be able to…

There was at Manila airport an executive lounge which had just opened when we went on holiday; they had actively been promoting it at that stage and for a very reasonable sum one could use the lounge – unfortunately we hadn't then had time. Anyway, an expat thought only First and Business Class travellers were allowed to use it, so I'd asked Pat to ring Thomas Cook up there and find out – they were the Company travel agent. The upshot was that they rung the airport and even the airports authority didn't know if I could use it or not. If they didn't know, who the ---- did know? Had a nasty feeling I wouldn't be allowed but was keeping my fingers crossed. It was just so difficult getting information or decisions from anyone about anything.

Next morning I made a sleeveless T-shirt then to Shell Club for Ladies' Club committee meeting – my last till after my leave. Afternoon to Hospital to take two sacks of towels donated by Pat's Chinese business associate, who turned up in evening and told us that, hopefully, the photographs of the Hospital project launch would be in the Philippine Star again. Fingers crossed!

8 September. To UK! Pat works the morning, has the afternoon off so he can take me to Manila. Our bedroom has French windows, un-curtained onto a side balcony, which is normally quite private. So at 7 a.m. I get up, put on a mud face-pack, and nothing much else, and potter onto landing to do my e-mails. Clatter from balcony just outside French windows. Peep round door; find ladder up to balcony, workman on the balcony just outside the window painting. Great. Deshabilee and face-packed as I am can't go and get my clothes from bedroom, or go down to ask guards to tell him to wait till I'm up. Stay marooned on landing till face-pack dries. Find P's voluminous bath-robe, creep through bedroom to bathroom remove face-pack, grab clothes while workman's back is turned, and go down to ask workman to wait. Phew! It gets the adrenaline going for my usual singing session. Imagine, the neighbours can lie-in next month while I'm away…

Pat gets home earlier than expected; driver takes us to Manila. Early flight tomorrow; we stay the night in airport hotel – not recommended. It's awful – dirty and run-down, and the ladies loo is dire, but it's near the airport…

Summary: So, dear friends, who knows? It's possible that when I come back from UK, we could be half-way through our stay, so this may be a good time to sum-up my impressions of my stay here so far in B.C. I don't like the lack of good food, the humidity, or the superstitious approach to religion. I hate the corruption, the apathy, the inertia, the sense of hopelessness, the pollution, the poverty, the attitude to animals, the insects, the disregard for safety – one's own or others', the lack of a concept of good citizenship. I still relish the 'differentness' of the place and enjoy the incongruities. I love the vegetation, the views of the mountains, the sunshine, the luxury of having maids, drivers and guards to look after us. We're very privileged and we let these people know that we appreciate them. I enjoy meeting local people with whom I have something, especially music, in common, like Jinky and Tony.

What else can I say? I wanted to be with Pat, but the first few months were incredibly difficult for us both. In all, it's been a very interesting, very challenging time, and I'm sorry to say that I often gave Pat a hard time. I've worked really hard on my music; I've discovered art in a big way (thanks to Gerry and Ben for the present of all the art kit to get me started), I've read loads of good books, we've both met lots of lovely people, local and expat, and last but definitely not least, we've been able to help a little bit where we could.

Back again!

I arrived back in Manila on 15th October, having had a good leave in UK with family, friends, and lots of music, all of which I would miss. Had to say that, as the plane descended, so did my spirits, but it was absolutely lovely to see Pat again. He was fighting off a really bad cold/bug, and had just finished a 71-hour week, but was otherwise fine, and was delighted to see me! We stayed for the weekend at the Peninsular, our favourite hotel in Manila, and did a spot of shopping before returning to Batangas on Sunday afternoon.

I hit the ground running, as they say. Seemed to be fortunate in that normally, in spite of the seven-hour difference, I wasn't too bothered by jet-lag. Anyway, I went down to the market children with Ronnie and five other expat regulars. They, but especially Ronnie, were working wonders with the children; I could really see a difference in their competence – and their confidence - since I'd gone away. Afternoon Aisha came in for a chat, and I half-made two pairs of light-weight cotton trousers for Gerry and her friend Debbie, who were coming out at the end of next week. They were apparently short of trousers…

Ladies' Club coffee morning at Dunkin' Donuts (sic). Eighteen of us there; good fun and I caught up with some of the news; Hilary came back for a chat.

Spent the afternoon finishing afore-mentioned trousers; they turned out quite well. I was supposed to make them each a grey pair (these were black) but I wasn't sure if I'd have time as already things were getting busy again… Jinky should have come round but phoned to say her children were ill so we re-scheduled for the next week.

I joined group of other ladies going again to see the market children – this time, Carol's idea, specifically to make papier-mache masks for Halloween. The children were really excited as we arrived and hung out of windows shouting 'hello'. The session was chaos, with children, balloons (on which we modelled the masks), torn-up paper, and wall-paper paste everywhere. Usually Vaseline is used so that the finished mask slides off easily, but in the absence of Vaseline I donated Q10 Night Repair Cream, which I felt should provide a somewhat superior finished product. It was too hot to use it on my face at night as I would probably have slid off the pillow and that would never do…

Shopping at Pic n' Save in the afternoon, and to Shirley's for party in the evening. It was the eleventh anniversary of her starting her computer business. There were lots of people there, mainly Philippinos, including a well-known 'Singing Priest' who did a couple of Karaoke spots. About ten expats including ourselves – we spent a pleasant hour or so.

Next day was great. I went up with two friends to Alabang, to the home of one Liz, an expat lady, for a charity piano recital, which we all thoroughly enjoyed. Only ten of us plus two children in the audience (in spite of their club having two hundred members), but it was very informal and fun and gave us a chance to chat with some new people in very civilized surroundings.

Dinner with some FW colleagues, plus visiting security consultants. Very interesting evening; really enjoyed it, and hey, guess what, the meal was also very good – and hot too! Months of constant requests and explanations on the part of us all were starting to pay off. When things went well, as they did on this occasion, we made a point of complimenting everyone concerned.

On 20 October we had a Ladies lunch – very good - and hot – and a really interesting talk: an expat lady came down from Alabang to tell us about her fascinating – and harrowing – experiences as a voluntary prison visitor to expats in gaol. Some of them had been framed, including one very famous case where a totally innocent Brit had been on Death Row for some time. It had made all the national press both in the Philippines and in the UK but thankfully he'd been released. Some of them may well have been guilty including one guy who was a drug pusher, but some had been guilty only of stupidity and gullibility…

Had my first lesson with new Bel Canto teacher. She was really nice, good sense of humour and obviously knew her stuff but I didn't really enjoy it; I needed time to get used to working with new people. I was sure we'd get used to each other though…

Dinner with Nigel and Halima, who was a brilliant cook and who managed well despite half a day with no electricity. The whole of Luzon, the largest island, had had a long 'brown-out' – no problem without lighting, but try managing without fans or air-con when temperatures are in the thirties with high humidity!

There had been rallies and demonstrations in Manila over the previous few days against President Estrada, who'd been impeached for a particularly bad gambling and corruption scandal. There were stringent calls for his resignation but so far he was sitting tight.

Saturday. Pat is as usual working most of the day; I spend the morning preparing for dinner party tonight with Carol, Hobby, and T. Purita, bless her, insists on coming in to prepare her famous spring rolls for starters. Come the evening, just as Pat and I are going out to the English Mass, the power goes off. We go down to the Basilica anyway and spend twenty minutes, waiting, by candlelight, for the emergency generator to be started. Finally go home as Mass still hasn't started and decide to go on Sunday instead.

Power stays off all evening, but thankfully I have cooked literally everything in advance. We cook by gas so it's no problem to heat everything up in the dark. We lead everyone upstairs by torch and candle and through our bedroom on to the balcony, where we spend a very pleasant evening. Dinner is piping hot and, in spite of the brown-out, is actually very good.

There was an earth tremor next day as I was sitting up in bed having a cuppa. We'd been told what to do (if necessary a safe place is in a door lintel with a cushion over your head, though I think this advice has since changed) and we weren't supposed to hang around, but P wasn't convinced, so, pausing only briefly to have a quick trip to swaying loo, (weird sensation!) flinging on a caftan and grabbing my handbag(!) we went downstairs to see the chandeliers swinging – a cast-iron sign. Heard later that it was 5.7 on the Richter scale; the epicentre was just 25 odd kilometres away. Oo-er!

Brown-out continued on Sunday. We spent the morning at the Shell Club, where we had a lovely swim. I did twenty-odd lengths of breast-stroke then worked on my crawl, which was starting to come together. Coffee and sunbathing, home for lunch. Met Isabel, expat from other company. She'd had no water in her house for a week, and now no electricity. With three small children, her husband's company were doing nothing to help...

Afternoon in, then church in evening, option of going to hotel as we still had no electricity; most other FW personnel had already done so. We opted to stay in the house as long as we had water and in fact our two nights without fan or air-con were not as bad as they could have been.

Next day we still had no electricity and now no water. (No problem with drinking water – we all got that in large containers.) Opted to go to hotel tonight if there were still any problems. Morning was Ladies' Club committee meeting at Shell Club where it was nice and cool, but just before I set off, friend Elisa phoned for a chat in what was to her the wee small hours.

Afternoon in: bingo! we had electricity so I made remaining two pairs of trousers for Gerry and Debbie. We were told that the electricity could go off again – no-one really knew for sure – there had been no official announcement and no-one seemed to know anything officially. It was incredible.

Seen recently by Pat and/or myself: Twice – a jeepney, crowded as usual, but the people are on top to make room for the pigs inside… A commercial vehicle in Manila with a small TV for the driver's seat, angled so he can watch it when he wishes… Ice-cream vendor selling ice-cream in bread rolls… Jeepney loaded with long bamboo poles. Large bemused goat is perched precariously on top of the bamboo and another one is being hoisted up…

24 October. Pleasant morning; Jinky comes in. It's lovely to see her; I haven't seen her since I came back so we have lots of catching up to do. We plan a duet for Friday and a run-through on Thursday. Jinky leaves at 11 so I go to Shell Club for lovely long swim and sunbathe. Crawl still improving! Spend afternoon making extra bikini for Boracay next week with Gerry…

Learn from Pat and others that a detachment of Philippine National Army on Monday found a Communist terrorist stronghold only about 8 miles away from here. There was a shoot-out and at least eight terrorists were killed plus 2 PNA. Another similar incident yesterday when four Philippino soldiers were killed.

It was the monthly craft bazaar in Manila the following day; Dodong drove Aisha and me. We met up with Carol and she and I went round some of the traders asking for donations of gifts to be raffled for charity at the Ladies' Club Christmas party. They were very generous and we were delighted. To Alabang for lunch and shopping, home about 5.30.

Jinky came over during the morning next day; we were arranging a duet together for Friday's Music and Fun. It was, in fact, 'Louise' as in 'Every Little Breeze' and we'd arranged it as a duet with a little dance. (I didn't get out much…) We had a ball! Carol and Shirley came over for a meeting re the Christmas party; we spent a very pleasant hour or so.

After lunch Carol and I went over to Caltex Club; Trish had been asked by the Manager to invite some friends to check out and comment on his new chef's new menu, which we did. The food was in fact good – some of it very good. What a pleasant way to spend time… Next tasting session would be Monday in the evening, but we were going to be busy with Gerry; would rather spend the evening with her.

Carol and I spent a fruitless morning next day checking out dance music for the Christmas party. Had hoped one of the local college bands would turn up trumps as P and I had heard them and they were excellent, but it couldn't be arranged and so it was back to the drawing board on that one.

Jinky phoned to say she wasn't very well – had slight sore throat and fever. Not sure if she'd make it for the afternoon but was desperate to do so. I took honey, and zinc lozenges up to her in tricycle and kept my fingers crossed. We were both keen to do the duet; thought it would be great, if we got a chance to do it.

The music afternoon was pleasant but a bit low-key, if you'll pardon the pun. I had to rush off pretty sharpish after in a tricycle to my session with Christine, Bel Canto coach. Had problems as the main bridge had collapsed between the house and the Site, causing major difficulties for traffic but especially for the heavy Site traffic. Apparently the river-level rose ten feet in half-an-hour…

Anyway, we collected G in spite of chaos (surprise surprise) at Manila airport. Non-travellers were not allowed in airport, and we had to wait on other side of road under appropriate surname initial, while arriving passengers scanned the milling crowd opposite. It was less than helpful to have a busy road in between with vehicles continually depositing and collecting passengers so you couldn't see in between the vehicles. Couldn't help getting irritated but cheered up when we met up with G. My baby! Good journey back to BC.

Seen by Pat/me over last day or so: Guy in middle of road having shower and shampoo during heavy rain, traffic dodging all around him… Chap sitting on chair on pavement outside barber's, heavily draped in towels having haircut and seemingly oblivious to the traffic. Driver on moped battling, whilst driving, with brolly turned inside-out Mary Poppins style. Little boy delighting in paddling through deep floods just kicking up water. Heard that during the day FW engineers had put up scaffolding bridge for pedestrians but that heavy Site traffic would continue to pose a problem.

Halloween! Ronnie, other expat regulars, Gerry and I, all went down to see street children for Halloween party. Eighteen children there as school was out and wow! What a party! Donuts (sorry, yes I know!) on strings, apple-bobbing, singing activities, not sure who enjoyed it the most, the children, the helpers, or the fifteen to twenty passers-by who stayed glued to the windows throughout, laughing uproariously…

P told us at lunchtime that BC was designated a 'catastrophe area' with seven homes destroyed, including, we heard, that of an FW driver, and worse, several locals missing. An official request had been sent requesting the army to build a Bailey bridge where the bridge has collapsed.

During afternoon I took Gerry, by prior arrangement, to see T. She got the tour of the house and the private, impromptu concert on his lovely old Steinway. He insisted that we sing 'our' duet – 'All I ask of you' from Phantom. He always requested it – it was about the fifth time now!

Jinky popped in later to say 'hi' and to meet Gerry. She brought little Philippine cakes which were delicious – and incredibly fattening. We spent the evening packing to go to Manila next day, where Pat had some appointments, then to Boracay on Thursday. Yeah!!!

Boracay

We were back from holiday in Boracay – one of the most beautiful beach destinations in the world. We'd had a super time; it was horrid to be back and I was going to miss Gerry so much, but no doubt we'd settle down again. Pat should still have been on leave but had a summons to get back to Site as one of the Philippino managers was in hospital and Pat was needed.

Back to the beginning: to Manila, where G's friend Debbie met us at the Peninsula hotel – our favourite – and after two nights there, the four of us flew to Boracay, a holiday island South of here. It was gorgeous. Ben had stayed there last year with a friend and loved it. It had a long sandy tropical beach with fine white sand and was very quiet, not much to do except for water-sports and bars. A rocky outcrop just metres from the beach had a statue of The Virgin. We used to swim out to it but never ventured onto the tiny island…

Boracay Beach

We swam every day in the sea – sometimes all day; went out in a boat and snorkelled; in one place hundreds of brightly-coloured fish came swimming to us for bread – magical! Coming back boat engine packed in, so we were drifting along, fairly near the beach but too far to swim. Happily, along came a boat full of divers to rescue us.

As usual, unable to refrain from drawing attention to myself, I made a spectacular exit from the boat: stepping down to wade ashore I caught my foot and fell backwards off the side, disappearing in a whirl of arms and legs and laughing my head off. Not very dignified, but then, what's new?

Next day was a quiet one at home until late afternoon, catching up with phone calls, e-mails, and unpacking, then to Christine's for my Bel Canto session. I liked her a lot and we were getting used to each other; she obviously knew her stuff but I still missed my UK music scene. Aisha came in for a chat after; I cut out a dress and made chick-pea curry for supper – really nice! With rice and tinned spinach; just wanted to share that with you. I don't know how you would manage without my little culinary tips and recipes…

Saturday 11 November. Pat leaves for work at 6.15 a.m. I lie-in till 7.15 then discover there's no water as tank was leaking yesterday. Workmen turn up at 8 and do grown-up things with oxy-acetylene welding (I think) and singing a happy oxy-acetylene welding (I think) song. Pat has really busy day ahead. FW are launching a major basket-ball competition today with local students, and there is a motor-cavalcade with streamers and banners, plus ceremonial freeing of four white doves (who presumably fly back to base to be sold again – hmm… this sounds like a good business proposition. Remind me to look into this), apart from the usual cheerleaders, interminable speeches, invocations and so on.

P had come back from hol to find that the basket-ball court had had the roof blown off and it was covered by water and debris, and that no-one had even thought to check it out. But hey, what's a small detail like that between friends? So long as the banners and the razzmatazz are in place, the rest doesn't matter too much…

When P comes back after the festivities, he tells me that the cheerleaders were absolutely fantastic – forming human pyramids, throwing girls back and forth above the boys' heads and even doing somersaults in mid-air. These are just school-children but they are, he tells me, totally professional.

Carol and Hedi are back from leave, hurray! Shirley and I have an informal meeting to catch up arrangements for programme for Ladies' Club Christmas party. Didn't want to be back but there are some compensations; apart from being with Pat of course, there are some really nice people here so I can't complain about that.

I have a lovely, relaxing, solitary swim at Shell Club during the afternoon. On the drive there, it's the first time I've seen where the bridge has collapsed. The debris, a colossal amount of it, is still in the river-bed, and the existing bridge is temporary, arranged with local contractors by FW. Pat reckons, and I bet he'll be right, that it will still be in place when we leave. Coming back traffic is heavy and so we take an alternative route through outskirts of BC and over a small bridge that I didn't know existed. We live and learn!

Have twice recently seen a lovely sight: carabao are large black animals – oxen maybe, or buffalo. Anyway, have twice seen them recently in mud-holes, with mud right up to their eyes, getting cooled off. You could just see the very top of their shoulders and backs, and their eyes above the mud. Hardly noticed them at first, they were in so deep…

After English Mass in the evening Heidi and Tim come over for dinner. As we are just four we have dinner on the balcony; very cool, pleasant and civilized.

Sunday we had a lie-in till almost 8 a.m. then finished washing-up from the previous night. Shell Club with P for a lovely quiet swim and coffee. Shopping to Pic'n'Save then home for lunch. Spent afternoon preparing dinner; Nigel and Halima, Des and Aisha came in for a meal. Nice evening. Food quite good in spite of being, for the second night running, almost exclusively from the store-cupboard. One hundred and one things to do with a cabbage. Or something…

To see street children following morning. We spent the morning measuring each child – sixteen of them today – with a view to getting them new t-shirts and flip-flops. They just loved the attention they got from the expat ladies and were really responding to Ronnie and her activities. They absolutely loved their Monday sessions and it was obvious that the staff were learning a lot too.

Back home for a very quick shower and out again; this time to Shell Club for meeting re Christmas party. Good meeting – everything seemed to be going according to plan. Except, that is, for the entrance of a gi-normous cockroach – like a three-inch job, which climbed up the wall of the room behind us. I practically went into orbit but Carol gave chase and did the biz, when I almost freaked out again. Calmed down with a cup of coffee and it was back to Shirley's for a quick look at music for said 'do'. I prefer being busy but it was just amazing how quickly the time went, and how difficult it was to get 'chores' done sometimes.

Jinky came round next morning; it was so nice to see her. We had a fun time chatting and re-rehearsing (so to speak) 'Louise' duet for Friday, which I repeat somewhat immodestly, was rather good. (You know me! Never backwards in coming forwards...)

Afternoon was meeting here of ladies who helped with the street children, to discuss issues like the forthcoming Christmas party, allocation of children's names for whom the ladies will buy new clothes – T-shirts, shorts, and flip-flop-type sandals, who should we invite to be Father Christmas, and more long-term issues. (Sorry, have I destroyed an illusion?)

Phew! No sooner had everyone gone than I had to rush around making couscous, tidying-up (Oooh shame, has Purita gone home then?) and getting ready for the evening's meeting/discussion/preliminary rehearsal of cabaret for party. First proper rehearsal was to be on Sunday.

With Aisha to Val's the following morning to prepare for Bring and Buy in aid of street children, then it was the actual sale in the afternoon. Good fun, well supported and we all came away with bargains of one sort or another – edible, wearable, useable or smell-able (if there is such a word). Val phoned later to say she'd taken 8000 pesos - brilliant. We'd certainly be able to put it to good use.

Evening Pat and I went over to Caltex Club to another trial tasting session with the new menu. On the way there we saw a guy working on a food stall at the side of the road casually using his food-preparing knife to pare his nails. Yuk.

There were about twenty of us, most of whom I knew. We had about seven new dishes to try then make evaluation comments on our sheets. Good fun and though the food was not as good as hoped for, nonetheless the Manager deserved supporting in his efforts to improve and extend his menu. When we left he was poring over the evaluation sheets with his staff...

16 November. Shirley has organized an exercise session over on the Caltex compound, with possibility of a swim after. I'd love to go but this week has been so hectic I haven't done half the things I should have, so give it a miss and do odd jobs instead. Not as much fun but it 's great to tick things off my lists.

I manage to do letters, e-mails, alter a skirt for a friend, start some long-overdue sewing, and fix up a meeting between Romil, the little boy singer, and Jinky who specializes in teaching children to sing pop. Some of the ladies said ages ago that it would be good to organize some singing lessons for him; Jinky is happy to meet and assess him. We'll see what happens – his family is very poor and they supplement the dad's meagre income with Romil's performance money so hopefully this will have a positive spin-off.

Afternoon I go next door to Mah Jong at Aisha's. First time since before my UK leave that I've played so feel quite rusty, but we have pleasant time. Twelve of us there. Back home to resume chores, including my second singing session of the day. FW have a number of bags of provisions left over from a recent workers' celebration, and as none of the other FW ladies are available (they're at beginners' bridge which doesn't interest me), Pat and I take it to the Centre. Not many children in today so we leave with the helpers; some children will take theirs today, some on Monday when the Centre re-opens after the weekend.

On then to a local shop where we buy a complete Boy Scout uniform for one of street children, one of the few who go to school and the only one therefore who has access to a Scout troop. It will be his Christmas present from the ladies; the other children will get ordinary T-shirts, shorts and sandals each. Total amount of the uniform is the equivalent of less than seven pounds sterling; how sad that it's beyond the reach of many of the people out here.

Visit a fabric shop and buy red fabric and white fur edging – I plan to make a sort of mini Father Christmas outfit to sell raffle tickets at the Ladies' Club party. Had been asked to wear the cabaret outfit which I wore for my 'I'll make a man of you' at the last cabaret but we don't want to repeat ourselves, do we? We have our standards to maintain…

Afternoon I have my singing lesson with Christine, which goes well and which I enjoy. As usual I take a tricycle up which I don't really like – the air is so polluted that it's not very pleasant, but walking back later is even less pleasant with crowded pavements – where they exist— in addition.

Fiesta Fast Food

Saturday. Most other FW ladies went to Alabang to do some food shopping - we could certainly have done with some perishable food but we'd be up there again on Wednesday for the monthly bazaar anyway so I opted to stay at home and do sewing, e-mails and phone calls. Boring, but I felt so much better for getting down again to some long-outstanding chores. I seemed to have so many balls in the air at that stage that they were in severe danger of crashing down...

Pat got in at 3.30 p.m., earlier than was usual on Saturdays. We went to 6 p.m. Mass as usual, the English Mass, taking a new guy who'd only been out a few days. After Mass we went to Aisha and Des's for the evening as we'd arranged for Benji, the DI, to come and do a dance session with us. That evening it was cha-cha, swing and tango, which had now become my favourite in place of boogie! Dinner after, with Nigel and Halima there too: a lovely evening.

Lizards and Loos

Sunday was a gorgeous day, blue skies and really hot by 9 a.m. Lovely swim at Shell Club where we also met a new lady, French, Michelle, who was just visiting for a month. Sun-bathing for a while after, and coffee in the sun – it was a far nicer way to spend a November day than shivering in the UK.

Pat took me to see two different venues for future reference, one of which was modern, and which we'd booked for the Ladies' Club party. Just as we appeared round the corner of the disused swimming pool, we saw a large lizard, about two feet long, disappear into the undergrowth after taking a drink from the pool. We discovered that the gents' loos were not working, and were not expected to be working by the time of the party. I passed the info on to Carol, who promised to check it out the next day. More about the gents' loos later!

The other venue which we visited was particularly nice. It was modern, but traditionally built in bamboo and was absolutely charming. P tentatively booked it for a FW party on 28th. Saw one of our favourite carabao lying down in a muddy pool, up to his shoulders in water…

We did some shopping in Caedo and bought some new furniture – rectangular rubber-wood dining table and chairs – very plain and stylish – and two sort of padded director's chairs, folding. The big glass-topped table on the landing seemed to be infested with some sort of tiny mites so we'd asked the landlord to remove it; this light modern stuff would really brighten up the landing and make it more comfortable.

Evening we had a rehearsal for the cabaret. We were pleased to have Carol and Hobby on board; they didn't want to participate but helped us to pool our ideas and we got at least a bit further forward.

Spent most of the following day at the Regional Hospital, painting one of the rooms in the children's ward with other expat ladies. When I arrived at 10 a.m. the place was so dirty I didn't know where to put my bag. This low level of cleanliness wasn't appropriate in any public building – even in a bus shelter it was hardly acceptable. But a hospital? The walls were peeling, the four wooden lockers had cobwebs behind, the bedsteads of the six or so beds were grimy, the one lavatory didn't flush, the tap-top had been removed, and the only way to get water was to place a bucket under the waste outlet from the sink and turn on the stop-cock. On the bright side, I thought they'd made more effort overall to keep the corridors clean; someone was cleaning and polishing – first time I'd seen that. First time also I saw no stray cats; I thought the stray dog in the men's surgical corridor had probably chased them off…

Carol arrived a few minutes later, and, normally full of energy, took one look at the place and just slumped on a chair. The other ladies arrived with scrubbing brushes and scrapers, and seven of us worked like crazy for a couple of hours. Nathalie, very much to her credit, started with the loo and went crazy with bleach and brush. We couldn't do the ceiling but that wasn't too bad anyway. Just concentrated on the walls and iron-grilled windows. Scraped off loose paint everywhere, wiped dirt off window grills, and when Carol and I left at 12 midday it was ready for painting. Home for snack, back in the afternoon and there were a total of twelve of us doing the painting. By 4 p.m. when I left with Carol it was finished bar the details; the others stayed on to finish as the staff had to get patients back in there this evening and free up the other room for painting tomorrow.

I imagine that I speak for the others when I say that I was totally exhausted – it was not just the physical work with temperatures in the thirties and no fan or air-con - for me at any rate it was partly the dirt and, to be honest, also the feeling of frustration and resentment against the people who let it get like that, and against those who pressed their noses against the windows to watch us but didn't lift a finger to help…

Carol was horrified to learn that men's loos didn't work in Christmas party venue, and that they would not be operational by the due date. Arranged to talk with Manager tomorrow and I took Carol to see other venue which Pat showed me the day before. She agreed with us – it was lovely, though more expensive. Pat promised to get his assistant, who came from that barangay, to help us negotiate.. P had a fair bit on his plate at that time, including a strike of workers of one of the contractors 'cos they hadn't been paid by the contractor…

Back home to prepare supper. Prepared delicious vegetable curry with rice. Thankfully realized just in time that wild rice does not normally climb up the sides of the saucepan (think about it) so slung same into rubbish and cooked plain boiled rice instead. A narrow escape!

November 21. The others are painting the second and last room today at the Hospital, but I'm not free and to be quite wimpish just don't think I could cope with it again. Jinky should be here to rehearse for Friday's Music and Fun, but she's ill with another throat infection and can't make it. She had to see the doctor yesterday and is quite worried as her voice is her livelihood.

Come lunchtime Carol and I, with Pat, go to check out the famous men's loos again in the party venue. Guy is late arriving (I discover later that in fact he just doesn't turn up) so before we push off we walk round the back of one of sports halls in the complex, to discover that the path between the rear of building and edge of steep ravine – about twenty foot down to river—is just crumbling away. Its widest point is about four/five feet, in places it's considerably less, and in one place the path has crumbled away right up to the building. P puts his foot to the edge to test it and a shower of earth and stones go crashing down. This is a new complex… Carol tells me later that the loos have been out of action for a couple of months and till now the men using the complex have been peeing in the bushes; definitely not acceptable for an expat do. Whatever next!

Evening we have rehearsal with them thespians wot are doing the cabaret for the party. We pool food and have a really nice supper first, then rehearsal. Some numbers shaping up nicely; am a bit concerned that my Prima Donna sketch with 'workmen' isn't really gelling yet, but hopefully it'll be all right on the night. Nice evening anyway!

To Manila with Hedi and Lek; first to the monthly bazaar for a couple of hours, where I bought lots of bits and pieces, then Alabang for lunch and food shopping. Out from 7 a.m. till after 6 p.m. – a pleasant day but a tiring one…

Funniest sight today was a bus (single-decker as they all are) pulled up at the side of the road with a flat tyre. Driver was jacking up his vehicle with a couple of blokes helping/supervising, and as they jacked it up there was a head poked out of every window watching. I could never be accused of being mechanically-minded but it seems to me that the bus would have been a lot less heavy and easier to lift without a full complement of passengers. Or not? Pat gets home at 8 p.m., having been out since 7 a.m.…

Much-needed morning in the following day doing odd-jobs – e-mails, sewing, tidying-up. Asked Purita if she'd be kind enough to go out for some Christmas decorations which she did. We put them up and it looked very nice. P and I both found it strange to see and hear around us all the preparations for Christmas – in bright sunshine. Weird! In Pat's lunch-hour we went up to Tony's office and collected the painting of his family home which we'd commissioned; it would certainly bring back some pleasant memories of Tony and his music when we were back in UK.

Wash-Day

Music and Fun

It took me all next morning to get ready for 'Music and Fun'. Lovely smells from downstairs where Purita was baking cakes – it sure smelt good. Mmmm!

First, the bad news: Jinky rang to say that she was getting better but had a rehearsal with the choir she was training and choreographing for a big school re-union tomorrow, so couldn't come. We were both disappointed but this was work for her whereas I could please myself what I did. Second problem was that Christine, my Bel Canto coach, didn't turn up; I discovered later that she wasted two hours sitting in a traffic jam and fuming...

Anyway, the afternoon was fun. Ten ladies of eight different nationalities. I did four numbers, two of which I'd planned as duets with Jinky but which I did as solos. 'Never Say Never', 'Thoroughly Modern Millie' 'Louise' and 'Chatanooga'. Couple of silly games, and Carol's hat competition. The outright winner was Bruni, a German lady, who was wearing an absolute masterpiece in straw, almost completely covered by leaves, flowers and Christmas decorations. A Father Christmas camel surmounted the edifice, and a pink fabric piggy sat on the crown with knife and fork rampant beside! Afternoon tea, or rather merienda, completed the festivities.

Off to Christine's for my lesson, which was fun and helpful. At my request Christine just listened, and prompted if necessary, while I rehearsed 'Art is Calling for Me' to backing tape prepared by the Maestro. It was difficult anyway singing to tape, and this one was particularly difficult if I lost my place, so I was glad of her support. This was in preparation for Saturday's cabaret...

I walked back home braving the traffic, the pollution, the open drains, the broken paving stones, the holes in the pavement – it was like going back in time to the seventeenth century. (P told me that Arab countries were even worse). I was exhausted by this time and fell asleep in one of our new chairs on the landing for a little while, and looked forward to a quiet evening. Not to be: Pat had to go to a local restaurant, to hear a band, possibly for the FW party the following Tuesday. Arrived at 9 p.m. as directed, band set up 9.30 ish and started to play at 9.40 by which time I was almost asleep. Very young, competent, but unbelievably loud – so loud the sound was almost distorted.

We left as soon as we reasonably could.

P told me that the strike, about which I wrote fairly recently, continued, and was quite serious. The contractors, as I said, hadn't paid the workers, although they themselves had been paid. (P surmised that perhaps they used the money to pay off people higher up who are more powerful). Problem was that the strike was in the ship-yard an hour's drive away, where some of our managers worked, and FW couldn't get out the steel and materials that were needed on Site, because of the strike. Attempts had been made day before to 'smuggle' out a barge with materials, but it had been intercepted and stopped. Promises were made, which were not fulfilled, (surprise surprise) that it would be ok, and on Tuesday the strike actually went official, which meant that the Government had to take over the situation from the local officials who were then dealing (or not).

Apparently it would be impossible to resolve by Tuesday, so anything might happen. Think the Government had their hands full at that time with President Estrada's impeachment proceedings, the frequent political demonstrations, and the fall of the peso...

Saturday 25 November. Lovely solitary swim, coffee and sun-bathe at Shell Club. Great to be in the open air: I always feel good after a swim. On way back I see near the river a beautiful bird, about the size of a jay, light, bright blue – iridescent like a kingfisher, but more turquoise than blue. Absolutely beautiful – Lito tells me they used to be common but now there are not so many.

We get another glimpse of the local fauna when Pat leaves home again after lunch: there's a two-foot dead cobra at the side of the house. The guards saw it trying to get in through the French windows and killed it. Photo call with Willy and Eric the guards, with me, holding the offending snake draped tastefully over a stick. They retain their venom for some time even when dead – the snake, not the guards. At two-feet long, it was just a young cobra, so there must be a nest of them on the waste ground next door.

P tells me two funny stories – both true – about the Philippino propensity for sleeping. Going into a Government office yesterday he found seven workers asleep at their desks, and late afternoon, taking a group of important visiting German dignitaries around the Site he was amused to see that when everyone went to listen to a presentation, the Germans, who'd set out at 7 a.m., were still bright-eyed, bushy-tailed, and asking intelligent questions. The local Philippino dignitaries, from the Mayor's office and local government offices, grabbed and ate all the cakes they could get hold of, and, five out of six of them just went to sleep! So the Germans, the British, and two Dutch Shell managers were there discussing problems of the Philippines and how best to help, when the would-be recipients were doing the thing they do best…

Individuals whom we know personally – T, Aida, Purita, Jinky, Christine, our guards, are great. Absolutely charming and with a very strong work ethic. On Boracay, Gerry and Debbie met a Philippino who had three jobs and who was studying for a degree too. Those Philippinos who go abroad to work really graft to send money home to support their families, but so many of them here are just downright lazy. They sleep anywhere; they eat five times per day. They don't see beyond the next meal for themselves and their families, let alone the next day. Poor, yes. There's lots of poverty but I don't think there's any starvation here - food is cheap and plentiful. Could be even more if they just got off their butts and cultivated the land.

When in Boracay we were chatting to the French proprietor of a restaurant on the beach; he has five more restaurants in the Philippines, has been here fifteen years, speaks fluent Tagalog, and has spent a lot of time studying Philippine behaviour. He told us of one instance where one of the girls working for him had a chance of a job in Hong Kong, but didn't have the right experience. He encouraged her, helped her, and was delighted for her when she got the job. Before she left she asked Greg to take care of her parents, who also worked for him and he said that of course he would.

A few weeks later, the father gave notice for himself and his wife, and when Greg asked why he explained they didn't need to work any longer, as the daughter was sending them cheques from HK. So the poor girl was working terribly hard to better herself while her parents were sitting in the sun waiting for her cheques… He had a Philippina girl-friend who worked for him. When he found she was stealing from him he understandably dismissed her. Couple of days later, her brother, who also worked for him came and gave in his notice, explaining that although he liked working for Greg, he had to leave, because the family would lose face if he continued working for him when his sister had been sacked. So Greg asked him what he'd do – he just shrugged – what about his two children he needed to keep in school? Shrugged again.

As several times this week, torrential rain starts completely out of the blue. Good thing is that it really freshens up the air. Lovely fresh smell... Coming back from Manila the other day we drove through really bad floods which similarly seemed to appear out of no-where...

Mass in the evening and then Jo, the new guy, comes back with us for a meal. Pleased to say that he's passed the rigorous selection procedure and has been unanimously cast as the third little maid from our Mikado sketch – i.e. he was available and couldn't think of a good enough reason why not...

Sunday started with a swim for me, but P was getting over cough/cold so just enjoyed relaxing in the sun. Was fascinated to see a three foot lizard waddling down the drive in the club-grounds - largest I'd seen, and the closest.

Quiet afternoon in the house making, among other things, three 'Japanese wigs' out of black card and tapes, dagger and other assorted props. We had a rehearsal in the evening when we worked on, and vastly improved, both 'Three Little Maids' and my comedy number, 'Art is Calling for Me'.

Nigel told us that he'd had an awful weekend. Yesterday he'd had a phone call from his house in Sarawak, to say that his new car had been stolen, and also yesterday he and Halima had set out to drive to Manila for the weekend, where they had tickets for Miss Saigon. The journey, normally two hours or a bit over, took over seven hours due to horrendous traffic, so they missed the show...

Next day we had a Ladies' Club committee meeting at the Shell Club; amongst other things we finalised the Christmas party arrangements. I was looking forward to it; should be fun. Afternoon in doing a spot of water-colour; first time for ages, and preparing props for rehearsal same evening. Managed to produce a 'present' (corn-flour packet in tin-foil, tied with red ribbon) 'piping/ engineering working drawings', with words and actions on the reverse, a dagger handle which would stick to P's shirt and from a distance (hopefully) would look like it had sunk into his person. Ho yus! A merry little afternoon and a productive one. Actual rehearsal, which we did in the venue, went well and Philippine care-takers enjoyed it too and laughed in (some of) the right places.

Ladies' Club coffee morning in Dunkin Donuts. Yes well, we went into all that before, didn't we? Not as well-attended as last time, but pleasant nonetheless. Afternoon in, then in the evening we had the Company Christmas party. The venue was the traditionally-built bamboo function centre which Pat had discovered the other week. It was delightful with fairy lights everywhere. Two hundred and fifty people at the party, which went well, but I didn't really enjoy it very much as Pat was busy for much of the evening. We'd be using this venue for the Ladies' Club party at the weekend; thought it would be a great 'do'.

The ladies were painting the last of four rooms in the children's ward next day; they moved the children out when we arrived – into the corridor where they stayed whilst we were painting. We discovered that the room in question was the typhoid ward, and that the children just outside in the corridor were typhoid patients. Confess that I wasn't over-keen on being so close to typhoid cases, but I'd had my jabs, as had the others except Halima, brave lady, who opted to stay anyway.

The room, like the other room I helped with, was filthy. In general, though, the hospital looked cleaner – certainly in the corridors as we passed through, and we only saw one stray cat. Went with Carol to see the Deputy Chief, who told us that the watchers were still helping with the cleaning – sometimes in exchange for free medicines – nice one! But they didn't like wearing the tabards. I could live with that, as long as some good persisted from our project.

Anyway, back to the ward. Nine of us, and by midday the room was almost finished. I heard later that by 12.30 they were moving the patients back in. I understand that, like the previous week, they hadn't cleaned the floor before so doing. It had been filthy before we started, and even filthier afterwards...

I felt really tired so had an afternoon in. Brown-out 8 a.m. till 5.20 p.m. so I couldn't do much; it was just so good to relax. Time was whizzing... We had a very quiet evening; P was exhausted and went to sleep in his chair straight after dinner.

30 November was a national holiday today, so-called 'Heroes' Day'. Jinky came round this morning and we had a lovely long natter – hadn't seen her for a couple of weeks. Pic 'n Save in the afternoon, and, first time for a long time, P actually got home early – about 5.30 p.m. Watched a fascinating TV programme about Kimodo dragons. Otherwise, not a very exciting day, but in fact I got down to some more art too, and enjoyed the peace and quiet.

Dinner on the patio upstairs. We'd sort of re-discovered it when we'd been forced to eat out there in the forty-hour brown-out some weeks ago. It was cooler than in the house, and was quite pleasant; we planned to get some orchids to put out there which would smack even more of gracious living.

Best of Friends

Cabaret

We had another typhoon on the way, but were not troubled by the wind (!) yet – just torrential rain – again. I was always pleased when it rained 'cos it really did freshen up the air. Didn't like continual rain though – so hoped it didn't persist. I would have liked a swim but there was no fun in swimming if you couldn't relax in the sun after.

I had a quiet morning: just popped out to see T, who had expressed an interest in the street children, and who would be coming to the party on 12 December. Also invited him next Wednesday evening; we were having a small-ish party before Hedi went back to Hungary for the festivities. Lots of ladies had left already for Christmas…

Afternoon was lesson with Christine which I enjoyed; I invited her to party Wednesday next. Evening was dress rehearsal for cabaret, which went suspiciously well. Ho hum, this was worrying. Didn't like the feel of this at all.

The Big Day! Pat was working as usual; I went over to the party venue, Villa Fransisca, in the morning with Carol and Hobby to get things under way. Caterer arrived soon after and what amounted to a military operation ensued: two lorries and a veritable army of workers turned up with one 'Juan Carlos' (his real name is Alex. Don't ask me…) They brought in tall ferns and palms, potted plants, life-size Fr Christmas, two resin statues, lights, streamers, the lot. Plus chairs, tables, cutlery, crockery, booze and food. It was just fascinating to watch and I was most impressed.

Afternoon passed in a frenzy of activity – rounding up of last-minute props, showering, altering, in a last-minute panic, both the dress I suddenly decided to wear and the Fr Christmas outfit I'd made. This was necessary as I couldn't find white fur trim, so had used a cotton-wool border, and guess what? It got fluff over everywhere – I looked as though I'd been out in a snow-storm. Or a chicken-plucking factory. Or both.

We arrived at the party to find everything looked absolutely wonderful. I sold raffle-tickets dressed up in my tasteful little outfit and then went 'backstage' with my co-thespians to check last-minute cues and music etc. After meetings and greetings came dinner, then the famous cabaret. It was a riot! The four items which we did all went really well and by the end of the show the audience was in hysterics – one lady laughed so much she had to take a headache tablet… It was the first time I'd directed a show and I was delighted. A brilliant team! Everyone had come up with ideas and suggestions, some of which had worked, some which hadn't, but it had been great to brainstorm and try things out. After dinner we had dancing; we'd arranged for our two favourite DIs to come so I got my favourite boogie and tango.

Sunday. We're both very tired from yesterday and lie-in (!) till 8.30 a.m. Then after a wake-up cuppa we start to put away all the dozens of props and bits-and-pieces from last night. Pat gets called round to a colleague's house on business and is away about an hour. Quick cup of coffee and off we go to meet Purita, who has arranged for us to visit her sister-in-law to buy some orchids.

Orchids are very common here, and very beautiful: they can either be grown in lumps of charcoal in pots, or grafted onto driftwood branches. Pat has wanted to get some for some time, to put on the balcony upstairs, so now he's getting his wish. We choose, and take, six in pots - white, lemon, mauve and purple, and choose two taller versions on tree-stumps, to be collected in the next day or so. Pic 'n Save next, to collect booze for Wednesday party, and more wineglasses, and salad/fruit bowls, of which we seem to be pitifully short.

Tagalog Mass in the late afternoon as we were out yesterday evening, then home, where I cook a 'roast' with roast potatoes and pumpkin, carrots and spinach, apple sauce, and tinned M & S turkey, which we can get in Alabang. We both fancy something sweet, so have also managed to make a sort-of iced jam sponge cake – not as light as in UK as the flour is so different, but not bad.

I was quite wheezy when I woke up next morning; something had been brewing for several days and Pat had had a chesty cough for about a week, as had lots of the other expats. Felt fine, though, and at least I'd managed to get through Saturday night party without mishap.

Went to see the market children with a slightly depleted gang of expats, many of them having already left for Christmas. The Drop-In Centre comprised two rooms with a small lobby in between with a sink, where, balanced on the draining board, the helpers cooked the children's lunch. (A small portable gas cooker was balanced, not the staff.) Anyway, that day apparently there was a brown-out in the social welfare offices, so the staff had come to the Drop-In Centre to cook lunch for the welfare staff. They were cooking masses of food in a large wok on the said gas cooker, and, guess where they had located the cooker? On the floor in the lobby, which is effectively a narrow passage between the two rooms. Call me quaint and old-fashioned but with ten children around aged 6 – 15 I couldn't imagine a less safe place to locate the cooker. I gently told them so and they moved to a safer place...

Tried to teach children 'London's Burning' as a round – their first to my knowledge. Literally couldn't sing – my voice came out as a croak - (what's new, I hear you say!) but Jean and Nessie arrived and we got them singing in four parts in just a few minutes. I wanted to start some harmony with them after Christmas. Snack lunch with Pat, then we dispatched Purita with Tom, driver, to collect remaining two orchids – the two grafted onto tree stumps. Shame we wouldn't be able to bring them back when the assignment finished; they cost a fortune in UK.

To digress completely for a moment or two: our armed guards had sawn-off shotguns, which they carried casually under their arms when they walked around or rode the bike round the estate. No untoward incidents yet, but Carol told us that one of their Company guards had got a bit bored the other day and had just started shooting into the air! No-one had been hurt, but he got the sack. Guns were common: even Mcdonalds had armed guards outside...

Nigel and Halima popped in for a quick drink; we arranged to go with them and others on Saturday, to see the Bauan dancers, whom we'd seen months ago – they were absolutely brilliant and we were already looking forward to the show.

Here's a very heart-warming story which I now have permission to tell you, but I've promised not to reveal names: an expat couple who are very good friends of ours have a delightful maid who is married with three small children. The maid and husband are both very hard workers, and extremely hard-up, but they decided that, as she has a steady job as a maid, she should go out to work, and the husband should look after the children.

They also grow a few vegetables on their small patch of land where they live as tenants. Every morning they get up about 4 or 5 a.m., pick what vegetables they can, and the maid takes them to the market to sell, before going to work at 7 a.m. with our friends. As I say, extremely hard workers.

Anyway, our friends discovered that their ambition was to breed pigs for the table, and, guess what? With the help of Tony, who has done all the legal work free of charge, they bought the land and house, assisted in measuring up and planning, purchased the pigs, helped them find all the information and advice that they needed, and have set them up as pig farmers. The eight pigs are flourishing and the maid and husband are taking the greatest care and pride in them. Every morning the maid goes round the other maids in the expat compound, and collects the food left-overs, in insulated containers which she bought herself, and every afternoon the husband walks over – maybe a kilometre - to collect the two or three heavy buckets to mix with the proprietary pig-food. These people deserve to succeed – they are such hard workers – and I know they will succeed.

Isn't that a story to warm the cockles of your heart? Such generosity – and they have grown-up children in their own country, who have whole-heartedly agreed to the scheme. It's been a privilege to know these people…

Heidi and I went to Alabang next day - long day but very enjoyable; I left the house at 6.30 a.m. Mainly shopping for the party next day plus bits and pieces. Tried to get a salad spinner but the one model I saw wasn't what I was looking for, so got a bookcase. As a bookcase it was very nice – rubber-wood, quite plain and stylish, but for washing salad it was hopeless. I should have known!

Lunch break at Deli France and a good journey home, arriving at 5.30 p.m., happy but tired after an eleven-hour day. The guys thought they had it hard…

Dinner watching first half of the film 'Remains of the Day'. We'd got half-way through once before and had never got round to finishing it so hoped we'd do better this time. Had read the book in the meantime which I thoroughly enjoyed.

More Christmas Festivities

6 December. Dee dee di dee dee! Party day today, party day today! Ey ay ey ay party day today. They don't write songs like that anymore, more's the pity. (She's finally lost it, I hear you say. How can you tell?)

Favourite sort of morning – in fact day – preparing for party. Purita and I do lots of food between us but several people have offered to bring things, including Carol, bless her, who's bringing a twelve-pound ham which she home-smoked herself. Isn't that wonderful? Prepare for one or two silly games (I know you'll find that hard to believe, but try), lay the table and so on.

It's sort of de rigeur here, it seems, to have Christmas lights outside and they're certainly cheap. Some of the houses have incredibly elaborate displays which rival Blackpool, nay, put it into the shade, if you'll pardon the pun. So, Pat dispatches Philippino contact to buy more outside lights to supplement the ones I bought yesterday. And hey presto! In a twinkling (get it?) we have Christmas...

Afternoon is like the morning, only more of it. Shirley sends round copy of the video from Saturday's cabaret, which I can't resist seeing. The cabaret is surprisingly good. And the party? Well... It's great. Not an enormous gathering, about twenty of us, but everyone enjoys it. Carol and Hobby stagger in with the twelve-pound joint which Hobby proceeds to carve with much ceremony, and which, I have to say, is absolutely delicious. Other people bring food too, and it's all delicious. I plate up two meals and take them out to the guards, only to find someone's driver is waiting too, (did you notice the way I dropped that casually into the narrative? Impressed?) so I plate up a third meal for same.

At the party there are Brits, of course, an Aussie, a Hungarian, Malaysian, Singaporean, and a Thai, two Americans, and five Philippinos – Shirley, Jinky and Mario, Christine and T. It would have been lovely to have made music but we just don't have time, as parties out here break up incredibly early by UK standards. We have a couple of silly games, though, which go down extremely well, and the last to leave, the 'cabaret crowd' all watch the video of last Saturday's antics. Everyone is very pleasantly surprised...

The following morning Pat had a lie-in and went to work at 7.30 a.m.(!) I staggered downstairs and started to clear up. Usually this was when I did my singing but I was a still a bit croaky and wheezy and gave it up as a bad job. Anyway, I worked for nearly an hour then Purita came in early and took over. (I know, you don't have to keep telling me...) I spent the rest of the morning in; had toyed with the idea of a swim but was too tired after the party and was quite pleased when it started to rain so I didn't feel too guilty! Pat came in early for lunch, and both then and at dinner we ate the day before's left-overs. Doesn't sound very appetizing but in fact they were delicious. Mah Jong in afternoon...

Over dinner we finished 'Remains of the Day' which I thoroughly enjoyed. There were only slight departures from the novel.

An interesting anecdote for you: I wrote recently that Pat had had to go round to a colleague's house. The reason was that the colleague had had an argument with a Philippino and had (supposedly) reversed his car towards the man with the intention of killing him. The Philippino in question had gone to the Police who'd served the FW guy with notice of the complaint. He had to report to the Police Station within ten days to answer the charges. There had been meetings between the Company and the other parties; it transpired that the 'victim' was a member of an influential local family who were trying to make money out of the situation. FW had persuaded them to drop the charges, but the Philippino mentality was such that there could nonetheless have been reprisals against him...

Jinky came round next morning to help prepare some music for the street children's Christmas party on Tuesday. It would be the social event of the year! Lots of the expat helpers had already left for UK and other destinations, so not many of the group would be fortunate enough to attend and to see the children's faces. I was one of the lucky ones.

P went off to work at usual time on Saturday; I lay in till almost 8 a.m. Short vocal session (voice was almost completely better now) - would do more later. Off to Shell Club for a swim which I enjoyed – my wheeziness, preparation for last week's party, and heavy rain the last few days had prevented my swimming for two weeks. The water was, for the first time, actually cold, and I was into my fourth length before I warmed up. Coffee and a read in the sun after – bliss!

Had been reading even more voraciously than usual: 'The Shipping News', a rather off-beat novel about Newfoundland by Annie Proulx, and 'October Sky', an autobiography about some young boys who teach themselves to become rocket scientists, also 'The Debt to Pleasure' by John Lanchester which is seriously weird and which I'd loved – once I could get into it. All quite unusual, and all thoroughly enjoyable. Just started 'Lucky Jim'... Don't remember having read Kingsley Amis before.

We had a disappointment in the evening: a group of us had arranged to drive over to Bauan to see the dancers there – they were senior high school students who sang and danced all over the world. We'd seen them soon after we'd arrived, and they were truly fantastic. Anyway, we had a message to say that the show was off as there was a typhoon warning. (It didn't materialize, but that was another story).

Pat, Jo and I went to Mass then Caltex to sample new menu. Our meals were really delicious, but, with the exception of the soup, were not hot, just about warm in fact. (Alex, the Manager, was off-duty, which probably explained it.) Staff couldn't heat them up in the micro-wave as the meals were beautifully presented and arranged on white china plates with silver trim... As we got up to leave, Pat glanced through the swing doors into the kitchen, and was amused to see one of the kitchen staff standing up, draped over the hotplate, fast asleep.

Sunday was a lovely day, really hot by 8 a.m. Pat and I went to the Shell Club where we swam, sunbathed, and drank coffee. Back home for lunch on the patio, which was looking so exotic since the advent of the orchids, then packing for our Christmas leave. It was dreadfully hot and oppressive; at one stage I felt quite overcome by the heat and I had to go and lie down with the air-con on full.

Over dinner we started to watch 'The Talented Mr Ripley', which had very good reviews, but we both thought it was unconvincing and self-indulgent so gave it up as a bad job. Early-ish night, but we both woke up in the night as the promised (or threatened?) typhoon struck. Out of no-where we heard a loud, low, menacing noise like an explosion, (Carol said later she wondered if it was a small tornado) and then within a couple of seconds the rain thundered down like a waterfall – we'd never heard rain quite like it. Within minutes the temperature had dropped by several degrees, and there was a delicious fresh smell in the air.

By morning all traces of the typhoon had disappeared. Spent the morning with the street children. Everyone was excited about next day's party and guess what? Father Christmas had kindly offered to drop by. Thinks, had I been a good girl or not? Watch this space…

During the afternoon I made a 'fairy' outfit so that tomorrow I could sing 'Nobody loves a Fairy when She's Forty' for the children. Droopy, off-white lace skirt over white T-shirt, Carol's Wellington boots, a long grey cotton mop-head for a wig with a glittery headband, and a silver wand (which bent to order) completed the ensemble. A distinct improvement, I hear you say. Must remember this outfit next time we went to an expat party. I would wow everyone. In the evening we went to Nigel and Halima for dinner, with Des, Aisha, Jo, and a new FW couple. Halima, a brilliant cook, excelled herself; we had a wonderful meal and waddled home groaning quietly…

12 December. Am horrified to see young guy in flip-flops scything heavy underground on the waste patch between Des and Aisha's house and our own. Horrified on two counts – firstly flip-flops don't seem such a good idea while he's wielding such a sharp blade, and secondly, we know there are snakes there. One of them, a cobra, ended up at the side of the house a couple of weeks back.

Lovely party this morning with the street children. When we arrive, half-an-hour early, the children – twenty-five of them today, word has got around – are already sitting in a circle waiting for the festivities to start. It's chaotic of course. We have lots of boisterous games, which they love, goodies to eat, I do my fairy number, they sing and dance for us, and then Father Christmas arrives.

Traditionally here, as elsewhere in Asia, people do not usually open gifts on receipt. They open them later in private, in case, we're told, they don't like them and they, or the donor, would then be embarrassed. Anyway, today is an exception. They open the presents straight away and there are inevitably a few hitches. Two of the older boys positively glower as they don't like their T-shirts. One or two T-shirts are too small, ditto a pair of shorts and a pair of flip-flops. The young lad getting the Scout uniform informs us that it's the wrong colour – he's been given the uniform of older boys – which the lady in the shop sold us in good faith. No problem, it can be changed and we explain this. There's a bit of judicious trading and most people end up happy, thankfully.

We end up hot, sweating and exhausted, but delighted that it's been such a success. It's particularly good that Carol's pastor from her Baptist church has turned up to meet the children, also T. Think both were impressed and we're optimistic that these contacts with 'good' influential local people may lead to other things for the children, some of whom have unbelievably sad backgrounds.

Pat, when he comes home, tells me that he went into a Provincial Government office this afternoon, to find three out of the four employees fast asleep and the fourth one was eating take-away noodles. Three o'clock in the afternoon. Because labour here is cheap, and because jobs mean votes, employees are recruited for whom there is virtually nothing to do. The strange thing is that we have almost never – maybe once – seen a Philippino reading while he or she has nothing else to do – they just sleep, anytime, anywhere. Weird.

Next day I had an early start and a long day: Dodong collected Aisha and me at 6.45 a.m. then it was off to get Halima, and up to Manila for the monthly American bazaar. Had a nice couple of hours there, meeting a number of Batangas friends, and the three of us drove to a ceramics factory shop which I'd been trying to get to for weeks. There was lots of nice stuff there, including lots of seasonal goods, and we all came away loaded. Or rather, laden but no longer loaded if you know what I mean. Over to Alabang for lunch and shopping, home about 5.30 p.m. Good day!

Amusing sign outside food eatery: 'Goodish Fast Food'. Hmm, tempted but decided to pass on that! Thanks all the same...

Vets and Vocals

Jinky came over next morning and spent an hour teaching me some very specialised warm-up and vocalisation exercises. We had a lovely morning, and Mario brought the children for merienda. (Midmorning/afternoon snacks).

In the afternoon Purita and I took Orlando to the vet's to have him 'done'. I had to leave him and collect him two hours later; was somewhat surprised, on returning, to find the vet's office windows open, and the room full of dense, white, foul-smelling smoke from a bonfire outside. It was horrid, but the two women working near the wide-open windows didn't seem to have registered it and they didn't even bother to look up from their work, let alone close the windows...

Back to the patient: he was terribly groggy and could hardly walk – he staggered around all over the place but managed to follow me upstairs, which was somewhat surprising. He finally went to sleep and slept most of the rest of the day. We were supposed to keep him in for several days but I suspected that would be too difficult; we would at least try to do so that day and the next.

The landlords came in the evening to discuss certain electrical and decorating jobs we'd like them to do when we were away. We were fortunate in that they did anything that we needed as quickly as possible, in contrast to some landlords about whom we'd heard. Cesar told me that, during the recent typhoon, one of the local streets had been flooded to a man's chin height; the locals had had to fix a rope along the street so people could pull themselves along.

Next morning, as was my wont, whilst washing up last night's dinner things, I did my vocalizing and for the first time I tried Jinky's new vocal exercises. After making loud, growling noises for a few minutes I suddenly registered that someone had been knocking at the door. It was the landlord to start some repairs. Was quite mortified - wouldn't have minded if it had been angelic noises, but loud growls? I don't think so...

Did a bit of running around – not literally – I had a driver - delivering pressie to Tony, changing wrong bits of Ruel's Boy Scout uniform, which I then took to

Drop-In Centre for him to collect, hopefully early the next week. Over to Shell Club for a swim, though not a quiet one: eighty disadvantaged children from the area were having a Christmas party hosted by Shell.

In the afternoon I re-packed my suitcase from scratch – again – and did Jinky's physical and vocal exercises to prepare for my session with Christine, which I enjoyed. Wouldn't be seeing her again for some weeks; she said that she'd miss me. No accounting for tastes!

Pat and I had to make a duty appearance at drinks party for some local dignitaries. Deadly dull. I asked Pat how we could tell that it was a party. We popped in at Jinky's to say 'hi' – she'd invited us to a family get-together but we couldn't stay long. We were actually due at another duty party but P was absolutely shattered and had an early start and a busy day tomorrow, so we decided to go home after Jinky's. Pat immediately felt asleep in the chair…

Saturday. I take P porridge in bed, made with oats I found the other day in Pic 'n Save. Healthy start to the day, huh? Frequently we have a bowl of fruit salad, as I do today. That's something I'll miss, the abundance of tropical fruit. P trots off to work at 7 a.m. Had considered a swim but I'm too tired so I have a morning in finishing the re-packing, making bread and on the computer.

We're at the stage now of having to use up food – tee hee – only three days to go! I make soup with carrots, lemon, onions, loads of seasoning and a good slosh of sherry. It's delicious… Aren't I good to share these ideas with you? I'll bet they've totally enriched your lives! Not…

P comes home from work about 3 p.m. and we do a mega shop so that he has lots of food for when he comes back from UK. Go to 6 p.m. Mass as usual but for some unknown reason there isn't one. Back home for dinner, and Benji, DI, comes to give us a private dancing lesson: the idea is that it will help bring P up to speed – I've had a number of lessons with Benji already. We concentrate on swing and then tango. Good fun – Pat has a superb sense of timing and movement and now he has a good idea of the actual steps too. Nigel and Halima come round for a drink and we sit on the balcony where it's a bit cooler, as it has been extremely oppressive today.

Sunday should have started with 8.15 a.m. Mass, but there wasn't one; didn't know why so finished packing instead and went over to Caedo to get a ballroom cassette so we could practise. Would have loved a swim but it was more important to get organized for our leave, as P would have no time tomorrow. Finally made Mass at 4.30p.m. then it was home for vegetarian curry, which was very good. P started watching 'Evita' on the TV and it was fatal – we didn't get to bed till after midnight, which, in the Tropics, with a 6 a.m. start to the next day, was a bit of a mistake...

Purita came in to work as usual next morning, but brought husband and little girl to say 'hello'. Lovely little girl, lovely family.

Pat rang to say we had to leave at 10 a.m. tomorrow for our midnight flight(!) as FW drivers were busy ferrying folk to the airport. No problem; we'd go to the New World Hotel for a few hours (don't I sound grown-up?) and have a nice relaxing time up in Manila. Could do a spot of retail therapy, though our luggage was fit to burst, or maybe we'd go to a museum. Tony's niece had an exhibition there of Philippine clothes and artefacts which had been extremely well-reviewed and had just come back from NY. Either way, it would be a nice day.

So, back to that day: street children in the morning. Only seven expats left but Ronnie could have managed alone: we all played just supporting roles. At the end of the session the children presented each of us with beautiful small ornaments made with stiff, folded, glossy paper; we parted with promises to be back after Christmas. It was just wonderful to see what changes had been wrought in the children during the last few months – who knew what might happen in the future?

The afternoon was finishing the packing, doing Jinky's exercises, pottering with some water-colours, and generally tidying up. We'd asked the landlords to decorate our bedroom while we were away, so I packed away our many photos of family and UK friends. Then in the evening P brought a bit of work home which he did after dinner, so we could make our getaway in the morning. I'd probably continue my memoirs(!) when I went back but this entry was going to be the final one for my year in the Philippines.

Christmas Letter

As I write this in December, the temperature is in the 30's, and outside the window I see the tropical vegetation – coconut and banana palms, a ten-foot poinsettia over the road and a papaya tree on the waste land next to our house. Pat and I are in the Philippines, where Pat is working on the Malampaya Project, and have been here for fifteen months (Pat) and eleven months (me). I can't imagine where the time has gone; in retrospect it has just whizzed by. Once the first few months, were over, when, you may remember I had been extremely unhappy and depressed, time had just flown. Such a lot had happened. How to sum up? Difficult to say; my feelings were mixed:

B.C., where we're based, is not an easy place to live. It is, on a good day, just over two hours' drive from Manila, and on a bad day, depending on traffic and on road conditions, anything up to seven hours. (That's the record, achieved recently by a FW guy who completely missed 'Miss Saigon' because of the traffic.) Anyway, back to Batangas. It's industrialized and extremely polluted. Food shops are no more than adequate, and there are no consistently good restaurants, nor anywhere decent even to have a coffee. However, we keep busy and we make the best of a difficult situation; more about that in a minute.

Pat is Training Manager on the Project here and does a great deal of local liaison and P.R. Like the other guys he works a minimum sixty-hour week, and often longer, including most Saturdays. This is a difficult place to do business. Although many of the local people work incredibly hard, there is an air of lassitude and inertia about the place. Local attitudes sometimes make us wonder if people actually want work, and when over half of the fifteen young people selected for training recently just fail to turn up, we get quite disillusioned.

The political scene is facing even more difficulties than usual: proceedings are going on at the moment to impeach President Estrada on particularly serious corruption charges. Feelings are running high; there have been a number of anti-Estrada demonstrations in Manila and other cities – even down here in B.C. The economic situation, bad at best, is worsening and the peso continues to drop.

We live in a large, pleasant house, on an estate behind the local Basilica. (The Republic of the Philippines is the only Christian country in Asia). Marble floors downstairs, polished wood upstairs, and chandeliers to boot! As with most expats we have a maid – an absolute delight. Purita works like a Trojan, never stops and is an excellent cook. She takes great care of us both, as do our guards.

Yes, we have armed guards (sawn-off shotguns!) two by day and two by night. They're based outside our house, and patrol also the other FW houses on the estate; FW arranged for them when Pat and I were drugged and burgled soon after coming here. It's good to know they're there!

I feel sometimes that I'm living in an adventure story – sort of Indiana Jones scenario: over the last few months we've had several typhoons, floods - one occasion the local river rose ten feet in half-an-hour and swept away the bridge, earth tremors, couple of shoot-outs about ten miles from here, between Communist guerrillas and the Police, with several fatalities both times, strike at one of the contractors' yards, and so on. We've had incredible electric storms and one evening saw the roof of the local Basilica struck by lightning twice. (No apparent damage; it's been there since the sixteen hundreds and I'm sure will be there a whole lot longer.) There has been sabotage/bombing at a bus station about ten miles away – the list goes on, but as expats we can normally manage to stay outside all this action…

County Living

Post-UK leave

Well, here I was back again in the sunny Philippines, after a long leave – I'd stayed on in the UK after Pat had gone back. Sadly my lovely Dad had died at Christmastime, so even more than usual, our leave hadn't really been a holiday. Thankfully though, we were in UK and my brothers and I had managed to be with him and to support my Mum: I was very grateful for that.

I'd been confronted by at least two hundred bills, invoices, bank statements, insurance queries etc., all of which had been piling up for the previous three months or so, and all of which had needed attention. It had taken me days even to open them – that was before I started dealing with them just a few at a time!

We'd been trying (from the other side of the world!) to buy a small terraced house in Reading to rent out and by the time I arrived in UK we'd almost lost it – everything hung by a thread which had been in perilous danger of breaking. Those of you who know the cumbersome, problem-fraught system of house purchase in UK will understand A crack in the rear wall (could it be subsidence, etc.) and the fact that it was to be let, had created all sorts of extra complications.

To cut a long story short, I managed to cajole, entreat, talk nicely to, etc. lots of people and we managed to complete on the house a couple of weeks into my leave. That's not all: within the three weeks after that, I'd arranged building repairs on extension (no it wasn't subsidence), total internal decoration which was a major job (formerly pink/purple walls in one room, green and yellow stripes in another, bad surfaces, etc.), overhaul of all electrics, new carpet throughout, and furnishings. From a grimy, dark little house, it was transformed into a light, bright, welcoming house I'd have been happy to live in. Oh, and I gave the garden a cosmetic job. The agents moved tenants in three days later. Not bad, huh?

Another priority for me, apart from seeing Gerry, Ben and spending time with my Mum, were several singing arrangements I'd made. I spent a day singing in a number of classes at the prestigious Croydon Music Festival (and came away with a second) and at the small Tilehurst Eisteddford (don't laugh) where I managed a joint third, but distinctions in my three classes. Also did a couple of gigs for elderly people, as I used to, with my friends.

It was difficult going back, much though I wanted to see Pat. Anyway, I had a good journey and a pleasant long weekend with him in Manila before returning to BC. Went to a Ladies' Club coffee morning the day after I arrived (after two and a half hours' sleep!). I spent a day or so feeling very depressed but was soon feeling much better after friends to supper and a dinner party. I had several swims during the week and got involved with the street children again.

In my absence the expat scene had changed; lots of FW people had left/were already leaving as the end of the Project was in sight. We didn't know when we would be leaving, but certainly within the next few months; we hoped that we'd get a few weeks' notice of our demob, at which stage we'd need to send off our boxes, as they would take some time to clear Customs and arrive at our home.

The time started to fly. Another Mary, a friend, and I, had finally found a Fine Arts student who gave us art tutorials on Saturdays in basic art techniques. So far we'd done sketching and pastels, with oils and water-colours to follow. It was surprisingly difficult, as I'd just experimented, and done my own thing so far... We both thoroughly enjoyed our art lessons, and the student tutor loved the lunches we all had together!

Whatever happened to us next we had a lot of ends to tie up, so about this time I stopped doing the journal on a regular basis - the packing would be a huge job, and I'd also wanted to do a French business course on-line, though I never actually got round to that. I continued, of course, to paint...

Taal Basilica

Easter

One or two very special memories remain with me from that second year: in the lead-up to Palm Sunday, the Sunday before Easter, families came in from the country and installed themselves in the Basilica car-park where they sat and made intricate palm crosses ready for the festivities. Each family had their own pattern and style, twisting, folding, pleating and plaiting the palm leaves into intricate designs: it was fascinating and colourful, to see... We counted five balloon sellers, and people selling little garlands of sampagita, the national flower, which smelt just lovely – a bit like lily of the valley.

Saj, our good friend and a good Muslim, asked to come with us to the Easter Vigil, the most important ceremony of the Christian liturgical year. The three of us gathered in the darkness with the crowds outside the Basilica around the fire; the Paschal candle was lit, and thousands of us trooped into the dark church carrying our candles. Pat, Saj and I went up to the dusty, cobweb-festooned choir loft and watched the darkness turn into light as more and more worshippers thronged in with their candles... It was very spiritual.

Which reminds me: Before the visit of St Therese's relics, there was a sign outside Mcdonalds, 'Mcdonalds welcomes the relics of St. Therese. Beef-burgers only 35 pesos.' For All Saints: 'Come and celebrate Mass for your dear departed. Courtesy of Coca-Cola.'

One particular Monday about this time was Ronnie's last day with the street children, and it was a very emotional one for everyone, Ronnie included. The children did songs and dances and one lad did a spontaneous spot: he staggered in with Ronnie's carrier bags and proceeded to imitate with her mannerisms and her words. He brought the house down, which was just what was needed to lighten the atmosphere. I said that I'd take over, with the expat ladies to help, but Ronnie would be a very hard act to follow.

Already we were in the throes of sorting and packing – I was due UK leave again and brought as many clothes back as possible, as if they came in the boxes we could have been without them for months. We had so much to bring back apart from clothes: furniture, karaoke-machine, TV, video, dining table and chairs, comfy folding chairs, paintings, about two hundred books, all my sheet-music, tapes, CD's mini-discs, all my art stuff etc. etc. We had somehow, as I said to Ben, contrived to have houses each side of the world, each packed to the gunwales (whatever they are) with our things…

Back again to BC after my leave, where the expat ladies were continuing to work with the street children, but thankfully most of the children were now in school, and as yet not many more had replaced them. One of the older lads, Frederick, who was fourteen, wanted to go back to school (he'd been at one time, not sure when or for how long) so we were giving him extra help and hoped he'd pass the entrance test.

I'd been asked to do another music afternoon for the International Ladies' Club the next week, and a pianist friend in Alabang was determined that I'd do a 'Swansong' concert with her before we left. Life was hectic!

Finally we got our date: we were to leave the Philippines two weeks' hence, which was fairly complicated anyway, but to make matters worse we had to move house for the remainder of our stay: the contract on the house was up and the landlord needed it back again. So, we duly moved to the other house where we camped out with minimum of stuff till we left. It was a very pleasant light, modern house, which we enjoyed, but it didn't have the style of our last house, with its beautiful polished wooden floors and wide staircase – plenty wide enough for two to descend elegantly and gracefully. Not that we had ever done elegant. Or graceful. But we could have.

So, travelling light as usual we dispatched 35 packing cases to our already full UK address, just leaving essentials like my sewing machine and box of fabrics, karaoke-machine, bulging file of music and over sixty practice tapes (stopped to count them just to add impact! - keep your priorities right, that's what I say) – two huge suitcases of clothes, two medium suitcases of miscellaneous and innumerable cartons of ditto. Things were manic.

Finally, in October, we sent off the rest of our freight – 8 more boxes which brought the total to 43. Average shipment was 12 – 15 boxes - we seemed to have created a new record… It had been a strange time, but I didn't regret it – this had been a unique place to live and unless you'd been here it would have been almost impossible to understand the contradictions and the practices. It was totally infuriating and frustrating; after nearly two years, Pat, normally the most placid of people, still just couldn't figure out what made people here tick, and it still drove both of us crazy.

The worst things were the poverty and the deprivation, and the corruption which caused them. It was a vicious circle: many of the people, including Government employees, were paid so little that it was a struggle to survive and they had no option, as they saw it, but to cream off a little. Bearing in mind that a large proportion of the huge population was doing this, it was creating more poverty in its turn. The small middle class seemed to guard carefully what they had to help their families – immediate and extended—there seemed to be little concept of citizenship and helping the community at large. As in other places (but it was worse here than most), many of the people who went into politics did so from self-interested motives and seemed largely lazy, arrogant, totally self-complacent, and frequently impervious to the problems of the poor. It didn't take long for power to go to their heads. Local people told us that Batangas was the most corrupt place in the Philippines; I could well believe it.

That was the negative part. On the plus side, the people individually, especially those who'd worked with and for us, like drivers and maids, were delightful – charming, appreciative, loyal, honest and hardworking. It seemed a culture of extremes…

I'd continued to study my music throughout, I'd read voraciously as usual and had done dressmaking too, which I loved, but rarely had time for in UK. We'd entertained expat and Philippino friends as frequently as possible; I'd taken up art and had become particularly fond of water-colours. Like my singing, I would definitely continue with that. I was so grateful that I'd had interests and hobbies: some of the ladies must been found life very tough there. We'd been very privileged to be in a position to help some of the local people while were in BC; we'd continued to work with the street children; it was great to know that some of the little ones were back in school, with one of the older boys revising for his entrance exam so that – we hoped – he could do the same.

Pat had worked even harder during our second year: his 60-hour week had increased to six/seven days so he was looking forward to a proper break. He'd got on extremely well with the local people, which was just as well as a large part of his work had been PR. The office girls called him Daddy Pat…

The busiest week of all was when President Gloria Arroyo and ex-Presidents Corry Aquino and Ramos came down officially to open the Plant. They were using seven helicopters instead of the expected one, so that created a major security headache. There were both Muslims and Communist guerrillas in the hills near the Site but there had been a big security drive to clear the area for the visit.

To digress slightly: a little while before, there was an accident involving a local bus company and some of the communist guerrillas, at least one of whom was sadly killed in the accident. The following day there were reprisals: the guerrillas lay in wait for the early-morning bus from said bus company carrying workers. They got the workers off the bus, torched it, and then – the worst bit of all - they gave the passengers breakfast to demonstrate solidarity with them!!!

I'm pleased to report that the handover festivities and celebrations went off without a hitch, which was a huge load off everyone's back, but especially Pat's who'd master-minded most of it. We had a super long weekend in Manila as Pat and other managers had to go up there for a celebration dinner: four of us wives went up too and we had a really good boozy dinner in La Souffle, an extremely prestigious restaurant in Manila, with two of the wives from Alabang. Pat had a curry lunch on Friday at the Manila Club so I had a swim, a pleasant lunch and did an hour of painting - I thoroughly enjoyed myself.

On Sunday, the Commercial First Secretary from the Embassy took us to the Manila Club for lunch; we met some really interesting Embassy staff for an informal lunch party – it was like the good part of being back in the Army!

My last Monday with the street children was a party at Mcdonalds: twenty children, six helpers, four expats. We had a suitably boisterous time and everyone was kept busy so there was no time for tears.

Farewell to BC

Last entry for Philippines: October. So, some of the more astute among you may have noticed that I haven't mentioned much about our next assignment. Well, as I write, it's probable that we're going to Alexandria, in Egypt. It's apparently a beautiful place and we understand that the package is good. We're coming back to UK first and Pat will find out first-hand more from FW Reading. We leave on Monday, in the small hours, and are having a few days in Hong Kong en route. We'd very much hoped to go via the States, visiting friends in Virginia and incidentally finishing going round the world, but they want Pat 'as soon as possible' – this after keeping us waiting so long for news! Just like being back in the Army again…

We had a big party in the garden of our ex-neighbours/friends next door, and just about everyone came – engineers, managers, drivers et al. We had loads of booze to use up – it literally filled one of the cars, so what didn't get used at the party was divided amongst friends. The silly thing was that soft drinks and mixers were more expensive than spirits here!

We took an emotional farewell of Purita, and we made provision for her and family to the best of our ability. She has been wonderful, as was Aida before her – I would have hated to have managed without them. Lovely ladies, both of them…

After a short night's sleep following the festivities, one of our favourite drivers collected us at crack of dawn and, even though we had plenty of time, drove like a maniac to take us to the airport. It was only later, several weeks later, that we discovered why:

Early-ish one morning, back home in Hamilton Road, the phone rang and I answered. A distant man's voice announced himself: it was Ken, Pat's boss from the Philippines. I called Pat who, half-asleep, staggered to the phone and took the call. I couldn't help over-hearing and I heard him say 'Yes Ken, of course I remember the party' followed by a surprised denial of something unknown to me. The mystifying conversation continued for a few minutes and he came off the phone to explain that one of the local managers had filed a complaint against Pat for supposedly beating him up at a party. We remembered well the night in question: he and I had been looking after the guest of honour, a charming, famous young pop-singer and we had both therefore been pretty high-profile all evening. The strange thing was that the accuser's cronies all seemed to remember the incident, but no-one else had noticed!!!. The alleged attack must have been very quiet indeed…

This was apparently a common ploy to make money out of an expat company: one of the staff was falsely accused of something, usually on a Friday so the Police arrested them and kept them in custody over the weekend, which gave said company time to make arrangements for transfer of money to settle the matter. It had actually happened to an Australian manager of one of the oil refineries here. It had taken the refinery in question weeks if not months to get him released…

Our lovely driver had got wind of the plan and had literally whisked us off before the Police could arrest Pat – hence the crazy driving to Manila. Even crazier than usual, that is. He hadn't even told us as he would have known how worried we'd be… We owe him big-time!

Eventually back home in UK our boxes arrived and we found ourselves totally surrounded by packing cases which filled our lounge in Reading. One of said packing-cases was large and tall-ish and we couldn't remember what was in it, as most were labelled but this wasn't. We opened it excitedly – it felt like Christmas - and found, appropriately enough, a huge Christmas decoration - a parol, hanging in solitary splendour on its own coat-hanger on rail. Parols were very large and very traditional – you saw them all over the place in the Philippines at Christmas. Gaudy but gorgeous, if you know what I mean… Typical of the Philippines, and a lovely memento, but maybe not worthy of a specially-constructed packing-case to bring it right across the world…

So now, we were ready for the next adventure. We were off to the Land of the Pharoahs – Pat first to get established, and me to follow him after a suitable interval.

See you soon! You don't get rid of me that easily…

EGYPT

Villa Mariem January 2002

Well! This is certainly not what I had in mind. I'm sitting at my newly-installed computer, huddled over a not-very-effective heater (more about that later), clad only in a t-shirt, jumper, fleece of Pat's, tights, long socks and trousers, and I'm still cold. Very. But not freezing, so that's a major improvement on yesterday, the day before, and the few days before that. It is unbelievably cold – the locals say it gets this cold maybe every ten years – and of course we had very few warm clothes with us, and the houses aren't built for the cold.

When Pat came out he warned me it was cold but at least it was mainly dry and bright; the last few days it's been just above freezing, with sleet more than once, (as I write in fact; it's like pebbles being thrown against the window), heavy driving rain much of the time, and last night, lightning, and thunder which literally rattled the windows. We've been out and bought sweaters, warm dressing-gowns, (which we have more than once worn over everything), tracksuits, and the afore-mentioned heater. We've had our bacon saved with the discovery of two beautiful warm blankets, synthetic fleece – about half-an-inch thick and at least we're warm in bed, even if I need the hood up of my track-suit jacket to drink my morning tea!

Pat of course spent two years in Oman, and in Army days had a posting to Aden (was there for British Withdrawal, but that's another story) so he knows how cold it can be in the Middle East, 'specially at night and in the desert. But this is something else; last night it was 6 degrees above freezing in London, only 2 degrees above here... Heard a rumour the other day that it gets quite warm here in the summer but neither Pat nor I can believe it. We think it's just an urban myth put about by the Egyptian Tourist Board.

But back to the beginning. I had a good journey out, albeit Economy, (how the mighty are fallen!) and apart from having my Swiss Army knife confiscated 'cos it was in my cabin luggage, and having to pay 160 pounds sterling for excess baggage (you know how we Colbecks like to travel light) there were no mishaps.

We spent a couple of nights in the hotel in Alex, then took the train up to Cairo. First class; not the Orient Express standard I'd hoped for, tho' not bad, shabby but clean, and both journeys the trains departed and arrived on time. Take note BR... Contact in FW had arranged for driver to meet us and look after us for duration of stay; said driver was very knowledgeable, reliable and pleasant.

Our hotel was actually just outside Cairo, in Giza, and was superb. Best hotel we've ever stayed in. Room comfortable, original part of hotel had been a palace and it was just sumptuous, like walking into a thousand-and-one Arabian Nights... Our garden room had a delightful view marred only slightly by two strange pyramid-shaped objects a few hundred metres away. Tee-hee! What a view! So near! And at night they were illuminated.

Girl-Talk

We got corporate/local resident rates for the hotel. Hanafy, driver, took us round the site; we saw the three larger and several smaller pyramids – largest of all being the so-called Great Pyramid, Cheops (pronounced kyoops for your info). We didn't go inside this time as there was so much to see, but saw the famous King's Boat, made out of five-thousand-year old cedar of Lebanon, and visited the Sphinx. Another day we visited the Citadel, a beautiful fort and mosque.

In the Cairo Museum of course we saw Tutankhamen, but in general that museum left me cold (literally!). It's very gloomy and old-fashioned and was very much like the museums that completely put me off museums as a child.

We saw the Changing of the Guard at the Tomb of the Unknown Warrior, where the guards insisted on posing for a photo with us (imagine what the Lifeguards would say!) and the ceremony was a hoot – but it wasn't meant to be. Hanafy thought it was the bee's knees so we couldn't say anything. There were two lots of guards, one dressed as Pharaohs, the other in what looked to me like Turkish uniform with fezzes, jackets and baggy trousers. They did a sort of (un) synchronized marching drill and some of the Pharaohs were continually out-of-step and changing. It was awful, but great fun as there were no other tourists there, which made us feel very privileged. Also visited the Coptic area and museum , currently undergoing extensive renovation. Again, not many tourists and we just wandered round looking at exquisite scrolls, parchments and priceless antiquities – several thousand years old and in the case of the parchments, the colours still glowing and bright..

Saw also, thanks to Hanafy, King Farouk's mausoleum in the City of the Dead. Incredible place with ivory inlaid chairs, chandeliers and icons, and the door just secured by a single padlock. Deaf-mute gentleman looks after the place so of course we rewarded him for his troubles. It seems that Hanafy and friends sort of look after him as he's so poor…

Luckily we'd both read in the Lonely Planet about the scams perpetrated by just a few individuals on tourists (most of the people are absolutely gorgeous, friendly and very welcoming indeed). Anyway we were both chortling away as we experienced first-hand some of these scams but remembered our homework and didn't fall for them: The first one was when the 'Director of Botany' for the Cairo Museum stopped to chat. (Sometimes it's a 'teacher' or other 'professional'.) He'd studied at – what nationality were we? – Kew Gardens – surprise surprise!! No doubt he had suitable names for French, German, Italian tourists…

When we explained we were living in Egypt he lost interest and turned his attentions to another European couple a short distance away. Much animated chat then we saw him usher them across the road to his shop. No obligation, you understand – just to look…

Second scam was in hotel car-park. Well-dressed, well-spoken guy starts to chat. He has a perfume shop locally and, surprise surprise!! Produces essentials oils for Anita Roddick of Body Shop fame. Were we interested etc. but you know the rest.

Third one was leaving the Coptic area. Shopkeeper strolls up and says (word-for-word quoting from guide-book!): 'What nationality? English? I have a letter written to me in English – can you help me translate it please?' Very aggrieved when we say 'So sorry, we live in Egypt and our company driver (sounds more impressive!) is waiting…'

Again to quote the guide-book, most Egyptians were charming and hospitable, and that was certainly our experience. On two occasions locals drove a long way out of their way to lead us somewhere when we stopped to ask directions and no-one was surly or unhelpful.

So, back we came from Cairo, arriving late afternoon, picked up car and e-mails at hotel, did some basic food-shopping, arrived in villa about 8 p.m. to discover that it was not really ready for habitation, in spite of obvious efforts on part of Menem, the caretaker. Freezing cold, loo in main house leaking and seat inoperable. So, undaunted we camped out in small guest villa across garden where we had hot water for shower but no shower-curtain. Made up bed, put in hot-water bottle (we Colbecks knew how to travel) and fixed make-shift meal. Pat, bless him, remembered matches but I forgot loo-roll. Happily found half box of tissues and P promised to nick some loo-roll from work next day. (We were nearly an hour from Alex and proper shops). Phew! Panic over.

In fact we had to camp out there for several nights but finally plucked up courage to come across to main villa in spite of no hot water for much-longed-for bath (water was tepid at best) and we had the loo fixed. One step forward…

So, first morning in villa, Pat disappeared for work leaving me determined to restore order out of chaos. Not so easy. Firstly I locked myself out of the main house as we only had one set of keys. Menem, who spoke not a word of English, kindly entered house by secret (not really) spiral staircase to roof, entered house from roof area and let me in. Useful object lesson.

Bristling with enthusiasm I entered kitchen to find only cold water for sink, no heater installed. Undeterred I boiled up lots of water ready for cleaning and unpacked single pair of precious Marigolds, only to find that the packet, marked 'medium' contained one medium and one so small it practically cut off my circulation.

Anyway, the villa was nice. Main building had large open-plan living area with sofas around two walls, and open fireplace; kitchenette led off it as did dining room (heavy Belgian-type dining set and the largest sideboard we'd ever seen). Two bedrooms, and all painted white, with black and white floor tiles. Nice. But freezing cold.

There was a very pleasant garden with small swimming-pool, and at the other end of the garden was the pretty, apricot-painted, guest villa, which had one bedroom with two beds, en-suite shower room, and pleasant living room on ground floor. On top of the main villa was a large sort of studio, very light and airy. Perfect for my music and my painting. Sorted. When our boxes arrived with our stuff. (We were told it could be ten days plus, but one couple had been living out of suitcases for three months...)

So, first morning, there I was in my ill-matched Marigolds, using a chiller tray from the fridge for washing-up as I couldn't find bowl, when I heard a bird quite nearby. Had already seen egrets, hoopoes and large grey and black crow-type birds; this one sounded quite like our own cuckoo. Dashed out of kitchen, hurtled round corner of living room to rush into garden, and en route discovered cuckoo clock on wall...

There was Menem, caretaker (boab in Arabic!) who came with the place, and we found a maid, Oma Ahmed. (Mother of Ahmed). She, like most of the maids and boabs around here, was a Bedu. The Government had re-settled a lot of them in this area and you saw them sitting in gateways, selling fruit and vegetables, minding goats and so on.

Neither Oma Ahmed nor Menem spoke a word of English, so I started trying to learn some Arabic – not easy for me as it has no Latin root. Initially I learnt about sixty key words and phrases and tried to learn a couple more each day – in context so I remembered them easier. My miming ability came on no end; no doubt my performing would benefit as a result. That had to be good, I hear you say... Menem knew what to do; he'd worked for the landlord for some time, but Oma Ahmed was another story. She seemed pleasant, willing and hard-working but needed direction, which was understandable – these Bedu were extremely poor and it was difficult to imagine the conditions in which they lived – and I wasn't sure if she had worked as a maid before.

Out and About.

No rain! Alex harbour had been closed for several days due to the gales and heavy seas, but today it was blue skies, and it being Pat's day off, we went shopping in Alex where we shed our fleeces for an hour or two. This was better!

The day before we'd had dinner with some people we knew in Batangas; another BC couple were there too and we had a pleasant evening. They were living in Agamy, small town near here which was badly flooded; we'd had to drive through deep flood-water on a number of occasions to get there. The rainwater was bad enough, but there was raw sewage too to contend with. Thought we'd stay put in our villa, thank you very much – it was a bit isolated but the immediate area wasn't bad, was not flooded with rain-water or otherwise, and the villa and garden were very nice.

Sunday saw a sunny day with lovely blue skies – chilly in the villa and out of the sun but very warm in the sun. We had coffee by the pool. Our pool. Small, but perfectly formed… Mass in the evening with Pat in Alex in the same church as last week – Mass in Arabic, as English Mass was a bit too late for having a meal and travelling back here. We had a Thai buffet at one of the local hotels; last week we'd had Italian. Nice to have a choice of restaurants again…

At this point the days seemed very long, although they were two hours shorter than BC. It was a bit boring but would improve when boxes the came and when I got to know more people; some people had leave at Christmas and New Year and had not yet returned. FW ladies had started weekly cultural trips and there was an American Women's Association which met weekly and which I would try out. I was still trying to train the maid and every time I went out I had to tell her not to come in, as I wasn't sure how or if she'd function when I wasn't around. I had application forms from the British Council and I was considering applying for part-time English teaching, but I wasn't sure how things would develop and whether I wanted a regular commitment once I inevitably got busy.

I was very reluctantly having an enforced and prolonged break from my music. Couldn't bring my trusty karaoke-machine out (which I'd used most days in BC for vocal exercises and singing) but instead brought out Walkman, speakers, and repertoire on both disc and tape. Managed to burn out my Walkman— sob sob, cost 200 pounds sterling and I couldn't replace in Alex – limited electrical goods and very expensive—cos I hadn't read the instructions on the transformer I bought out here. The music centre in the villa was elderly, decrepit and one-speed. Bit like me really. So, I was lost till the boxes arrived with their two cassette players. It was so frustrating…

Likewise, I had very limited art stuff with me, only acrylics and three canvas boards (thanks Gerry and Ben!) of which I'd used two and was saving the other for when I got desperate. Was now reading my third and last book till the boxes came – we couldn't wait – it would be like Christmas. Were told it should be soon. We had two satellite TVs on the premises which we had not yet been reduced to watching.

Back to the Arabic: One day the previous week I'd learned a new word. In context. It was 'far' and it means 'rat'. Told Menem who hopefully would deal, but I had to say it was sleek and quite pretty (another expat said the same of one she'd seen in her garden). I hoped that desert rats (as opposed to dessert rats!) were somewhat different to sewer rats…

Freezing Cold in Alex!

We went to party one night in Alex; mainly, but not only, FW people. Nice, friendly and welcoming. The place certainly had possibilities and I hoped it would be a good posting. Also went to Alex one day with one of my few FW neighbours (five minutes' drive away; too far to walk). We'd had a pleasant morning with shopping and coffee; she was a mine of useful information. Alex was almost an hour's drive away, but I planned to go in there with the local FW ladies at least once per week; in fact I was meeting some other ladies the next day and going shopping with them. I was looking forward to that!

Saw a lovely sight the other day, local herd of about forty goats, attended by small boy near the entrance to our estate. There was a particularly huge villa there on the corner, surrounded by ornamental wall, sort of scallop-shaped, topped by an over-hanging, neatly-trimmed, hedge. The tallest goats were lined up along the wall munching the greenery, the medium-sized ones jumping up between them, and the little-est ones were at the back, jostling for position...

Two evenings that week we'd had a short drive after work along the desert road towards the coast, where I had seen my first herd of domesticated camels – not like the ones we'd seen round the Pyramids, but dark brown and woolly…

The previous evening we'd got as far as the coast, about half-an-hour's drive. Checked out the Hilton Beach Resort but in fact we hadn't been impressed – there was a lot of accommodation for not much pool or beach – must have been awful in summer. Still, it would be nice to have the option of driving out for a meal after work and, living as we did on the edge of the Western Sahara(!) it was great to see the scenery – couldn't wait for a photographic trip one Friday.

Went on the weekly food-shopping trip recently with two other ladies. Pleasant trip, nothing exciting to report except for a delicious strawberry juice in a restaurant in town.

Food in general seemed good. There was a good range of fruit and veg (though I thought that in the Philippines it was even better) and there were dry and canned goods both local and imported, of good quality. Bread was good – the Arab unleavened breads were delicious – but it would be nice to have my bread-machine again even though I couldn't get the same range of suitable flour. No margarine either although apparently one supermarket twenty minutes' drive away did have limited amounts of Flora very occasionally—I was working on it… The olives were a real disappointment. They tasted as if they were pickled in Dettol (maybe they were!) and, call me quaint and old-fashioned if you like, I wasn't too keen on that. I'd managed to get some salmon fillet the day before and some free-range chicken fillets – till then we'd been living on pulses, canned fish, and spicy home-made soups. Humous was popular of course, and other vegetarian dips like babaganoush (aubergine) and different sorts of foul (cooked white beans) but I still missed my range of vegetarian options in UK...

Had by now seen several of the other expat villas and a number of them were absolutely palatial - one had six bedrooms, six bathrooms and a large pool! Made our property quite humble by comparison, 'tho in fact it was nice (except for the main bathroom which was somewhat basic) but ours was reasonably priced so I think Pat made the right decision.

On Friday the afore-mentioned goats were milling round our gate, attended by several neighbourhood urchins. Rushed inside for camera and took some photos, which caused a lot of laughter, shouting, pushing and generally showing off. (And that was just Pat and me!)

Went for a drive round our compound again the other evening. First tour had been less than successful as far as I was concerned as the local butcher had been killing goats, which rather upset me. (The goats weren't too pleased either.) This time there were no such mishaps...

Bearing in mind that the country was predominantly Muslim, and that this compound was well out of town, we had been surprised to find a huge Coptic church complex, new, all gleaming white with fantastic staircases, balconies, crenellations and the like. We had just been having a look round when a group of nine or so young male students, possibly seminarians, materialized, greeting us, trying out their almost-non-existent English and generally being really pleased to receive visitors. They were just delightful, so full of fun, and insisted on taking us all round. We planned to go back and take them some goodies.

The funniest thing happened one Thursday; Pat appeared at lunchtime as usual bringing one of the big bosses out from Reading, pleasant guy by the name of Paul. Apparently all week Paul had been drinking tea during the morning break, but that day the tea-boy had offered cappuccino and he'd accepted. The cappuccino was a long time coming; Paul had wandered down to the kitchen to see what was happening. The tea-boy was standing at the work-surface with a cup of instant coffee and a drinking straw and HE WAS BLOWING DOWN THE STRAW TO MAKE THE FROTH................

Pat's day off, we went into Alex supposedly for an hour to get some stuff for the house. We got totally and completely lost (for once we had no map with us), in slums and narrow streets with rubbish piled high all round us; it was just vile. Anyway, eventually we'd found ourselves out in the country, with no main streets to follow – just narrow passage-ways between the houses. Found a motor -way under construction and drove down it till we came to a dead-end.

Turned back and drove down another road which got narrower and narrower; we passed earth-trodden courtyards with small dwellings around and chickens and geese waddling in the dirt. Brightly-clothed Bedu women balanced large bundles and containers on their heads, and children played everywhere in the dust – it was all truly medieval. In one filthy courtyard we saw a lady walking very gracefully through the mire with a bucket balanced on her head. We got a quick photo, which resulted in a small oil-painting 'Grace in the Barnyard'...

No-one spoke English but eventually we found a young student with a limited amount of English; he wanted to visit his brother in Alex and hopped aboard to direct us. As he obviously wasn't a driver, he took us the way he would have walked. Once again we drove through narrow streets with market stalls on one side and worshippers kneeling on mats the other – at one stage the road was so narrow we knocked down some woolly hats piled on a road-side stall. The mode of transport here was old, brightly-painted, sort of covered horse-drawn wagons. Incredible! Then someone, very good-humouredly, indicated that we were driving the wrong way up a one-way street

After two hours, we got back to Alex where we fell on hot coffee and tuna croissants in the Cecil Hotel. So there we were, sitting in the Cecil after our traumatic experience being lost in the slums of Alexandria, just sitting quietly relaxing, when up ambled a middle-aged gentlemen, reasonably smartly dressed but unshaven. He stopped by our table, didn't say anything, just pointed to my glass of water and indicated he wanted a drink. No waiters around. We were both quite stunned; Pat said 'No!' but he'd already touched the glass, so I indicated he could have it. He just took a sip, put the glass down, and ambled off. Seriously weird!

Telephone line has been down again this morning. Last time Menem went up on the roof and did something technical to the line, which was looped around drain-pipes and washing-line-posts and in places almost trailing on the floor. As his cousin, Fathy, who with his wife seemed to be part of the menage, was on the roof earlier fiddling with bits of scrap iron, I wondered if he had dislodged something. Hoped M. could sort it. Later – he did! Very quickly. Definitely Fathy was the prime suspect…

We had a pleasant day on Sunday: our boxes arrived, and after Pat finished work we went into Alex to Mass and then had dinner with a couple we know from Batangas days – he was on a short contract with the Project and his wife Pat was visiting on a month's holiday. Went to quite a prestigious fish restaurant; the mezze was delicious and there was loads of it fortunately, as I'm not very keen on fish. It was good to catch up with Pat and John and hear all the news.

While I think, back to Mass; we'd gone to an Arabic Mass: anyway, we were amused to hear that one of their hymns was set to the tune of 'Lemon Tree' ('Lemon tree very pretty, and the lemon flower is sweet, but the fruit of the poor lemon is impossible to eat'). Was it sung by Peter Paul and Mary? Think it might have been. Oh yes, and even funnier, another hymn, believe it or not, had been sung to the tune of 'Puff the Magic Dragon'. Honestly!

So there I was, sitting in bed the other morning with my cup of tea when suddenly everything started to shake, and the windows began to rattle. I called to Pat who was performing his ablutions at the time but he hadn't noticed: yes folks, we'd had an earth tremor. Apparently the epicentre was in Crete, 6 point something on the Richter scale and we were just on the edge. Not as impressive as the 5 point something in Batangas, though, when we were only a few miles from the epicentre.

We regularly saw funny sights out here, especially on the roads: a lorry with high, precarious load of cardboard boxes, man sitting atop them as the lorry lurched down the road. Another time we saw a flat-bed cart carrying a load of sacks –of vegetables maybe – with a layer of fodder on top maybe two or three feet high and another layer of fodder. On top of that a boy and a goat were balancing precariously… Then one day we were amused to see a donkey sedately pulling a dilapidated cart on which was sitting a young lad attended by two large sheep. The sheep were indolently reclining, just relaxing and gazing at the traffic as they passed…

One Saturday, it being a workday for the guys, I'd invited a load of the FW ladies over for the day. I'd made an enormous pot of spicy lentil soup and lots of goodies and after lunch we played Occupations' and 'Taboo'. They all departed saying what a lovely time they'd had and I really enjoyed it too. I hadn't known many people very well but really felt I was starting to belong. Only problem with the FW ladies was that we were quite dispersed; there were three areas where we lived, each about forty minutes from the others, so it wasn't quite as easy to socialize as it might otherwise have been.

Pat and I loved people-watching, and in Alex it developed into almost an art-form. There were sophisticated city-types, both men and women, in fashionable clothes and lots of jewellery: our lawyer landlord visited one day bearing a Versace bag and sporting Ray-Bans. There were the Muslim ladies in head-scarves, and the traditional full-blown ones in the full kit with just their eyes peeping out – I saw one of the latter type wearing spectacles over her eye-slit – right down to the country-people and the Bedu such as where we lived. The Bedu women wore bright clothes and different head-scarves, and the Bedu men and countrymen wore flowing robes and turbans – it was all incredibly Biblical.

Short skirts seemed to be taboo, as I'd heard, and when the summer came I'd been told that sleeveless dresses weren't normally worn. In public, that is – in private homes and clubs, and on private beaches, any clothes, including bikinis, were acceptable. There was a very nice Swedish lady who went onto the beach last year near the hotel in Alex where she and her family were staying, and stripped off to a bikini. She was absolutely mobbed by the local men jeering and hissing at her. The Police had to surround her to protect her from (verbal) abuse, and word got back to the hotel who sent someone over to rescue her.

Another expat lady who wears short-ish skirts has complained of the unwelcome attention she's received, and yet another lady, friend of mine, walked along the sea front one day modestly dressed in trousers and got hissed at by a group of workmen at the fact she was out alone. Probably down from remote villages up-country –as I said earlier, most people were absolutely delightful and helpful.

Monday 28th Jan. After Pat finished work yesterday we drove to Alex to church; we could see pretty impressive storm-clouds building up. While we were in church there was almost continual thunder and lightning – one crash was so loud I thought the church had been struck. It reminded us of BC when we twice saw lightning strike the dome of the Basilica...

It had also been raining and sleeting heavily, with high winds, and when we drove home - we decided for once not to stay in town for a meal – the traffic was appalling, and there were widespread floods on the roads. Along one stretch of the central reservation the hailstones had piled up like snow; people couldn't believe it and inevitably we saw numerous shunts and minor accidents – including one guy who'd just driven straight into a lamp-post – all obviously staring at this strange phenomenon. One of the expats told me they saw tyre-marks in the hail-stones just like in snow, and we heard that we're having the worst weather in living memory here...

Grace in the Barnyard. See p.203

Retail Therapy

Egypt being predominantly a Muslim country, it was difficult to buy booze. There were however three places, one in Alex, two in Agamy, where we could buy a limited choice – each place being about half to three-quarters of an hour's drive away. So, one Friday, Pat's precious day off, we drove into Alex specially to stock up on booze, only to find the shop was shut. We should have thought and gone in the evening instead – most shops stayed open very late, and some, but not all, were closed earlier in the day. So, it would have been an abortive journey but we happened to see a perfume shop selling proper French perfumes – not 'Channel No 5' 'Asian-Asian' or 'River Gorge' (made those up, amusing huh? Just think about it). So all was not lost – I treated myself to some Burberry, as I hadn't brought my perfume out with me and I hadn't had time to buy any at the airport.

One particular Tuesday I went on the shopping bus and bought more things for the house – sheets, towels and lavatory brushes – a girl needs a little luxury now and again. Had one of my favourite strawberry juices, and a delicious tuna croissant in the Cecil Hotel. Pleasant day, but somewhat marred by three incidents which distressed me quite a lot:

I twice saw donkeys who were lame – one of them badly so and virtually hopping on three legs– still having to work pulling carts, and then later we saw a man on a donkey cart with the donkey trying to get purchase on a stony surface to pull the cart over a ridge at the side of the track. The donkey kept slithering and the man was hitting him with a stick – he couldn't even be bothered to get off and lighten the load. I banged furiously on the window of the mini-bus and shouted at him – asked the driver to get out and remonstrate with him. Don't know what he said but then ladies shouted at him to drive on, as in the past when this has happened the owner has actually taken it out on the animal. Suffice to say I was very upset…

One Friday we did a bit of food shopping and went to check out the Alexandria Country Club, about twenty-five minutes' drive away. It was a large club with extensive grounds, a gym, TV/video room, French restaurant and swimming-pool – the pool was pleasant but not quite large enough for serious swimming, but we thought we'd join (FW would pay half) as it was near enough to pop into the gym a couple of times per week and have a good meal. (As opposed to home cooking!)

Speaking of which, we ate Egyptian last night at home – spiced fish – they spiced it for you if you wished in the supermarket, as a helpful Floor Manager explained. (He also told us how to cook it – in the oven topped by a layer of tomatoes.) With it we had aubergine pickle and Egyptian rice which we'd bought ready-prepared, cooked with sultanas, pistachios nuts and spices, and Arab bread. Mmmm! Nice...

Going back to yesterday; it was the first day it had been hot enough to sunbathe, which we did on the roof. Very hot up there with just a slight breeze – we played safe and just stayed on the roof for half-an-hour. By the way, in case you're worrying, it was a flat roof, not a pitched one! (Visions come to mind of Mary and Pat, clad in not very much, clutching the ridge tiles with one hand and nonchalantly trying to apply sun-tan lotion with the other.)

The rest of that week was pleasant – couple of shopping trips with the ladies and on the Thursday we had friends in whom we'd known in Batangas and who were on short-term contract. A really hilarious evening and the food went down well. Sometimes it wasn't so easy, entertaining in those far-flung places, as many of you may remember from my Philippines journal. The day went something like this: Put bread-machine on early so that was out of the way; it would look after itself. Not. There was a very brief power-cut half-way into the programme so it switched itself off at the dough stage. Too late into programme to go back to square one so removed from machine, shaped into rolls and cooked in oven.

M'Ahmed, the maid came in so I had to abandon the kitchen and keep out of the way for a couple of hours to give her a clear run. Amused myself with e-mails and my Italian course on CD-rom which I'd bought in UK and which was really excellent. Basic, but extremely well-designed.

Dispatched maid with cries of 'Shukran!' (thank you) 'Mumtazz'! (excellent) and 'mish bukra' (not tomorrow) as next day was Friday. Impressed so far? Don't be; my Arabic was still at the one-word, max two, per-sentence stage. Anyway I digress.

Returned to kitchen. Prepared bread-and-butter pud with marmalade and popped in fridge to stand. Mixed chicken casserole with just a hint of hint of ginger and fresh chilli, celery, onions, carrots, courgettes and sweet potato.

Incidentally, here I go again, it was free-range chicken. Not easy to get when your Arabic is limited and your miming ability ditto. I said in supermarket, in English 'chicken please'. 'Yes madam', pointing to chickens. (Many people spoke some English.) I said 'free-range chicken, please'. 'What madam?' I drew a cage in the air and said vehemently 'la, la' (no, no) whilst shaking head and making negative gestures. 'What madam?' Clucking noises followed. (From interested spectators.) Then I had a brainwave. 'Shams!' This meant 'sunshine' - the nearest I could get to saying 'out-of-doors'. I followed this with running movements with my fingers and pointed to imagined sun. Repeated negative cage procedure and went again through 'Shams' routine. By this time I think that they thought I wanted a chicken with a sun-tan, (optional as far as I was concerned) but the penny dropped and I got my free-range chicken fillets.

So, back to kitchen. Seasoned layers of potato, onion and courgettes with the chicken, tuna dip with crudités for starter. Hey, notice that accent on the crudités? Wow it's done it again – what a clever computer – it did it all on its own – I didn't even know I had an acute accent in the machine. Marvels of modern science etc. Let's try it again – crudités, crudités, crudités, hey, isn't this fun? (I don't get out much). Try it for yourselves. That's about all I could say really about the menu. Relief relief I hear you say – but it was a nice meal and a really good evening.

The next Friday we went with the same friends to El Alamein, an hour's drive away. An interesting day; first to the museum then to the British and Commonwealth War Cemetery. Beautifully laid out and landscaped; it was very moving – so many of them had died so young… Coffee on the way back and a quiet evening at home.

The weather thankfully was improving by the day and was quite hot in the sun – cooler in the shade and in the villa but even that would change soon. We started to think that there might be some truth in this tale about hot summers in Egypt. Yup folks, summer was definitely i-cumin in. Just wished it would be i-cumin in just a tad quicker so we could swim… Gerry was coming out to see us in four weeks' time, just for a week; we were so excited! Then hopefully other visitors would be following in hot pursuit. Ben was back-packing with friends; had just spent three weeks in Thailand where he had a good time except for having his designer sun-glasses, and money, stolen. He'd just arrived in Sydney, which I knew he was going to love. He planned to be away up to a year so may not get to visit us; I was thinking of going to Sydney to see him if he was there long enough and if he wanted his Mum to visit…

It wasn't easy at the best of times for Pat or for me to be so far away from Gerry and Ben, but the worst occasion was one particular day when each of the four of us was not only in a different country, but on a completely different continent: Pat was in Egypt, (Africa!) I was on leave in UK, Ben was in Oz, and Gerry, who then worked for an investment bank in the City, was on business in New York. We missed the 'children' so much…

I'd been wanting for some time to try Kushari, a local street-food dish, and got my chance the other day. It was basically two sorts of pasta and two sorts of pulses, cooked together with fried onion and spicy tomato sauce. Mmmm… delicious. And healthy to boot.

Typical Village Scene

Traffic Jam

One Saturday night Pat and I'd gone into Alex. Tried unsuccessfully to get some ID photos done for the country club, had a walk along the sea-front, and finished with a strawberry juice in a traditional old restaurant. Then the fun started:

As were driving back to the villa we joined a bad traffic jam so that the traffic on our side of the road was gridlocked. Everyone got out of their cars peering into the distance; the jam stretched ahead as far as we could see. We waited a little while. Nothing happened. Vehicles at the back of the jam started reversing, turning if they could, and most of the traffic, ourselves included, drove across the central reservation where we drove, albeit slowly, on the wrong side of the road. Traffic on the wrong side with us built up to five lanes on a three-lane highway – all going in the wrong direction and completely blocking the road for on-coming traffic.

Finally pressure from would-be-oncoming traffic built up to the point that some of the traffic going the wrong way, including ourselves, slowly had to drive back across the central reservation – lorries, cars, coaches – leaving just one lane going the wrong way. It took ages but we made it and joined the nose-to-tail queue on the correct side. Our progress was hampered by the fact that some oncoming traffic from the other side of the highway had come across to our side and was now driving the wrong way towards us. This made two three-lane highways either side of central reservation, each with two-directional traffic.

At one point all the traffic stopped completely again just as 'Twist and Shout' came on the radio, so we turned it up loudly, opened the window wide and treated the nearby drivers to a little display of hand-jiving and jigging in our seats. I leant out of the window clapping along with passengers from the bus two lanes to our right and taxi drivers were hooting. It was hilarious! Discovered later that the jam had been caused by a multiple pile-up but most vehicles had got off reasonably lightly.

I went into the British Council one morning to whom I'd applied with a possibility of doing a bit of work for them at some juncture. Observed one lesson, which I really enjoyed, and would be teaching the same class, an intermediate one, the next Wednesday, for an hour, as part of the interview process. If they offered me work I really only wanted to do one session per week and this might not be enough for them. I was keeping an open mind… Back to Mass in Alex with Pat then met friends for the Sunday roast at the Ramada—very pleasant evening!

Monday was an irritating day. Transport was a problem so it was wiser to use drivers who'd been tried and tested. I'd arranged for a known driver, via one of the other expats, to take me into Alex to the American Women's Association, for the first time. Addresses didn't mean very much there, as they didn't in the Philippines – it was 'turn right at the rusty sign, left at the abandoned oil can, past the three palm trees, opposite the Bedu hut' – that sort of thing, which was difficult enough to explain to another expat, let alone a local guy.

I'd arranged that Pat would pop back from the Site, five minutes' away, collect me, and drive me to the Refinery where said driver would pick me up at the main gate. With me so far? We waited ten minutes in the driving rain, (happily in Pat's car). I couldn't get driver on his mobile. Gave up. Asked Pat to drive me home from where I could ring other Pat, friend whom I was supposed to be picking up in Alex en route and who'd now have to make her own arrangements.

Finally made contact with driver who says 'Car, madam. Mechanic. Car stop'. It was still pouring with rain, wind lashing, just as you'd expect in Egypt. Pat drove me home where the boab said in sign language that he knew a good taxi locally. 'Ok', I said and I waited. Pat returned to work and rang to say that he took Menem, the boab, up the lane and dropped him off at the main road where presumably he'd gone to look for said taxi. I rang friend in Alex and explained, and waited. And waited. It was now too late to get to the AWA anyway and not worth going in for the little shopping I needed, but as Menem had gone to so much trouble over taxi felt that I should go, if taxi turned up. It was now an hour since I should have left…

Taxi, and Menem, finally turned up at quarter to ten, but meeting started at ten, an hour's drive away. Could have gone for last hour, but didn't fancy the journey in the inclement weather conditions and in an unknown, private, car. Car didn't look too bad outside, but was decidedly shabby inside. Probably wouldn't have baulked at short journey but thought it better not to risk it under the circumstances, so explained that it was now too late for meeting, thanked both Menem and driver profusely and tipped them both generously. Retired indoors, disappointed but brave, with lower lip trembling only a little...

Christened my music studio one day, up on the roof – windows all round and lovely acoustics. Normally I worked on my music downstairs while I was working in the kitchen but I took the opportunity of a good old bellow up there that afternoon. I hoped that the locals didn't find my singing as unmusical and discordant as I did theirs!!! (But they probably did.) Tried to work on my music most days, as I did in Batangas...

I was also doing an interactive Italian course on CD rom; it was absolutely brilliant – so cleverly designed. It was basic conversation really but it was such fun and I really enjoyed it. Also had a two-hour taster course in Italian with Michel Thomas, who's now very well-known; I'd seen him on TV. His methods were revolutionary and I'd been very impressed by the programme. Hadn't got round to doing that but planned to soon. I'd always wanted to learn Italian!

The following Wednesday I finally gave my lesson in the British Council. It was a very small class, only six students, and I wasn't at all nervous till the very last moment, when I realized that the Assistant Director of Studies would be assessing, and not the usual class teacher. Anyway, it wasn't perfect, but it was fun and the assessor said he was 'impressed'. (No accounting for tastes!) The students volunteered that they'd enjoyed the lesson and one of them gave me a tape of a famous Egyptian singer. Sweet! Downside is they rarely had daytime work which was all I was prepared to do - Pat worked six days per week and so I didn't want evening work. Still, a useful professional challenge for me...

That Friday we had a Valentine's buffet for FW. The place was packed; very friendly and we enjoyed ourselves. Heard afterwards that several of FW managers were off sick for several days as a result. Don't know what they ate but we'd been, as usual, very careful, and we were fine...

On Sunday I spent most of the day in Alex. Went in with small group of the ladies to do a painting-on-wood lesson given by a lady from Nova Scotia. They were into folk art in a big way in the States and it was fun to try new things. Definitely not as easy as it might look, but I enjoyed it and we were going to make a recipe holder when we'd mastered the basic brush-strokes. I was hoping eventually to paint a clock with Egyptian numerals and scenes – including the Dalek-shaped pigeon roosts which were common locally... The apartment where this lady lived was over a cookie shop on the Corniche, and had a magnificent sea-view. Access was a bit scary though – eleven floors up in a tiny, ancient lift which took four of us crammed in like sardines. Walked down again after on the pretext of needing the exercise; interesting to see the others did too...

Evening Mass in Alex. The church was beautiful: traditional, ornate, marble pillars and chandeliers. Left-hand side of the church was, as usual, almost completely taken up by children of varying ages, all black – we wondered if they were refugees - from Nubia or Aswan for example, where a dam project had made a lot of people homeless.

After Mass we joined our ex-Batangas friends for the famous Sunday roast in the Ramada, then went carpet-hunting. The carpets in Egypt were famous, and beautiful, and we hoped to bring one or two back with us at the end of the assignment. It was just a preliminary sortie and I could see we'd be spoiled for choice when we finally came to decide.

Monday was an interesting day. I was trying out a new driver – not a full-time one, but one I could use occasionally. This guy seemed ok; I'd give him a bit longer before I decided finally. Anyway, an expat lady out there was learning the violin and she'd managed to find details for me of a contact who was a Bel Canto teacher. I rang teacher, and made an appointment to visit. Road conditions and traffic were unpredictable, so I allowed plenty of time to get to this lady's apartment and the new driver arrived exactly as requested, but in fact there was no problem and we got into Alex twenty minutes early. A pleasant residential area - in fact the flat was above the Rumanian Embassy – but no restaurants around where I might have killed some time, so I went in about twenty minutes before I was due. My mistake.

An elderly, wizened gentlemen, with a face as brown and wrinkled as a walnut, and clad in flowing robes and large turban, escorted me upstairs in an even more ancient lift than Patricia's, all wrought iron, curlicues and with an uneven floor and no light. Oo-er! He indicated Madame Titi's(!) door with a flourish, graciously accepted my tip, and was ready to depart when the door opened. Said Mme Titi, in fetching pyjamas and dressing-gown, but without teeth, poked head out and informed us, in French, that she'd had a crashing head-ache all night and couldn't sleep; could I please come back in half-an-hour?

I apologised profusely and offered to leave but she was adamant that she wanted me to return, so down I went again with the hand-carved gentleman. Asked driver, who spoke not a word of English, to take me to the Hotel Cecil, where I could have a quick coffee. 'Hotel Cecil?' I try 'Hotel Sofitel? (It was known by both names.) Blank expression. Had map, but didn't know name of Square where it was situated. Luckily I managed to direct him to the right place – more by luck than judgement. Ordered coffee, which I didn't have time to drink (it's the story of my life, that) and back we went.

Duty Policemen lounging outside Rumanian Embassy, all looking as alert as, well, wet lettuces, ushered me genially inside and into lift, which I drove myself this time, yes I knew you'd be impressed. Slight panic when the lift stopped as I was not sure how to open door but luckily I'd watched Mr Walnut and managed without too much trouble – it was a sort of dusty, creaking, lever, which slotted into a sort of loop on lintel (do lifts have lintels?) – just wanted to share that information with you, in case you're ever in that situation.

This time Mme Titi was fully dressed. She received me full of apologies; headache had slightly abated and she wouldn't hear of my leaving. What a character! Quite a formidable lady, but lovely and luckily we hit it off - spent an -hour-and a half chatting. She tried me out with a couple of scales; said I had 'a pretty voice' simper simper, and she'd very much to like to work with me. Wanted me to start off with her own basic breathing exercises, (though faster than a complete beginner, thankfully!) and scales to help my theory, as I'd been totally honest about my difficulties with same. Incidentally, the whole experience was 'en francais' so if nothing else it would brush up my French!

Very, very French – the influence in Alex was still strong, particularly amongst the 'old' Alexandrians, and Madame had been educated in France. A fascinating glimpse into life for the 'old order'...

If in Doubt, Follow the Instructions…

Back to Alex with Pat in the evening where he treated himself to a tracksuit, we had a short walk along the Corniche, and we bought an electronic fly zapper. This was hilarious; Pat and I were wondering facetiously to each other whether it would make toast and the shop assistants were on the point of rushing off to find a toaster 'cos it wouldn't. Well, obviously. As we left I mimed turning the TV off and watching the zapper catch flies, as alternative entertainment – that sort of transcended the language barrier and we disappeared into the night with them chortling away – no doubt about ze mad Eengleesh… (Why I wrote that with a French accent I have absolutely no idea…)

Got the zapper home and found it easy to use in spite of the instructions, which read as follows: 'Advice. Please conhect the grouhded wire before use it for gour safetybecanse its shell is made of the metal. don't toach the electriferous wike with the finger and electric club.' Ok, thanks, we'll bear that in mind…

The journey into Alex, going back a bit, had been a perfectly typical one, and the sights had included a fire on the horizon, a refinery (not FW!) flare actually on fire and assorted lorries, many brightly coloured and decorated and including some 'Chevorlet' (sic) all loaded with sheep and cattle for the weekend's forthcoming festival. One lorry even had two sheep on the roof of the cab – can't imagine how they got 'em up there. We imagined a sort of Gary Larson cartoon with one saying to the other 'Hey, Fluffy, we're expected at the Ahmeds' for dinner tonight'. Also saw a small flat-bed donkey-cart with the donkey (or maybe a mule) cantering along the road, and the young lad driving was standing up, feet apart and legs braced like a sort of modern-day Ben Hur.

Look Mummy, no
Hands!

The Festival, three days of it, was for the Prophet's birthday. (I think). Thousands of sheep, goats and cattle had been brought into the area from the desert. There were make-shift pens all along the side of the road, and flocks of animals watched by men or young children, with the occasional sheep in a shop doorway in the middle of town. Some of the roadside pens were sheltered by huge, brightly-coloured and decorated drapes over a framework of poles – the scenes couldn't have changed much for thousands of years.

So there we were, bowling along one of the main roads in Alex on the eve of the Festival in fact, when we drew up alongside a taxi. We both looked into said taxi, and burst out laughing – on the back seat was a very large, very dirty, very surprised-looking goat, looking somewhat bemusedly out of the window.

Friday was Pat's day off. We drove up half-way towards Cairo to check the road out before we went up with Gerry, who was visiting us soon. Had intended also to find a large Coptic monastery which we're told is worth a visit, but couldn't find it; will try again. We stopped for coffee at a small place, thinking it was the place recommended by expats, but it was sort of, er, local. No wonder there was only one other car there! Nice, friendly waiter, though. Found the right place a few minutes later – very upmarket, and we'll certainly visit again.

Home to sunbathe on the roof (here we go again!) but although sunny it was too cold and we abandoned the idea in favour of a hot cuppa and a good book each.

The next day some of the FW people who live in town told Pat it had been a nightmare, with sheep being slaughtered all over the place for the Festival. I'd been worried that, out in the country where we lived, we'd have had some unpleasant sights, but thankfully not so.

Seen on a menu: 'sandwitches' and in a supermarket 'artichokes bottoms' (ooh cheeky!) and along the canal bank a large white mule sauntering along tout seul and minding his own business. Owner came up behind to take him back and mule lashed out, kicking back at owner purposefully with its hind legs. I wouldn't have cared to be on the receiving end, but the owner seemed more concerned that his discomfiture has been witnessed by foreigners than by the incident itself...

Had a pleasant lunch on the seafront the other day in Alex, with some of the other expats. Fourteen of us in all, celebrating the birthday of one of our number. Food good, company excellent and view superb.

Am writing this bit at 3 a.m. whilst drinking a cup of tea. There's a very impressive storm raging – no rain, thunder or lightning thankfully, but extremely high winds. All the windows and doors are rattling and banging, and the ones upstairs in the studio, which never close properly at the best of times, are swinging loose and crashing to and fro - it's a wonder they're not all shattered to bits. We've both been awake ages but it's given me a chance to spend half-an-hour or so on my Italian vocabulary computer game which is absolutely brilliant, and on which I'm quite hooked! You just find yourself concentrating on the strategy and choosing the right word subconsciously.

Forgot to say that I heard, and saw, a thrush, in our garden the other day, and a sea-eagle flying over. Then last night in town, passing a park, we saw hundreds and hundreds of white egrets – in the trees, filling the sky – everywhere. They're slightly smaller, prettier, versions of storks.

Had a pleasant time on Monday. Went into Alex with a couple of the local expats to meet up for our wood-painting lesson. We were still working on paper but hoped to graduate to wood soon! Pleasant lunch together in Izzy's gorgeous flat – eleventh floor with a balcony, and it was all windows, parquet floor and paintings. Ladies took me to find a framing shop – it was apparently extremely cheap out here so I planned to take the opportunity to frame some of my 'masterpieces' – it was certainly not worth spending a lot of money on them! Found also a couple of good art-shops – not browse-y ones, smallish and a bit pokey, but with a surprisingly good range of art things. Canvasses dirt-cheap…

Saw a little boy in yellow print pyjamas pottering round the back yard the other day and it transpired that Menem has his family out from the town – presumably for a holiday as all the children seemed to be off school. Met an older son, Ibrahim, later, when he came to help carry stuff out of the car, and several unknown ladies were seen congregating round Menem's door. One of them detached herself from the group and Menem introduced her as his 'miree' – wife. They seemed like a very nice family.

Keeping out of Mischief…

Wednesday was a pleasantly busy day. Started when the new driver turned up an-hour-and-a-half early to take me into town. Obviously our combined efforts with English/Arabic weren't very successful when I made the arrangement. Roll on the Arabic lessons! Can't wait to start but things take time to arrange out here… So, Said, said driver, (pun?) waited while I got my act together.

Went to see Mme Titi. We chatted for almost an hour, worked on music exercises for the same and she extracted a promise for me to stay a bit longer next week. It was brilliant for my French, and I was sure would pay off with my singing in the long-term. She was red-hot on technique and had her own method; I really would have preferred to work on technique/repertoire simultaneously, but she was the teacher and certainly knew her stuff…

Back home early afternoon to find the water was off. Completely. Tried guest villa, no joy. Drinking water came in bottles so no problem there, but we had a dinner party that night. Ah. Luckily, had done as much as possible before I went out, but had had to leave a sinkful of dishes which now couldn't be washed. Oh. Menem mimed fractured pipe and informed me water would be on later, so I went and painted for an hour which I really enjoyed. I got withdrawal symptoms if I didn't spend some time painting when I was at home. Almost as bad as my music – I couldn't stop.

Water eventually did come back on so I abandoned painting and was just about organized when everybody turned up. Pleasant evening, company good, food not bad and plenty of booze was consumed by all. What more can I say?

Thursday night we joined about ten other expats for a drink and meal in a nearby restaurant. Food not bad and company excellent – as usual, everyone was very friendly and we planned more gatherings of the FW people in this area.

Friday, Pat's day off, we drove into Alex to the Montazah Palace and gardens, which were beautiful. Lunch in the Palace, now a restaurant, and came back early afternoon all psyched up for a swim. We got as far as swimsuits, and Pat got half in. I managed a toe and we abandoned the idea – it was freezing! Shame, I wanted to be able to boast about swimming in our own pool. Thinking of exercise, or lack of it, reminds me: we now had an exercise bike; bought it the other evening in town. I used the one in Batangas most days but we couldn't bring it with us. No excuses now not to keep fit!

Went into town the other evening to collect our membership cards from the Alex Country Club. They'd managed to lose our ID photos for said cards so we had to wait about twenty minutes while they (probably) panicked. Found 'em in the end, but it had been no problem to wait; we'd been looking out of the window onto the canal. We were entertained by the sight of an elderly punt-type boat being poled past, crewed by a country lady in long flowing dress and veil (not the most practical attire for boating, really), while her husband pulled in the fishing net (yuk, you should have seen the state of the canal!) while two small children in woolly bobble-hats reclined in the stern. It was just lovely.

Did some shopping for forthcoming curry dinner party next week, and home for spicy home-made lentil soup and home-made bread. The bread-machine I'd had in the Philippines had finally given up the ghost, but the new machine was doing sterling work. Arab bread was great with dips and the like, but, call me quaint and old-fashioned, you just can't beat a new, warm, loaf of home-baked bread…

Travelling into Alex on Sunday night, we spotted a lorry overloaded with wooden planks. Nothing new there, even the fact that the lorry was loaded to twice the height of the actual bed of the lorry. What was new was the fact that there was a row of four men sitting facing backwards, balanced on planks which jutted out at the back of the lorry, so they were suspended about fifteen foot in the air on top of a precarious load…

Monday was a fun-packed day, or at least a packed one: it started at 8 a.m. when I left with one of the other expat ladies to go into town. First I had a routine blood test for cholesterol. In the few minutes that Irene was waiting for me, she saw an amusing incident: a taxi stalled in the middle of the road, and the taxi just behind couldn't stop and bumped into him. First guy was annoyed and got out to remonstrate with guy behind, but in his agitation he forgot to put hand-brake on, and his taxi reversed into the taxi which bumped into him. He was quite upset and angry, so second taxi-driver put his arm round him and apparently said the Egyptian equivalent of 'There, there! Never mind, worse things happen at sea', and other such platitudes…

After coffee we went to the American Wives' Association coffee morning for another coffee and chat, followed by wood-painting session and lunch chez another expat, finishing with a spot of food-shopping before the journey home.

Visited Mme Titi on Wednesday. Her system was really reinforcing what I'd done already, and was extremely intensive. We were moving on quicker than she normally would; we would be starting on repertoire soon now that she'd assessed my voice and confirmed that I was a lyric soprano. My French was coming on in leaps and bounds! Hoped my singing would soon do the same…

Wednesday night was fun; we had friends in for a curry and we played silly games after - it was a very good evening. The best bit, though, or one of the best bits, was that I SAW A HUGE OWL! TWICE! I'd been so envious of Pat who'd seen it before. Yes, he was right – it was large, with a three to four-foot wing-span, and could be grey but against the street-lamps it looked white. Beautiful creature. Didn't know they had owls there, but then, why not? Looked like a snowy owl to me; decided to look up owls on the Internet.

Thursday was a quiet day at home, and Friday was a veritable flurry of activity getting ready for Gerry's arrival – buying bits and pieces to make 'her' room look more homely; there were even six original oil paintings on the walls. (heh heh) In spite of said oil paintings(!) it looked really nice, with white walls, rose-coloured bed-spread, and small Egyptian rugs on the floor.

The Old Fort, Alexandria

Gerry and Practical Jokes

I'm continuing this on Saturday morning; we took Gerry back to the airport at 5 a.m. after a really good week. She really enjoyed her stay and we've certainly enjoyed having her here. Pat had three days off work, and we managed to do a lot of tourist-y things, some of which we hadn't done ourselves. Her first day was just 'vegging out' here and relaxing, then in the evening we went into Alex to church and drove through the town just showing her the sights. We had dinner overlooking the harbour and we introduced her to the delights of 'mezze' – different dips and salads, mainly vegetarian, and Arab bread.

The next morning we had an early start and drove to Cairo where we stayed again at the lovely old Mena House Hotel in Giza, right opposite the Pyramids. Mr Hanafy did the honours again, drove us round, issued information and advice, and kept hasslers at bay. We actually went into the second Pyramid this time, which we hadn't had time to before and it was amazing. You go backwards, bent almost double, down a narrow sort of staircase, along a corridor, up another low narrow staircase, and find yourself in a stone chamber with an immense tomb. The walls are covered with hieroglyphics. Incredible!

As the other visitors disappeared down the passage, Pat insisted that I try the accoustics so I sang a few bars of 'Don't be Cross'. The accoustics really were amazing, and now I can say that I've sung at the Pyramids! It was great fun, and at one point climbing the narrow staircase bent double we passed other visitors trying to squeeze their way in – we laughed so much that Gerry jerked her head up and banged it on the low ceiling...

Had a full day in Cairo visiting the Museum, the Citadel, the Souk and King Farouk's tomb in the City of the Dead. This isn't normally open to visitors, and is not on the tourist trail but we saw it last time and knew Gerry would love it. An opportunistic Egyptian business-man saw us go in and followed – he was apparently a film-director and thought it would be a fabulous subject for a film...

The sight-seeing continued during Gerry's two days in Alex – the Roman Amphitheatre, Pompey's Pillar, the Catacombs, the famous Harbour and the Fort.

The Fort is on the site of the old Lighthouse which was one of the Seven Wonders of the World. It's a pleasant spot, right on the rocks. There were lots of local people there enjoying the sunshine and doing what, to quote Gerry, they do best – just milling around. It was amusing to see many of the ladies, partially veiled, and most of them in long skirts, paddling in all their clothes…

Had mezze again in a popular restaurant overlooking the harbour. After, we had an amusing experience: the car-park was packed, with a stream of cars trying to come in and backing up onto the main road. When it's busy, as yesterday, you leave the keys with the attendant who parks it for you – some cars in the streets nearby if the car-park is full.

So out we come but can't find our car. Car-park attendant gestures vaguely into the distance, so we assume that our car is parked nearby, and that one of the attendants will fetch it. We wait. And wait – good-humouredly, and I ask the attendant if it will come today or tomorrow – he laughs. We wait a bit more. The attendants push, manoeuvre and shunt the cars around in the confined space, as people come and go.

Finally see our car arriving so decide to tease the attendant, who prides himself on remembering which car belongs to whom. As he indicates the arriving car, the three of us say, with straight faces, 'No, no, that's not ours. Mish dee – not that one.' The attendant looks horrified and panic-stricken but only for a moment as we burst out laughing. He roars with laughter himself, and three Policemen who are also milling about in the car-park join in. We left them all standing in a row practically mopping their eyes…

Well! The last couple of days have been very busy and very pleasant. Not busy as in working, you understand, but busy as in enjoying myself.

Gerry left on Saturday morning and I'd organized in advance for some friends to come for the day on Sunday – I knew I'd need cheering up after she'd gone! So there were four of us here and we just sat by the pool (no, it wasn't warm enough to swim) and painted. It was bliss… One of the ladies is an extremely accomplished artist and presented me with her picture – a beautiful, bold, splashy, semi-abstract, spray of gladioli. Pat and I love it and I'm getting it framed later this week. Had a pleasant lunch together; Pat popped in for a quick lunch and brought two colleagues with him. It was quite a merry affair! In the evening we went into Alex to Mass and met two of said friends afterwards for the roast at the Ramada, which nicely rounded off a very pleasant day…

Monday went into Alex with two friends to the American Women's Association, where Pat, Shirley and I touted for custom for our forthcoming pot-luck lunch and entertainment. More about that in due course! Met up by chance with some other FW ladies and we all had a mezze lunch together.

Wednesday went to see Mme Titi as usual; a friend came along into Alex and we had lunch together where we met up with another friend, who took us to the 'Green Market' to buy fruit and veg. A bit, er, local, but good fruit and veg, and very cheap. I've recently discovered 'harankesh' (your new Arabic word for the day!) – which means 'physallis'. The fruit comes in dinky little gift wrappings – papery sort of leaves. They're delicious – the physallis, not the leaves.

Thinking of Arabic words reminds me that Irene, new neighbour and friend, is as keen to learn Arabic as I am, and frustrated that the lessons haven't yet materialized. We spent a couple of hours the other morning poring over a small 'Arabic for You' and listening to the tape. Great fun; we nearly fell off our chairs laughing at one point with different ways to remember Arabic words. We plan to do this regularly (study Arabic together, not fall off our chairs) if the lessons can't be sorted.

Random bits and pieces seen recently: in a local shop: prayer mats with built-in compasses, several carts pulled by both a horse and a donkey – as Pat says, one-and-a-half horsepower, and a lorry loaded with large formal dining room table and chairs. Seated on the chairs around the table, on the lorry, as it bowled along the highway, were half-a-dozen delivery men chatting away as if they'd finished a delicious meal and were just passing the port…

Friday was fun; in the afternoon we had a buffet at the Refinery Manager's house. Lots of people there, some I knew, some I didn't. Nice and friendly and the house and garden were lovely – T-shaped swimming pool with the stem right to the dining room windows, and the cross-bit enclosing two small wings of the house. Real 'Homes and Gardens' stuff…

We've had high winds for several days and nights which deposit Sahara sand everywhere (I just can't resist name-dropping!) and it's decidedly chilly; I have on a long-sleeved sweater as I write…

Life continues to be busy and pleasant: Last Friday evening we took a driver, so Pat could have a drink (or two!) and went into Alex to the so-called Portuguese Club. Every nationality under the sun there except Portuguese, so don't ask me. It's just the expat club. Anyway, we met friends there and had drinks and a quiz. In spite of having me on board we managed to come third, which was fine – second would have been better, but not first, 'cos then you have to organize the next quiz…

The rest of the week has been busy, with shopping and visiting Titi, but mainly because there was a lot to prepare for the pot-luck and 'informal entertainment' on Thursday last. A pot-luck, for the uninitiated, is where everyone brings some food; it's the best so far as I'm concerned, and the food was superb. Several friends helped me with loaning chairs, washing-up, and organizing in general.

Anyway, so many people were away for Easter that we seriously thought we'd have to cancel – we decided that ten people was the cut-off point. In the event there were thirty of us of at least eight different nationalities. Thank goodness there weren't more – I just don't know where we'd have put them!

The entertainment was fun (surprise surprise!) It took place in our lovely light, sunny studio, dubbed 'The Little Theatre on the Roof' for the day, and we had Pam Ayres poetry, a short, very funny recitation, Indian and Mexican dancing and Egyptian belly-dancing, plus my own vocal contributions. Everyone was laughing (in all the right places!) and chattering and it was a really nice atmosphere. We had with a musical quiz devised by one of group, a chance to join-in some simple belly-dancing steps, (great fun!) and finished with lunch. Friend Pat stayed for the evening; she and her husband joined us in eating the left-overs.

Religious Affairs

So, Pat and I used to go to a Catholic church in Alex, and Mass was in Arabic, which made it difficult to follow; we'd been religiously (pardon the pun!) been following the Sundays of Lent in our Missal. A friend had told us very recently that there was a small Franciscan chapel in Alex with an English Mass. We duly turned up yesterday for the Good Friday service, to find that, not only was there no service but, although it was Latin rite, they followed the Coptic calendar and that it wasn't Easter weekend at all – it was only the second Sunday in Lent!!

We were really excited; we'd just booked our long-awaited trip up the Nile. We were flying to Luxor on 16 April, cruising to Aswan over four days, and then flying Aswan to Cairo. Went into the local souk the day before and bought a black evening skirt for the 'black and white ball' as I hadn't brought any evening dresses out with me. I'd also now got my UK flights; was coming home 28 April and returning here 20 May. I was looking forward to that too, although I didn't like to leave Pat when he was so busy.

The day before, Saturday, we'd gone back to the small chapel at the Franciscan convent school for Mass – yes, for the second Sunday in Lent. About ten in the congregation and it included two friends so it was good to be with people we knew and to be able to celebrate in our own language...

Easter Sunday (or what should have been!) was cold, windy, and generally miserable – bit like the UK really!!! I spent a really pleasant day at home while P was working; got up late, did some music and some tidying up, and watercolours in the afternoon, then Pat and I drove over to Agamy after work to get some booze. It was a seafront town, a popular resort with Egyptians in the summer, but it was an absolute tip. Floods had dried up, but there were piles of rubbish in many of the streets. Anyway, we went for a walk along the beach; it was deserted and very bracing; the colours of the sea were deep jade green to pale eau de nil. Beautiful in spite of the very dilapidated buildings along the beach.

Monday went into Alex with friends to the American Women's Association. Pot -luck at someone's house – understand she was a diplomat and the house was suitably grand. Huge, all painted white, with oatmeal upholstery and curtains, parquet floors, beautiful rugs, original water-colours – very like the houses where the expats had lived in Alabang and Manila. (Not BC!) Just beautiful. Got quite a lot more, good, feedback on last Thursday's musical afternoon; they were looking forward to the next one. (No accounting for tastes!) Forgot to say that we'd had a raffle and collected donations on that occasion which went off to a charity looking after the horses and donkeys of the poorest people. So, by helping distressed animals, you're also helping the poorest of the poor.

We had lunch in Alex and I came home to prepare for the evening, when friends were coming to dinner. It was a pleasant if slightly manic evening; the landlord and agent arrived at the same time to discuss some work we wanted done. Suffice to say that the food, while not exactly burnt, was a trifle over-cooked…

Anyway, as with most of these expat do's we were a disparate (if not desperate) bunch: there was of course Pat and me who are, we think, reasonably normal human-beings, then there was Steve, a Brit, ex-BC who was married to a Thai. She, Lek, was in Thailand while he was packing up his Alex home as he's off to India. Then another expat friend, Indonesian by birth but quite Americanised, and his girlfriend from Uzbekistan or one of the other 'Stans', Irene, our friend and neighbour was there (husband on duty) – she was South African, and she brought her friend who was visiting from Saudi, although she was a Costa Rican. New readers begin here…

The weather had been decidedly chilly, with high winds and heavy rain, but it started to improve on Wednesday and it was set to continue improving. We hoped… Anyway, on Wednesday I went into Alex, collected our good friend Pat, who incidentally, was leaving on Saturday with her husband, sob sob. We did some food-shopping, had lunch, and went round Manshaya, the local souk. I bought a shocking pink galabeya for the 'galabeya party' on the forth-coming Nile trip, and a very nice white evening scarf to go with my black outfit for the 'black-and-white party'. Pat came back with me; her husband joined us for dinner and it was, as usual, a hilarious evening.

Thursday Irene came up for the afternoon; she was keen to start some painting, and already had a good eye for drawing, so we spent the afternoon by the pool doing water-colours. Really relaxing, especially as the weather is starting to improve; there may even be something in this supposed myth that it can get quite warm in Egypt... P and I drove into Alex later; met friends Pat and John again in a local restaurant for positively our last dinner together before they left on Friday. We'd miss them, but there was a chance that they'd be coming back.

Alexandria Skyline

Friday was a pleasant, busy day. Jobs in the morning, lunch, then into Alex for shopping with P. For once it was him making the purchases – shoes, galabeya for party on boat, and visit to the framer to collect Shirley's painting which she did for me the other week. They'd made a very good job of it, very inexpensively, and I left some of my own paintings with them for similar treatment. Felt quite grown-up! The shoes which P bought bore the following legend: 'Rocket Shoes Co. Which is famouse with International model's with hight quality and elegance it's model's from the Beast natural leather that Comfort for foot.' Well, that's good to know...

A gentleman visiting Menem the other night had the sweetest little donkey and cart. The former was in quite good condition, the latter was a bit ramshackle, like a small rectangular covered wagon. He was selling fabrics, unfortunately nothing I liked, but we took some photos, gave the donkey a carrot, and tipped him (the gentleman, not the donkey) so they both departed happily.

Night Visitors

One night we had some bizarre visitors: Menem gestured us round to the side of the house where there were three men, none of whom spoke a word of English. They had two green hessian sacks, and proceeded to unload the sacks. In the light of the lamp, they unloaded about thirty heavy pieces of brass, which they assembled into a seven-foot-high ornate lamp. It was surmounted with a sort of circular tray, around the edge of which were small candle-holders, with three huge candle-holders across the diameter - it was massive, and weighed a ton. Then they just stood back for us to admire it, which we duly did; obviously, they wanted us to buy it. Tried to ask 'where's it from?' and got 'Luxor'.

They sent for interpreter who informed us that it was about two-hundred-and-fifty years old, and seemingly came from a church. In pidgin Arabic we explained that it was very large and our house in England was very small so no, it was beautiful but we didn't want to buy it. They seemed surprised at our non-alacrity to snap it up, but it was all very amicable and we thanked them profusely. It could well have been stolen, as had Gerry said, and if so we probably couldn't have got it out of the country. In any case, we didn't want to be labelled as a soft touch for the future. Poor things - they then had to dismantle it and re-pack whilst we went back to our glasses of red wine...

Heard pounding and bashing from Menem's back-yard one night. Peeped out of window to see him and Mrs M, who'd been staying for a day or two, making Arab bread on the ground in the moonlight. Large rusty oven had appeared, obviously for cooking of said bread. Arab bread was very good, but in this instance thought I'd stick to my trusty Hinari bread machine, thank you very much. A girl should never travel without her bread machine.

The week had been busy and pleasant; shopping with friends, visit to Titi who was just recovering from a cataract op, wood-painting and lunch with other expats, and getting reading for Nile cruise the next week. Couldn't wait! Weather was really nice now and getting very warm; Pat even went in the pool the one night, albeit briefly – didn't join him as I'd just washed my hair. That was my story and I'm sticking to it...

Nile Cruise

Here we are back in Alex, after a superb holiday – not a rest – but a wonderful break. The weather is relatively chilly here, especially after last week. But let's start at the beginning: saw a delightful sight on the way to Cairo: horse and mule together pulling a small tanker of some sort. Nothing new, but they were so well looked-after, so glossy and proud – heads high and harness jingling, that we were captivated! Stayed a night in Mena House, which we loved and flew to Luxor following day to join our boat, the Oberoi Philae. It was an irritating journey: we'd allowed plenty of time to cross Cairo, chaotic at the best of times, and managed to arrive early at the airport. So far so good.

Our 10.45 flight wasn't posted on the signs so we asked and were informed that we were too early and were told to wait 'over there'. 'Over there' was in fact the Departure Lounge but as entrance was unmanned and x-ray machines unattended, we ambled in, sat down, and waited. And waited. Finally went back out to Check-In desks, past the now-attended x-ray machines, to be told that the flight didn't exist, but we were in fact booked on the 12 midday one. Great. We were supposed to join the boat at midday in Luxor.

So back to Departure Lounge, past the same people manning the entrance and x-ray machines we'd passed a minute or so earlier on the way out, only this time they insisted on x-raying our luggage even though they knew we'd been waiting in there. Rang Mena House and asked them to pass message to boat (both Oberoi group) that we'd be late, and arrange transfer from airport to boat in due course. Sorted. We'd chosen this boat out of all the others as it was one of the best on the Nile and it was just superb – wood-panelled dining and reception rooms, lovely cabins, each with a tiny balcony, and excellent food.

The sad thing was that, due to the political situation, there were not many tourists: the boat had a capacity of 102 passengers; there were only 35 of us on board – with 60 staff to take care of us! The day we left the boat there were even fewer arriving – only 10 new passengers. Sad for the tourist industry, but we revelled in the luxury. The staff were charming and couldn't do enough for us. Excellent food but I managed not to put on any weight - didn't lose any either, but that would have been almost impossible, given unlimited breakfast, lunch and dinner each day plus a light afternoon tea. In fact a colleague of

Pat's on the same boat a few weeks ago put on 5 kilos in 5 days, so I guess I did quite well. Otherwise my smalls would have become mediums or even larges...

Going back to the political and security situation, we saw no evidence of problems; admittedly there were Police everywhere, as in Alex, but we found that reassuring. The tourist industry was vital to the Egyptian economy, and everyone from President Mubarraq down seemed to be aware of the fact and wanted the system to work.

Our fellow-passengers were a fascinating lot – none of yer run-of-the-mill tourists with shell-suits and peroxided hair (we saw loads of those on our visits to the tombs and temples – most of them spoke with heavy middle European/ Russian accents, wore pop-socks on even the hottest days, and ate cabbage sandwiches in their packed lunches. No, seriously, only the last bit is invented, rest is true). No, we woz definitely a cut habove the rest. In fact, it would have been very far-fetched even had we been characters in a novel. Would have made super Murder and Mystery fodder. Read on:

There was a middle-aged, one-armed, millionaire owner of trawler fleet with young attractive wife and small son. There was a party of American journalists and tourist writers, including one spaced-out gentleman with small moustache, very tight shorts and a wiggle to die for. Pat was convinced he was CIA. That too. Then the mysterious French couple who kept themselves very much to themselves, travelling on our coach but always viz zair own private guide. Our theory was that he was a well-known public figure and was travelling incognito viz 'ees attractive mistress. (But she wasn't nearly as attractive as she thought she was). A retired Indian Admiral was on board, a charming old chap with excellent sense of humour, delightful wife, and two grandchildren. On one occasion, when we were moored in Aswan, he insisted on steering the ferry-boat across the river, to the consternation of the boat-man..

He, the Admiral, got a reputation for being the best at negotiating prices and we teased him continually about it. In fact, on one occasion, I negotiated a good price for something and we clinched the deal very amicably. The shop-keeper was quite miffed to hear the Admiral, who'd been standing behind me, say 'And I'll take two of those at the same price please'!

There were two hard-drinking, compulsively-card-playing expat couples from Cairo. Our own particular friends were a retired Bank Manager and companion from Shropshire, and a Bradford and Bingley Manager and wife, who co-incidentally had taught in BAOR a few years after us, just a few miles down the road from where Pat and I had met! The six of us spent a lot of time together and much of the time in tears of laughter. My eye-make up spent most of the week round about my chin(s).

Every day there was a visit to tombs and/or temples, including of course the famous Valley of the Kings. Philistine that I am, I didn't really appreciate the tombs, and was in fact not the only person in the group to suffer from information overload. I preferred the temples, which were beautiful, especially Philae, which had been moved stone-by-stone from its original position after the flooding of the Aswan Dam, to its present position on a beautiful small island.

Back to my earlier comment about the cruise not being a rest – the problem was that every morning when we woke up—very early—we just had to get up – we couldn't bear to miss the wonderful scenery. The scenery along the Nile was just beautiful. I can't do justice to it in words. Early mornings on the Nile were stunning: all pink and gold... All the tours were over by midday, though, because of the heat, so we had afternoons to rest on the sun-deck. I only read two pages of a book during the whole time, and did two tiny sketches. Had planned to do loads of painting but just sat and gawped at the landscape instead.

We saw, against the desert back-drop, date and banana plantations, cultivated terraces, a herd of camels sheltering under some trees, water-meadows with buffalo and cows, people riding donkeys along the bank, people messing around in boats – on one occasion we saw an old chap dozing in his little boat. A larger boat passed and we saw the wake and guessed what was going to happen. As it hit him he woke with a start and fell backwards in his boat with flaying arms and legs. Not terribly elegant, but awfully funny...

The funniest incident, though, was in preparation for the galabeya party (long loose robes worn by Arabs). The afternoon before the party we were waiting to go through some locks, when the boat was surrounded by almost sixty small rowing boats, each manned by two men. They were selling assorted galabeyas, belly-dancing outfits, scarves and tablecloths, which they bundled up and threw up to the passengers on the decks above them for inspection.

It was bedlam. Sellers shouting, passengers yelling, mysterious bundles flying upwards through the air and landing all over the place, with unwanted bundles flying back down to the boats, sometimes landing in the sea, boatmen balancing precariously on prows and almost falling in – no-one did, which was quite an achievement. Everyone was excited and the noise got louder and louder – all the sellers trying to outdo the others. I am now the proud owner of a black cheese-cloth tunic and baggy trousers with elaborate designs in golden sequins. Nice! Shame about the uneven hem and the ill-matched patterns of sequins on the trousers. And also a beautiful, elaborate, bright red beaded galabeya, about four foot too long and three foot too wide. My usual cry – 'but it was a bargain'…

It was a standing joke throughout the cruise, my love for a bargain. (You know me – I'd buy a bra with three cups if it was marked 'reduced' I'd find a use for it). One day I bought a blouse at a price only slightly higher than the maximum I should have paid. After I've scrubbed it up, as it's pretty grubby, shortened the sleeves, and snipped off all the loose ends it'll be as good as new. Well, almost.

The crew were brilliant. Every day when they made up the beds they made figures on the beds out of towels and whatever was lying around. We had a large swan one day sporting a boater, a croc with an apple in its mouth, two small swans, and a praying figure. We got our own back one day, though, and made a figure for the stewards, wearing a new navy trouser suit, sun-glasses and sun-hat, stuffed with pillows. Very stylish.

One day we travelled the short distance from the boat to a particular temple, by horse-drawn carriage. Pat and I, at the head of the queue of passengers, were detailed off in the first carriage, with another couple. The poor horse was unbelievably thin and I refused, managing not to lose my temper, saying gently to the owner 'Your horse is too thin to be working and we don't want to ride with him'.

The next carriage had a horse which had a large raw sore, about eight inches long on its flank. Similar, polite explanation and refusal on my part. Happily, the next carriage had a very nice horse in very good condition, and I praised the owner, but I was particularly pleased to see that the couple behind us in the queue had backed us up and also refused to ride with either of the original horses. I was annoyed, though, that our driver started to canter the horse (never canter on the road!) but he slowed down when I asked him to. The tour guide told us that the supervisor had really told the two men off afterwards. Apparently this often happened with tourists complaining about individual horses, and he and other guides were always on at the owners. He thought it was just laziness on their part, as there was free veterinary care available for the horses. So please, dear readers, don't accept, in Egypt or anywhere, this sort of situation. Irresponsible owners must be made to realize that eventually their income will suffer if they don't look after their animals, even if they don't care for the animals for their own sake. Here endeth the lesson…

On the Banks of the Nile

Back in Alex the weather was pleasant but not hot. It was still cool enough to use the exercise bike most days on the patio. At least I was getting a bit of exercise regularly: for four months, the only exercise I'd had was shivering.

In fact we'd gone up on the roof to sun-bathe the previous day, to face two problems: the parapet was about waist-high so we'd asked the landlord to put up a sort of modesty-screen so we could sun-bathe without scandalizing the locals. (A bare arm is a no-no here, and we'd planned to bare far more than that.) 'Modesty screen' had gone up, about eight foot high, with bright red striped curtains. Could cope with bright red curtains, but the screen was too high and blocked the sun for much of the day, which rather defeated the object of the exercise. The small remaining patch of sunshine lured us up onto the roof, and we crouched in the last sun-lit corner of the roof only to see the sun disappear, and stay, behind clouds. Oh well, I'd been spared one more wrinkle…The rest of the week would be spent getting ready for the UK on Sunday…

Post-U.K.

I had a pleasant leave, manic as usual. It was lovely to catch up with Gerry, my Mum, who came to stay for a week, and lots of friends. Not all of them I'm sorry to say – it took me a couple of days physically just to open the accumulated mail, let alone action it...

Spoke to Pat most days and although he was fine I knew he'd be pleased to have me back. I had thought we had marital dis-harmony, as the last week or so our phone conversations had been interspersed with 'Oh, just go away' 'Will you leave me alone!' and even more disturbingly, 'Will you stop nibbling'. It transpired that Menem had adopted a puppy and he was always up to mischief. The puppy, that is; I wouldn't know about Menem. Pat told me that the place had been a hive of activity: Menem and M'Ahmed had been giving the place a veritable spring-clean ready for my return. I was quite flattered!

The last week of my leave was particularly busy with last-minute jobs, and packing. Then unpacking and re-packing. Then weighing, unpacking, re-assessing, re-packing. And so on. At least four times. Finally I was finished and only a few kilos over-weight. And my luggage too.

Had two sobering experiences during my leave. The first, on Friday, was when I'd decided to colour my hair. 'So what?' you ask. Don't be so impatient; I'll tell you. So, I used my usual brand and colour ('to cover all grey'), and as I'd used it umpteen times before, I didn't bother to read instructions. Should have undone cap of first bottle, inserted into base of second bottle, clicked it closed and shaken well for one minute. Well, I got it almost right. It was just that I absent-mindedly unscrewed both bottles, got to the shaking bit, and realised I'd sort of have to jam them together manually, which I did, before shaking. (The exercise must have done my upper arms no end of good). Well, the colour turned out, as usual, to be very nice. Took very well too. On the floor, the towels, the walls, the shower, and the loo-roll. A bit even went on my hair...

The next one happened on Saturday: I was taking part in a singing workshop but popping out for an hour or so to enter a music festival, and then going back for the workshop concert. Did the afternoon workshop and it went very well. I enjoyed it, was optimistic for festival and concert. Left in plenty of time to go home, wash, change, and have butty. (Brussels pate with garnish of watercress).

So far so good. I was cool, calm and collected. Staggered out of house with bulging brief-case full of music, pair of good shoes as I was driving in old ones, handbag, jacket, and bottle of water. Opened passenger door, put in everything, including car-keys, and carefully pushed door-latch in to lock, and slammed shut. Ah. Spot my deliberate mistake. Not such a good idea. I was locked out. I immediately dissolved into a quivering, blubbering heap as I was due at festival shortly. So much for my sang-froid. (Hey, that's really exciting! I think that's the first time in my life I've ever actually used that word. I like that. Sang -froid, sang-froid, sang-froid. It has a sort of ring to it, don't you think?)

Just at the right moment up came a taxi, and co-incidentally dropped tenant who should have been out for day but who was ill (happily for me!) and had had to come home early. Grabbed house-key off tenant; rang daughter who had spare car key at her house. Daughter was on train half-way to London. Oh. Daughter thought quickly and suggested I got taxi to her place to pick up spare key. Tenant's taxi had just disappeared round corner. Rang taxi-firm in quavering tones and explained it was an emergency; could I have a taxi quickly please?

Ten minutes later, back came same taxi, drove me over to daughter's house where happily I found car key exactly where she said. Back to our place, but now time was too short and I was too stressed to drive so removed everything from car and taxi took me across Reading to festival. Story tails off somewhat lamely here; I have to confess that I didn't stagger home from festival laden with cups, although I sang like a bird. (maybe the adjudicator doesn't like corn-crakes…) I sang well, I think, but just not well enough to win. Still, a friend did win so the story does have a happy ending! And the concert? Well, let's just say that, as far as I was concerned, it was like the curate's egg…

Tuesday. And here I am, back in the Land of the Pharoahs. A reasonable journey; at least it's short – four-and-a-half hours instead of the seventeen hours to the Philippines… We landed a bit early; Pat was waiting for me, and we were back in the villa just half-an-hour after our scheduled landing time. Not bad, that. There was a reception committee waiting for me: I was greeted with handshakes by Menem the boab and Fathy, his brother-in-law, and kisses from Mrs Fathy, wife of same, and from somebody's little girl, maybe Fathy's.

Or maybe not. Maybe she's an intruder and everyone thinks she belongs to some else. Yeah, maybe. Last but not least there was the new canine arrival to the ménage. He's small, bit like a Jack Russel, really, fluffy, 'cos he's still not much more than a baby, mainly white but with a few brown patches; has one ear pricked up and one permanently at half-mast. Quite sweet. And very lucky – Menem's son Basim rescued him from a rubbish tip where he was foraging. Pat had sent him off to the vet's with Menem for his jabs, including rabies 'before Madam comes back'. Quite right too.

Montazah Palace, Alexandria

Mayhem with Mike

I hadn't been sleeping so well for the last week or so, and one day I woke early; couldn't go back to sleep. The Call to Prayer from two local mosques was very loud and there was incessant barking from some dogs nearby. I was also disconcerted by a rustling noise from inside our room, and saw something move out of the corner of my eye: a little fluffy ghost with one ear at half-mast quietly slipped out through the curtains and the security-grill at the French-window...

The previous week had been very busy and very pleasant: my brother Mike came to stay - he arrived here the day after I arrived back from leave. Two events marked Mike's first night with us: the first and more significant event was un-armed, bare-chested cockroach wrestling (but Mike wore a t-shirt), and the second was an earthquake, apparently six on the Richter scale, epicentre Crete. He was sobered by the first, un-worried by the second, and managed to enjoy his week with us anyway. The three of us were sitting by the pool one evening and chatting about our next posting – maybe China. Mike commented how weird it was to be sitting with us in Egypt wondering vaguely if we would next be going to somewhere as alien as China...

The three of us had a day in Cairo which we all enjoyed. Took Mike to the Pyramids at Giza and we went into Cheops' Pyramid, the largest of the three - also a first for Pat and me – it was great. There were still very few tourists around so we were very lucky, but it was awfully sad for the Egyptian economy. We had lunch in the big souk, Khan e Khalili and did some shopping. Great excitement – Pat and I finally bought a carpet – wool, hand-made, beautiful quality, and very traditional. We'd been looking for ages but hadn't been able to find what we wanted. Now all we need is a complete change of décor and furniture to our living-room in Hamilton Road...

When Pat was working I took Mike around. We spent a couple of days in Alex doing the sights: one occasion, walking along the Corniche, we saw a group of fisherman hauling a boat ashore. I indicated camera to ask if it was ok, ('Mumkin?' – 'May I?') and so Mike joined the group hauling in boat and posing for camera. Everyone was laughing – what lovely people the Egyptians are: they have such a ready sense of humour...

With the political situation there had been some local unrest, mainly amongst the students, but it's been mostly minor. There were banners the other day on the Corniche in Alex, anti-American and anti-Israel, but it was all reasonably good-humoured and there seem to have been no serious incidents.

The day before Mike was due to leave we went up to Cairo so that he could visit the Cairo museum; I declined to go to the Museum, and planned an afternoon by the hotel pool. We hired a driver (very nice but he didn't know Cairo) and set off. The arrangement, which we explained to Hamed, the driver, was that we'd drive into the centre of Cairo to drop Mike at the Cairo Museum, continue through Cairo to the so-called Swissotel near the airport to drop me, and Hamed would go back for Mike four hours after dropping him. We showed Hamed the Museum on the map, near the Nile Hilton, on the banks of the Nile. OK so far?

So we soared across the river on the overpass, and saw the Nile Hilton ahead on the right. Mike asked Hamed to drop him 'anywhere near here' as he would walk rest of the way, which he liked to do. No answer from Hamed; we continued on the overpass. Pointed out that we had passed where we wanted to be and asked him to turn round at next opportunity. Only problem was that this overpass crosses Cairo from side to side, and there were no-turns offs en route. Somehow we managed to pass over the main railway station twice. Ah, we'd have to turn round when overpass ended and come back. No problem. Much.

Some time and miles later, overpass ended, we descended, into solid, grid-locked, Cairo traffic. We inched our way forward, and found no-where to turn. Abdul asked pedestrians, Police-men and taxi-drivers as we edged along, and several times we heard the word 'Opera' so assumed that the Cairo Opera-house was near the Museum and a useful landmark. Remember that piece of information; you'll need it later. Time was getting on; it was after midday, we were lost, the wrong side of Cairo, still pointing in the wrong direction; Mike saw his time in the Museum disappearing, and I was worried about my afternoon by the pool. Finally said to driver, gently but firmly (you know me!) 'Hamed, we will find a taxi for Mr Mike to take him to the Museum because we are now the other, airport, side of Cairo'. 'Oh', said Hamed. 'Museum? I thought you said 'Cairo music'. Truly. Hence the 'opera' bit. Even given that, we were still miles out of our way and hadn't a clue where we were so I stuck to the taxi strategy.

Usually the taxis pestered you like flies but on this occasion they were all occupied. Hamed drew up alongside another taxi and again asked for directions. The driver was taking his fare there anyway, and we were to follow him. Hamed did really well, weaving us in and out of the Cairo traffic following taxi which was not easy as they're all black and yellow Ladas. Don't laugh; this was serious. The legend 'Batman' on the rear of said taxi was a great help. The taxi-driver in front finally got us to the Museum, gave a cheery toot and drove off. We deposited Mike near entrance, agreed collection time and set off again in direction from which we had come, to take me to the Swissotel. Remember?

Almost immediately we took a wrong turning. I saw a sign to the airport off to the right and pointed it out to Hamed, who peeled off left. Mike and I had swapped mobiles so he could ring Hamed if necessary without his calls being routed through the UK; I had his UK mobile and was reluctant to use it as now my calls would be routed via UK. Suggested Hamed rang his boss which he did, for directions, as the arrangement had been made with his boss. (Swissotel? No problem). This left Hamed with almost no credit in his phone, and we were still lost. Had another go. Passed railway station a third time. (I got quite fond of it.) Asked a few more pedestrians and Policemen for Swissotel. No joy.

Finally, in desperation, I rang Pat, via the UK, and asked him to find the proper address and directions, as the booking confirmation letter did not have either. Pat found the necessary information, and rang back with an Arabic lady who knew Cairo, who directed Hamed to the right area and gave him the address. Phew! However, our troubles were not over yet.

We found ourselves driving through slums – surely this can't be right? It wasn't. Rang Pat's office again, got re-directed. We were in right area but couldn't find hotel. Stopped yet again and asked a pedestrian, who leapt in and directed us to hotel. We arrived at the Swissotel, and Hamed gently pointed out that the name of the hotel was previously El Salaan, and everyone still knew it as such... Finally I got my lovely relaxing time by the pool, a swim, and a good dinner with Mike that evening when he returned, a bit Museum-ed out but fine; he'd had a good time. He left at crack of dawn the next day. And I had a thankfully-uneventful drive home with Hamed. And yes, I would use said driver again. He was so obliging and helpful and such a safe driver – I'd rather drive with him any day than a maniac who knew the area but with the wrong attitude.

Hibiscus

Pat and Mary in Giza

Below: Fabrics 'r' Us. p.228

Small boat-traders on the Nile. P. 233

Animals and Arabic

The newest additions to the ménage were nine hens, who wandered around Menem's yard and the garden. We were amused to find them all cosily tucked up the other night on the steps on the spiral staircase leading up to the roof, about six foot off the ground and seemingly oblivious to the drop. I had hoped Menem was keeping them for the eggs, but I have a nasty feeling that they are destined for that great stew-pot in the sky... Surprisingly, Mishou, the pup, didn't bother them, nor they him.

We had an unpleasant experience the other evening: Pat and I were driving through Agamy, having loaded up with booze, when we drew up behind a horse and cart. I could see the horse's head over the cart from behind, and knew from his action that the horse was very lame. Then as we drew level with him his hindquarters literally collapsed under him. We couldn't stop in the middle of the road, so overtook them and I got out to speak to the driver and companion. By this time the horse was back up again and as they drew up I stopped them.

Frustratingly they didn't speak English so I pointed to his hindquarters and said he needed a 'doctor'. The two men were pleasant but defensive, and I gave them my precious only card from the Brooke Hospital for Animals. It explained in Arabic and English that there was free veterinary care available for animals. We could only hope... I needed to get some more cards and couldn't wait to start lessons in Arabic (Thursday) so maybe we'd be able to get some simple, stock phrases ready. It was so frustrating that some of these owners at best overworked their horses and donkeys – why couldn't they see that in taking care of them they were safeguarding their livelihood for themselves and families???

Monday was Alexandria Women's Association. Went in with Irene, good friend and neighbour and Rena, ditto. Lunch after. I was very flattered: had just finished quite a large oil painting of Aswan, which Irene and Rena had seen the other day when they were over. Rena apparently spoke to her husband and has asked me to do a commission for her! Suddenly I felt awfully grown-up. And panicky...

We got up yesterday to see Mishou, who'd broken through the barricade, sitting one on of my bikinis which had been drying outside, and munching the other.

Pat rushed out clad in not-very-much and rescued both before any damage was done . My hero...

Wednesday was an irritating day. Should have been to see Titi and some shopping. Not to be. 'My' driver was not available, so agreed to use another, who would drive Pat's car. Pat, who had a business appointment, arranged to use another car. Problem: driver didn't show up. Rang his boss several times, got Menem to speak to be sure he understood where we live: 'Leave main road past Refinery, opposite water tank, at turning indicated by very large, very rusty sign in central reservation. Drive down road to first, main, albeit dirt-track, crossroads. Turn right; we're second villa on right, where boab is sitting in dust smoking his sheesha'. So now you know where to find us! I waited. And waited. And waited some more. Driver, boss, and unknown person who was 'sitting in his office waiting' (?huh?) all called, but still no driver. Finally, after waiting an hour I gave up and cancelled the whole expedition. Just wasn't worth the hassle sometimes, but I hated letting Titi down...

Pat and I the other day found Menem, his sister-in-law, and an unknown elderly lady clad all in black, sitting outside in the sun, watching an equally elderly, black-and-white, flickering TV...

We had our first, long-awaited, eagerly looked-forward-to Arabic lesson the other evening – Irene and I, her husband John, and Pat. What a disappointment. The teacher was absolutely charming, but her materials and her methods (if she had any) were completely out-of-date and totally ineffectual. Spent the first hour starting to learn the Arabic alphabet which Irene and John knew but which, given the limited time we had available, didn't interest me – I just wanted to be able verbally to communicate with people, on even on the most basic level.

This left half-an-hour for learning some simple questions and answers. Could have been fine but it was so random and unstructured that, from the whole experience, I gained nothing. Irene commented afterwards that she and I had learned far more when we'd studied with a tape together. We'd give it one more try, and I'd suggest some simple language repetition games. If this didn't work, it would be back to the drawing-board...

Gerry would be out again in ten days' time – yippee! – this time with Hugo, boyfriend, which would be great. We were so looking forward to it. Obviously Hugo would want to see Alex and the sights of Cairo and then we were flying up to Sharm el Sheik for a day or so on the Red Sea. It would be a first for Pat and me and he would appreciate the break.

Saw an amusing sight the other day as I went up on the (flat!) roof to hang out the washing. Opposite our house was a very large, very grand villa with a huge garden which was surrounded by a ten-foot wall; behind and against the wall was a line of trees about ten foot again higher than the wall. So there was a tall, angled step-ladder set up alongside the wall, with a barefooted guy up said ladder hacking with an enormous machete at the branches. Sitting on the pavement below and to one side was a line of local men, no doubt 'supervising' and dishing out advice, but immediately below the ladder was a herd of goats eating the branches as they fell – usually on top of them…

Menem presented me the other morning with a bunch of beautiful, full-blown, old-fashioned roses, in bright reds and pinks, obviously picked from a local garden, and smelling absolutely delicious. Irene told me that she met him on the way up the lane past her house, carrying said roses. She'd stopped to say 'good-morning' and he carefully selected two roses and gave them to her – what a gallant gesture from a humble little gentleman– she was very touched.

Tuesday night was our second (and for me, last!) Arabic lesson. It was awful again. You really have to work hard to make learning a language so boring. It got so bad that I went out, ostensibly to go to the bathroom (isn't that a lovely word – aren't you impressed? 'ostensibly', I mean, not 'bathroom') but really to find my mobile and to ring the land-line to create a distraction. Pat came rushing out to answer the phone, also desperate for a diversion, and saw me with one phone in each hand, immediately twigged, and took the imaginary call for a minute or two. We were both trying hard not to giggle. It was only temporary respite then was back again to lists of vocab and phrases which we could easily have found in one of our dictionaries. No interaction, no drills, no games. It was BORING and what's more it's impossible to learn a language like that. The evening finished more happily, I'm glad to report. We went down to John and Irene's, had a swim with them which was fun, and supper. That's more like it…

Thursday was a really good day: we had a painting day here. Lots of ladies were away, but there were still eight of us – two English ladies married to Egyptians, another English lady, me, a South African, two Americans, and a Dutch lady.

Mishou was delighted to see all these ladies, thinking they'd come to see him, but of course, understandably here, most people were wary of unknown dogs. The more agile of the ladies negotiated the anti-Mishou barricade, and the less-so had it removed for them. Peace reigned for a short while, then Menem appeared with a very nice blue leather handbag which one of the ladies had apparently dropped and which the naughty pup had carried away to play with.

I thanked Menem profusely for finding and bringing the bag back undamaged and thought no more about it. One minute later, all hell broke out. Mishou was yelping fit to bust and we all realized at the same time what had happened. Everyone was galvanized into action and we all charged through the barricade shouting 'No, no, no' and 'la la la'. Menem, who'd been very embarrassed by the bag episode, was even more mortified to see all these large European ladies bearing down upon him and shouting at him as he hit Mishou with some cardboard. Mishou, the wimp, slunk off, and we explained to Menem that he mustn't ever do that – firm 'no' but never beating him, even with cardboard…

Only three of us were painting, for various reasons, so the rest helped get lunch and did all the washing-up. Another painting day next Thursday at a neighbour's house – a new acquaintance, thanks to yesterday. And, great excitement! I've actually sold my first painting – a small water-colour of a beautiful local mosque to one of said ladies. I was chuffed to bits…

Little Bedu Girls

Summer

Pat and I went into Alex Thursday night – it was getting very busy with the summer upon us and the hordes out of Cairo. The beach was black with people; some of the men were in shorts or swimming trunks, swimming or playing football, and the others, and the women, were fully dressed sitting under umbrellas on the sand. Not my idea of a beach holiday.

There was, however, the most beautiful sky, and later sun-set. It had been a windy day and as we drove along the Corniche the sea was jade green and the waves were crashing in. The dark-grey storm-clouds were tinged with gold, and the sun's rays were reflected in the water and up into the sky. It was a real old-fashioned, children's prayer-book, God-the-Father sky – I wouldn't have been at all surprised to see Him sitting on a cloud.

Later, as we drove along the edge of the salt-marshes, the setting sun was huge and molten-red below the lowering clouds. It was beautiful to see it reflected in the water between the clumps of reeds, and the outline of distant, bluish, factory buildings and chimneys were such a contrast that they only enhanced the sunset...

Saturday evening was pleasant—drinks party at the British Consulate to celebrate the Queen's birthday, and belatedly, her Jubilee. I thought it would be quite stuffy and didn't really want to go, but it was excellent. The festivities were held in the Consulate garden, which was lovely – not that you could see much of it for the people jammed in – there must have been several hundred people there. The trees were decorated with tasteful white fairy lights (not vulgar coloured ones of course!) and a string sextet played everything from 'Eine Kleine Nachtsmusik' to 'La Paloma'. I was surprised how many people I knew – FW being in the minority – and it was a really fun, lively occasion.

So there I was, all soaped up in the shower on Sunday morning, when the water went off. Nothing daunted, I discovered that it's amazing what you can do with a face-cloth and half-a-bottle of drinking water – even though the latter entailed tip-toeing past an un-curtained window to reach the fridge... Pioneer spirit...

Monday I went to Alex Women's Association followed by lunch with friends and shopping. We'd just got out of the FW minibus: Diana was first, saw an elderly beggar lady and gave her some money. I followed her out of the bus, reached for my money, and she told me 'don't worry, I've given her plenty' so I followed her onto the pavement. There was a commotion behind, and it appeared that one of the young car-park attendants had cannoned into the lady and had taken the money which Diana had given her, and she was crying. We zoomed into action and confronted him to make him give the money back. A couple of men came to support us and our driver joined in the fray. Young guy gave the money back: hope he'll think twice next time. Rat…

Off to Cairo to meet Gerry and Hugo who arrived safely and who met us in Mena House, where we all stayed the Thursday night. They enjoyed their stay with us – once Hugo got over his shock at the appalling driving, that is; it was his first impression of Egypt. Gerry and Hugo did the Giza Pyramids the next day, and Sakhara, the oldest site, before we drove back here. On the way we saw a lorry in front, with, I noted absent-mindedly, six large heads on long necks lolling about above the side-boards. Just like meercats, I thought absent-mindedly, then realized they were camels, sitting calmly and enjoying the view.

Coming from Cairo Pat got stopped, and fined, for 'speeding'. (We're fairly sure he wasn't). So while the Police were checking out his docs for this imaginary offence, they completely ignored a small pick-up truck which was driving along the motorway with twenty to thirty Bedu crammed in the back and on the cab roof. Looked like the finals of how-many-can-we-squeeze-into-a -small-pickup competition, in which case, they would undoubtedly have won.

Like the Philippines, the driving is appalling, and no-one is worried about the consequences – it's all down to fatalism. 'If it's meant to happen it'll happen' mentality. 'Inshallah' in Arabic. So I'm driving an unlit bus the wrong way down a one-way street at night, and someone gets killed –well, it was meant to happen. Pat reckons that fatalism is one of the major problems in this country: that's fatalism, but then what can you do about it??? (Take your time…)

Dead snake outside the garden gate: driver confirmed it was poisonous, and that at two feet long, it was just a baby. He's seen them in the desert and they grow up to three metres long – let's hope this one's Daddy doesn't come looking!

Taking G and H around we saw a pathetic sight in a poor area: a small donkey cart coming down the hill towards us, laden with bricks. Cart was obviously heavy and sliding down onto the donkey who had splayed his legs and was trying to brace himself against the load in the traces. The two men with him had to try to hold it too; a passer-by seemed to be remonstrating with them. Even our driver, an educated man, just laughed until we took him to task, politely but very firmly, and told him that tourists don't like to see animals abused and if the poor people look after their horses and donkeys they'll get better service from them. Hope we got our message across: we were not amused.

On a lighter note, saw a lorry driving along the road with a man perched on the roof of the cab – nothing new there – and another man standing on the front bumper and holding onto the bonnet. We passed the vehicle, drove on a bit and looked back, to see the man from the roof rolling into the road, unhurt, but no doubt feeling as stupid as he looked…

We flew up to the Red Sea coast for a few days, to Sharm el Sheik, which was excellent. As we arrived my heart sank; it looked just like a large, admittedly up-market, and spotlessly clean, holiday camp, but the rooms were pleasant, comfortable and cool, the staff were wonderful, and the snorkelling was excellent. We were able to snorkel directly from the beach, and were swimming/snorkelling each day most of the day. Magic!

The beach at Sharm was busy but clean and pleasant, the snorkelling was wonderful and the reefs well-conserved. Highlights of our stay were a trip in a glass-bottomed boat, and people-watching on the beach. There were the usual skimpy bikinis as you'd expect, but also several ladies in the 'full Monty' - clad from head to toe in black, even for swimming and snorkelling. Honestly.

Gerry, Hugo and I spent their last night in a hotel near the airport, whence they departed at crack of dawn on Sunday. Stopping in the ladies loo at a 'motorway' service-station with Gerry, we'd been given our ration of loo paper by the attendant on duty, and had joined at least thirty other ladies in orderly queues for the three cubicles. Orderly, that is, apart from two large, elderly, black-robed ladies who elbowed their way from the door right to the front with all the style and expertise of an Egyptian driver weaving in and out of the lanes of traffic. They achieved their objective quickly and efficiently, and I was amazed at the tolerance and good-humour which prevailed amidst the melee...

Cooking and Cars

A friend of ours apparently delivered a large bone to Menem whilst we were away, for Mishou. There is no sign of it on the premises, and Pat and I are fairly sure that Menem misunderstood, and used it to make soup for the family. But, it was a beef-flavoured NYLON bone!

Pat was running a team-building workshop for FW the other day, which culminated in a meal for everyone. As a special ending to the meal the caterers produced a huge cake, ornately decorated and dedicated to 'Fooster Weller'…

Speaking of cakes makes me think of cooking and flour: (well, it would, wouldn't it?) We never had weevils in the flour in Egypt, whereas we frequently found them in the Philippines – maybe it was the humidity there, whereas it's dry heat in Egypt. Or maybe it's 'cos I don't make cakes and sweet things here; as you know, honey is the loot of boll weevils. Sorry, I just couldn't resist that – I made it up the other day and was well impressed with myself.

Forgot to say that I'd had a culinary disaster when Gerry and Hugo were with us. In my usual efficient way I'd made bread and a salad, defrosted some stuffed peppers and had a sudden brainwave: there was half a packet of pine kernels open which I tipped onto the peppers to add flavour, crunch, and a little extra protein. More than I bargained for in fact, as the pine kernels were absolutely teeming with tiny mites, all of which landed on the pine kernels. There wasn't much fresh food in to replace, as we'd just come back from hol, so Gerry and I had to pick over ten stuffed peppers and remove all the said pine kernels.

Those of you who are familiar with pine kernels will realize that it's not such an easy task; although yer average pine kernel is longer than yer average grain of rice mi lud, have you considered puny pine kernels which are shorter than their fellows? And rice grains which are somewhat over-developed? I consider myself to be an expert on such matters now. The stuffed peppers tasted good in spite of my ministrations, and suffice to say that in future I will never again leave pine kernels in an unsealed container in a hot climate…

Menem disappeared the other night. He'd borrowed Pat's car to take Mishou to the vet as he'd been throwing up – Mishou, that is, not the vet. Or Menem. Mind you, I wouldn't know – maybe the vet had been throwing up. Or Menem. How would I know?

Please do try not to interrupt. So off he went in the car but came back quite upset as someone had driven into the car and bashed it quite badly. (We're not sure if he actually got to the vet's or not). So Menem made some gestures to Pat and Pat said 'OK' ('go with the flow', that was our motto) and off Menem went again in the car, presumably, and hopefully, to get it sorted.

Three hours later we started to get worried. Another hour went by. His three teenage children, his sister-in-law, brother, and their child, who'd been staying, had all disappeared too – probably too frightened to face us. Then up turned Basim, eldest son, who'd had a message from Menem to say one more hour and he'd be back with car. One more hour went by. Still no car and no Menem so at midnight we pushed off to bed. When we woke at six the next morning, the car was back, with a new panel to replace the damaged one. So far so good, but unfortunately it was a totally different shade of blue, and it transpired that, being a French car, the paint was different too so we were going to have to shell out a bit to have the job done.

Menem, bless him, had been terrified and had offered to pay (how can he? – it would be almost two months' salary for him) but we reassured him and may be able to put it through FW petty cash, but if not, it's just one of those things…

Went out with FW colleagues for drinks the other night, and saw an Egyptian lady with a very small, skeletally-thin, Doberman puppy – about six weeks old. She told us she'd rescued him the day before from a cage in a pet-shop where they patently weren't feeding him. He'd be fine but it was very upsetting to see all these cases of ill-treatment, or neglect, of animals. Even if people don't like animals, if their livelihood depends on them in whatever way, it seems strange not to take care of them. Neither P nor I understood this mentality.

Went with four friends the other day to a market. Really local, and great fun, for the first hour that is. After that it got quite claustrophobic with people pressing on every side, cars passing literally inches away from your feet (I grabbed a complete stranger at one stage and pulled her back!) and incredible noise – shouting, someone banging a drum, and traffic. Bought two small bath-towels, two nice t-shirts, two house-dresses and a rather nice skirt for ten pounds sterling. You know me and bargains!

That night we went out for dinner with the art-group and there was also a dinner in Alex for the FW top management team. It transpired that afterwards, when one of them arrived home that evening, his home had been completely cleared – of everything – including his passport and credit cards - right down to the satellite dish on the roof. He'd left lights on and car outside so that it looked as if the house was occupied. Had to be an inside job…

Went to see Titi the previous week and had a different driver take me. This one didn't get off to a very good start: as I walked out of the gate towards the car he dropped a piece of tissue in the road. Pat's had a continuous battle against the indiscriminate dumping of rubbish here, so I picked it up and gave it back to him, whereupon he apologized. He spent the whole journey to Alex trying to ingratiate himself back into my good books – not very successfully – by quizzing me about the sights of Alex which I've seen (scored about 80% there) and testing me on my Arabic. Conservatively I'd award myself about 25% so that wasn't too good but then you win some and you lose some…

Out of Town

The Little Dead Hen Who Came Back...

Mishou was growing into a lovely little dog, full of energy and bounce; when Pat went out each morning he rushed round in excited circles. (Mishou, not Pat.) He disgraced himself the other day, though: Menem was out, and we found a newly-dead hen on the lawn. We were worried that Menem would be angry with Mish (he would have – that represented a lot of money to Menem) or worse, even thrown him out. Anyway, Pat took a very rapid executive decision and slung the dead hen over the wall into the normally-disused plot next door and we hoped Menem would think he'd miscounted. Then we felt guilty as maybe they'd have eaten the chicken, but as Pat pointed out, it wasn't Halal...

The saga of the Little Dead Hen continues: the more observant of you may have noticed that I said 'the normally-disused plot' next door. So yesterday, there it was, the same dead hen, back on our patio – definitely not newly-dead, but yer Honour, the state of the ahem! carcass was compatible with the length of time wot 'ad helapsed since the said carcass was slung over the wall yer Honour. (not that I can claim to be an expert on chicken carcasses.) Obviously someone had found it and thrown it back. Pat went out to dispose of it, with three stout plastic carriers, one for each hand and one for the offending carcass. Thankfully Menem was out carousing with his chums, smoking sheesha and quaffing orange juice so still doesn't know the depths of Mishou's naughtiness.

Pat and I popped into a small shop down a side street last week, to look at some furniture, both antique and reproduction. The helpful shop-keeper gave us his business card which explained his hours of opening: Biznes Time From 10 – 1 After Noon, From 5 – 9 Night, but that on Sunday he is Cloccis. Oh well, that'll save us a wasted journey then.

Menem's three teenage children had been staying for a week or so; they were very polite, a bit shy like their Dad, and very helpful. Yesterday, Mrs Menem turned up too and was apparently staying 'alla tool' – permanently. It was lovely that they were all together, but we were not sure what would happen to the children's schooling, as that was the reason they'd moved to Alex.

Then yesterday, another couple appeared who were unknown (to us!) with several children—seemed to be staying too. Bearing in mind that Menem's accommodation seemed only to have one basic living/bed room and bathroom with a couple of outhouses, we were not sure what was happening. However, this was the system, and they seemed pleasant too, so it was not a problem – for us, at any rate!

Last night there was great bustling, clanking of saucepans and jollity from them all. Pat and I went on the roof to put out the washing while it was cool (it's well over a hundred up there in the day) and peeped over the parapet. There was a wonderful sight – a group of people sitting on the floor, in the dust, around a circular mat, on which was heaped a variety of dishes. It looked a veritable feast, and it was such a happy innocent sight; I found it really moving. Then, to cap it all, as we pegged out the smalls, the mediums and the larges, what did we see? Not one, but two, TWO, large grey owls swooping, around the neighbour's roof. Flew over us a few times to check us out but thankfully decided that we didn't represent an owl's dinner. Three to four foot wingspan! Really awesome...

Thursday was a super day again. Some artist friends came for day and we painted, then in the evening we all went out with other another friend and her husband. Drove out to a hotel on the coast and we sat out on the terrace for drinks, then had dinner; it was cool, pleasant, and great fun – there were eleven of us.

Mishou was up to his chicks again – I mean tricks. Mmm, I don't know though: heard a squawk one morning, looked out of bedroom window, and saw Mishou munching on a chicken leg. Problem was that the chicken was attached. And live. I bellowed at him and he looked up in injured innocence, which gave the chicken a chance to run, or rather hobble, away, seemingly ok. So if you should see a chicken limping around, you'll know that Mishou is about...

Driving to Alex a few days ago, we saw a horse and cart. Nothing new there. Horse in excellent condition; cart brightly decorated. Excellent. Unusual thing was that the whole thing was being transported, lock, stock and barrel, on the top of an open lorry – horse still in the shafts and not batting an eyelid.

Post-Leave

Well, here I am, back in Alex, after a pleasant, but very busy, leave. Wish I could say I had a good journey to UK but that wasn't the case: Arrived in good time at the Borg el Arab military airport in Alex, which is the one BA uses. I checked in, as you do. No problems. I waited for boarding. And waited. And – you get the picture. Just a short while before we should have taken off, there was an announcement to the effect that the plane, from Addis Ababa, was waiting on the tarmac but we couldn't board 'cos the plane had a flat tyre. The authorities had to send to Alex civilian airport for another tyre. Now, Alex airport is almost an hour driving each way – could be more if traffic is heavy, and it would take, we were told, about half-an-hour to fix once it arrived.

We waited some more and were offered refreshments – complimentary coffee in plastic cups. Big deal. No sandwiches, biscuits or the like were available. An obnoxious small child threw an empty paper cup all over the place, running everywhere after it and shouting, while another couple of boys, admittedly a bit older, armed themselves with paper and pencils from parents and spent the whole time sitting on the floor drawing – a pleasure to watch.

Eventually, we were told the tyre had arrived but now had to clear Customs. Fair enough. We were allowed to board, everything was stowed in the overhead lockers, we were told to fasten our seat belts, and – there followed another wait, so we all un-fastened ourselves and got chatting. I had two pleasant Muslim ladies, one each side, and next- but-one was a young girl in her twenties, Emma, who'd been on the plane from Addis Abba and who informed me she was phobic anyway about flying and who was getting increasingly nervous…

Very little information from the Captain, but the son of one of the Muslim ladies, who'd been sitting at the back, came to tell his mum and a small group of us (I like to think of us as the 'In Crowd'!) that yes, the tyre had arrived. Yes, it had cleared Customs, but the tools had not been sent with said tyre, so the tools had to be sent for from Alex airport.

The transit bus re-appeared and the passenger-spy explained that according to his sources the crew were almost up to their limit with flying time and we might have to wait till the next day to fly. Uh-huh. We waited some more, and a tall rangy individual with a surgeon's face-mask paraded up and down the aisle. Don't ask me why – I really hadn't a clue, and to be honest, by this time I didn't care. If it made him happy, so what?

Any road up, finally, after a total delay of four hours, we had the announcement that take-off would be in ten minutes, and Emma (nervous next-passenger-but-one, who was already in a state), asked me 'Mary, will there be enough fuel, now that we've waited four hours with the engines running?' (It must have been almost a hundred degrees on the tarmac), and then, 'What's that funny noise?' Why I had been selected as aeronautical adviser for the flight I'm not sure - it could have been my loud voice and my officious manner. Anyway, suffice to say that I rose to the occasion with my usual aplomb and confirmed that everything would be re-checked including the fuel (how would I know?) and that seemed to help so that, although her knuckles tightened and whitened on the arm rests, in between the two audibly praying Muslim ladies, she survived take-off, and what proved to be an uneventful flight for the rest of the time.

The first week of my leave was lovely; my mum came to stay and we spent much of the time sitting out in the garden chatting. Or what I laughingly call a garden – some would call it a jungle, 'cos the gardener has done his back in, and apart from cutting the grass once while I was home he couldn't do anything. I had divided loyalties – was concerned for him ('Backs is 'orrid') but also for our lovely garden. I was lucky with the weather throughout – sunny and hot until the last day. The sun always shines etc.

Rest of the leave was manic: mountains of paperwork – some of it urgent, some just important, but all needing at least opening and assessing. Got the whole house decorated externally. (Not me personally, you understand, I just wrote the cheque, on Pat's behalf), un-blocked the fridge with a piece of curtain wire, a drinking straw and half-an-egg-cupful of hot water. Won't bore you with the details now, but I was proud of myself. Had a dinner party and a lunchtime soiree (chuckle) for fifteen friends.

I was rushing around that morning preparing food and the kitchen window was open as the painter was doing the window frames. He had the radio blaring out Women's Hour, which included discussions on the menopause, HRT, hysterectomies, and other small-talk topics in which a house-decorator might be interested. At one stage he popped his head round the window-frame and said 'Are you listening to this, love? It's quite interesting 'innit?'

Here's a handy little hint you might all appreciate; it concerns eating out. When in an Indian restaurant, or any other sort of restaurant, come to think of it, never tip a vase of flowers from the table, into your handbag. The flowers are easily removed - though they do seem to wilt quicker than usual for some reason - but, should you have any small black throat sweets loose in your handbag, you will spent the next week or so prising out noxious black lumps from lining of said bag. And mobile phones are notoriously difficult to peg on the washing-line...

I was walking through Boots the other day, feeling decidedly un-glamorous – even more so than usual, and with my arms as long as a gorilla's due to two large heavy bags of shopping, when I was waylaid, nay, accosted, by a perfectly -groomed, tall, elegant lady, a vision in French navy, with not a hair out of place. 'Madam' she intoned 'I have something here which may interest you'. Such was her authority that I meekly followed her to a counter with a sort of bar stool, on which she indicated that I should perch. With my short fat legs it would be difficult at the best of times but I did my best to wriggle upwards on to said stool, only to discover that I was still clutching my shopping. Couldn't get down so I had to drop it on the floor. Have you ever seen two heavy bags of freely-falling shopping dropping at a rate of thirty-two feet per second per second? It makes a great crash, I can tell you. I derived at least a bit of satisfaction from seeing the Vision jump like a startled hare.

Any road up, she got her own back by saying superciliously: 'You seem to have a shiny nose Madam'. (Who does she think she is?) 'I have a new product which I think will help you'. So I still have the shiny nose but I'm 19 pounds lighter. Sterling. I must have the most expensive shiny nose in the business.

Pleased to say I had a good journey back to Egypt. Was met by gentleman with clip-board who whisked me through Customs and Immigration by a back corridor and no doubt some backsheesh. Luggage came immediately, and we were out into the hot night air just as the hotel mini-bus drew up. Luggage briskly loaded as it was a no-waiting area, and I just about to board when the driver said 'Where's your husband?' 'In the hotel, waiting' I said. (It was midnight.) 'No, he isn't ' said the driver 'he came in with me to meet you' and off he went to the car-park to wait while Clip-board and I pushed and shoved through the thonging, sorry, thronging crowds, trying to find Pat. I eventually found him propping up an exit doorway and peeing, no sorry, peering into the airport looking for me.

Speaking of airports and crowds reminds me: there are a surprising number of Russian tourists in Egypt at the moment – maybe the largest national representation on the tourist front. The ones in Cairo tend to be large and middle -aged, with peroxided hair and pop socks (and you should see the women!) while the ones in Alex look younger. Two FW engineers out here have Russian girl-friends with them, who are definitely not of the peroxided-hair-and-pop-socks variety. Unfortunately however, short skirts, bare arms and cleavages mean Only One Thing over here, and last week one of them spent two hours in Immigration in Cairo airport while they checked out her credentials...

Had a lovely morning with swims – two – and sunbathing, before a nice lunch and coming back here to Alex. Was met by the usual reception committee and handshakes, multiple air-kisses and ankle-nibbling respectively from Menem, Ibrahim and Bashim (sons of), Murfa and unknown lady, and Mishou.

Alex Harbour - Lady in foreground seems about to do a cartwheel!!!

Rest of the week was busy and pleasant. Small dinner-party for Titi, Nellica and Ad, Dutch friends of ours, seeing friends in Alex on Monday, and washing, sorting, packing and re-packing for Oz on Friday. Plus my usual painting in the afternoons – I wouldn't dream of doing anything else if I was at home. How was I going to cope if we did go to China. (possibility for next posting...) Brrrrh! It would be Winter; I couldn't bear to think about it. Still, on that score, we'd just have to wait and see – there was still no news...

Holiday Down Under

I'd been back twenty-four hours from Oz; we had a lovely time there and spent most of the time in Sydney so we could see Ben. Ben was fine – now – but had been diagnosed with shingles while we were there, so we'd extended our stay by a few days to make sure he was on the mend. It can be such a debilitating illness that we wondered if he'd have to come home, but thankfully he caught it early and got to the doctor in time to nip it in the bud.

Pat and I did a lot of exploring whilst in Sydney; we walked for miles and tried to see and do as much as possible that we hadn't managed first time round when we'd visited Gerry. Went on a speed-boat round Sydney harbour. (Best bit for me was getting off – I was terrified!) Ben and I opted for oilskins, supposedly to keep us dry but in fact we got drenched – and stayed drenched throughout, so we had to walk home with soaking wet bums. Every time we passed anyone en route we had a loud conversation which went along the lines of 'I enjoyed the speed-boat, didn't you? But I'm still soaking wet' just in case they thought we had an incontinence problem...

Ben and Pat did the famous bridge-climb over the arch of the harbour bridge, all kitted out with natty climbing suits and hooked on to wires. My idea of hell, not having a head for heights – the thought of all those gantries and vertical ladders looking down through wire mesh into the bay just makes me shudder. They loved it though, and got certificates and group photos, just to prove they did it.

I loved the huge fruit-bats hanging upside down in the trees in the Botanic Gardens. Thousands and thousands of them. Every so often one would take off for some reason and fly to another tree – their wing-spans were between three and four feet. And their dear little furry faces – they were so sweet! Besides the bats we were fascinated to see sulphur-crested cockatoos everywhere, and ibis, huge, long-beaked birds which almost look pre-historic in flight. Only four (two?)-legged wildlife we saw were wallabies. We would have loved to see possums, wombats or koalas in the wild. We'll have to start saving to go again!

We also managed to see a lot of our good friends Trish and Col, who we'd known in the Philippines, and who lived on the outskirts of Sydney. We stayed overnight with them, went to dinner another night in a pub with alternative entertainment to follow – so ghastly it was hilarious – and took them to a Hari Krishna veggie restaurant recommended by Gerry and Ben, which had a private cinema upstairs with rows of futons instead of chairs. We saw 'Gosford Park' there but I was far too comfy and slept through the denouement. I can honestly say I slept with a friend's husband... Trish and Col took us out to the Hunter Valley one day for lunch and wine-tasting. In fact by the time we'd tasted cheese, sausage, bread and pickles, with some fudge samples to follow, we had very little room for lunch. It was so good to catch up with Trish and Col again.

The Blue Mountains beckoned us and we spent three days there. It was sunny but bitterly cold and we had to go and buy a windproof jacket for me – even so I hardly ever got warm there. But it was gorgeous; we stayed in a brilliant B and B. Had planned to stay there one night, move on somewhere else for a second night, and return to Sydney but it was such a wonderful place we stayed there three nights and used it as a base. The scenery was incredible; we went in a cable-car down to the valley, and back up on the world's steepest railway. We went on an old steam-train, the so-called Zig-Zag Railway, and we went to the famous Jenolan caves, which is a huge cave system miles from anywhere, with absolutely fabulous stalactites and stalagmites.

Must tell you a super website; it's www.wotif.com and it has last-minute, reduced-price hotel accommodation world-wide. Before the Blue Mountains we'd stayed in a rather shabby, down-at-heel guest-house in Sydney, but having been recommended wotif, on our return to Sydney, we found excellent rooms in a business hotel just round the corner from Ben which were marginally cheaper than the first. Can't recommend it highly enough – it saved us a bomb.

So, back to Alex. Menem and family seemed delighted to see us and I was thoroughly air-kissed several times by the ladies of Menem's household. Mishou was full of beans as usual and nibbled our ankles as we staggered across the lawn to unload the car. Back in Egypt with a vengeance: no hot water in bathroom, then the next day no water at all for most of the afternoon.

The kitchen and spare room had been infested with ants, and worst of all, we had a mouse in the house. Jet-lagged one night I couldn't sleep so sat at the computer throughout the small hours. Suddenly said mouse shot out from under my feet across the room. Needless to say, I shrieked. Went into the bedroom to find Pat and was not best pleased to find he'd slept through my crisis. Worse, he'd nicked my pillow. You can go off some people... Mousie had also demolished two new bags of flour so there were piles of white stuff all over the storage cupboard. Pat said that at least we'd be able to identify him – when we found him – by his white feet. Didn't want to kill him unless we absolutely had to, so we just hoped he'd go away...

Mishou had been up to mischief again: a batch of bantams had arrived and it had been too much temptation for our little fella. Pat found him hassling a bantam; bantam was alive, but clearly shocked, and Pat put him somewhere safe in the hopes he'd survive. Still, at least he (probably she) was breathing, or Pat would have had to try mouth-to-beak resuscitation.

The local people were very friendly and seemed to enjoy communicating with us: they had a delightful sense of humour. The other day in the supermarket we were at a check-out manned by a young man we knew. Our groceries moved along the conveyor, followed by a large sack of dry food for Mish. I very solemnly pointed to it, patted my tummy and rolled my eyes in ecstasy, saying, in Arabic 'Delicious!' Young check-out guy looked horrified then Pat and I burst out laughing. Check-out guy joined in, so loudly that the Manager came to see what was happening, and everyone around us was laughing too...

The Mousie Stomp

We'd just had Gill, a UK friend to stay for a week. Had arranged for her to be collected from airport the evening after our arrival back from Oz, and to be brought back here. Estimated that she'd be here by 1 a.m. and got quite worried when she wasn't here by 2 a.m. Even if we could have found the number, the airport would be closed and/or manned by, at best, cleaning staff. Couldn't ring transport firm at this ungodly hour, so we continued to wait. Phone rang at 2.15a.m. and we were mightily relieved to hear the boss of said transport firm asking for our address as 'the driver doesn't know your house'. (Addresses are no good here.) We gave directions and Gill arrived safely.

The mouse was in evidence during Gill's stay; I decided to deal with the problem one evening and mustered Pat and Gill to help me beat (as in grouse-shooting) the little chap out of the house. Mouse went behind cooker so we opened the outside kitchen door, lined up in the other doorway and in close formation stamped our way across kitchen, clapping our hands and chanting a mouse-beating song, hastily improvised for such an emergency. Not entirely, let's be honest, not at all, effective. Gill and I collapsed in hysterical screams of laughter, Menem's daughter took refuge in the outhouse from which vantage point she could observe this strange foreign ritual from the safety of the window, and the mouse stayed firmly behind cooker, no doubt, Pat acidly observed, terrified out of its wits.

Rest of Gill's stay in Alex passed more-or-less without incident. Well, except for the wine bottle incident, that is. Technically it was a dry society, though it was possible to buy limited kinds of beer and wine in a few places. So we'd gone into Alex to stock up on booze and went into the Cecil hotel just round the corner, carrying a sturdy plastic carrier with the week's supply of wine. I managed to knock the carrier over on a marble floor and smashed one of our precious supply. Wine flooded out. A waiter rushed over with a cloth and mopped up. I removed all the other bottles from the carrier and presented a security man standing nearby with the carrier holding the broken bottle and the rest of the spilt wine - with pleading smile and profuse apologies. This left us with no carrier to hide the offending remaining bottles from public view and the three of us had to leave the hotel loaded down with wine bottles. It wouldn't have been quite so bad except that we'd only gone into the hotel to use the loo...

A sad thing happened the other night: we had a party for Gill, and the first guests arrived with the awful news that there were some children outside with a very large – dead – owl. You may remember that we'd seen them once or twice since we'd been there, and once occasion saw two of them circling a neighbour's roof. It was the shooting season and this one appeared to have been shot – maybe, let's be fair, accidentally. Gill and I went out to investigate but everyone had disappeared. What a shame – such a beautiful bird. We were both really upset. The party, on a lighter note, was excellent, I'm pleased to report.

I took Gill up to Mena House, our all-time favourite hotel, for her last couple of days. We had an afternoon by the pool and a superb Indian meal there, and in Cairo visited the Citadel and the Souk. Our usual Cairo driver took us to the Pyramids and kept the hawkers at bay, with the exception of two delightful children who managed to sell us a few priceless objets d'art (!) before they were chased away by the Tourist Police. There was, how shall I put it, a slight incident with Gill and a photo-call with a camel in a split skirt (Gill, not the camel.) Anyway, Gill tells me it can be repaired, so that's all right then...

We finally had confirmation of our next assignment—China, as we'd thought, and thankfully accompanied again. Time was running out for us in Egypt: the packers were due on Thursday so there were piles of things all over the house – didn't know we had so much stuff with us. Very little food in house but masses of booze (nothing new there then!) so I thought we'd have to have another party – a please-whatever-you-do-don't-bring-a-bottle party!

Well, the packers have been and gone, but there are still miscellaneous papers everywhere and piles of things to be passed on to various people. This will be almost the last instalment from the Land of the Pharoahs. So much has happened in the last nine months... We've enjoyed it here and we've met so many nice people, both expat and Egyptian. We've had a couple of super holidays – the Nile cruise and Sharm on the Red Sea – plus we leave here on 25 September, have a night in Cairo then fly to Aswan where we have a night in the famous Old Cataract Hotel, then four days/three nights cruising Lake Nasser and going back to Mena House for our last couple of nights here.

It's a veritable social whirl at the moment as we've made a lot of good friends here . Had a Chinese meal the other night in the Ramada, Alex, with FW people and were amused to see from the menu that the hotel welcomed one Phil A, whoever he was, and 'fiends' to celebrate his birthday! There was a party at American friends' of ours last Saturday, we took a friend out to dinner last night and yesterday I had lunch chez Suzanne, a good friend, and other friends.

Our house-mouse is still in residence. He's obviously quite a feisty little chap and with expensive food tastes: I left an avocado on the kitchen work-surface to finish ripening, and came back later to find tiny bits of peel nibbled off and discarded, and tiny teeth marks on the flesh… He often runs behind the taps and Pat was afraid that he'd fall in and drown – not only for the mouse's sake, but for mine too - he could just imagine the racket if I found a dead mouse in the washing-up, so he left a sauce of water near his home behind the cooker…

I decided we'd have to get rid of him, but we couldn't bear to kill him. Suzanne lent us a humane mouse-trap which would only trap him, allowing Pat to take him away and release him. Suzanne had also had a mouse-problem, had caught the mouse and gave him, in a bucket, to the guard in the building next door asking him to take away but definitely not to kill him. What did guard do? He shot him. In the bucket. Painful. At least it was a humane end to the mouse but it didn't do the bucket much good. Suzanne was hopping mad on both counts.

So, back to the trap. A steel door on strong springs was held open by a wire, the end of which was threaded – just –through loop jutting out through top of cage and with hook inside the cage for cheese. The mouse was supposed to take the bait, which jiggled the hook, which released the wire, which slammed the cage door shut. It didn't work out like that, though: Pat baited the trap with jalapeno-flavoured cheddar and we left the trap in a suitable place and left it overnight. I had a sleepless night worrying we hadn't left water in the cage so he would get dehydrated and die, but in the morning the cheese was well and truly nibbled, most of it gone. The steel door was wide open and the mouse still at large…

Freedom of the Villa Mariem

There were some things we wouldn't miss, including the sheer lunacy which prevailed on the roads. Drivers hurtled along weaving in and out of traffic at high speed, squeezing between other vehicles literally with inches to spare, swerving violently, not slowing down to avoid pedestrians with a collective death-wish. Vehicles frequently had no lights and often drove the on the wrong side of the road; we saw a pickup the other week swing round a corner with both doors hanging open. The previous day there'd been road-works on the main road into Alex – totally without signs or warnings, so for almost half-an-hour we were inching along in heavy traffic in virtual gridlock. The two lanes of traffic became five, and in one place SIX when vehicles teetered along on the edge of the lake to get past the hold-up. We saw a heavy lorry driving along and the driver, for some inexplicable reason, opened his door and hung out looking backwards as he drove. Don't suppose it made much difference to his driving, come to think of it. Also saw the other day, two lorries driving about fifty miles per hour, one behind the other and nudging it along. Crazy.

I came back from Cairo in a taxi the other week, having seen Gill off, as the FW driver had forgotten me. (I frequently have that effect on people.) Driver was charming and courteous, and car was spotlessly clean but front windows had no handles to open them. Luckily rear windows did, so when he wanted to open the front windows he just leaned back, removed handle from my rear door, applied it to front window, and replaced in rear. Simple really! Original car clock obviously didn't work so driver had stuck purple alarm clock into clock space. I ask you, purple –especially as upholstery was mustard colour… Arriving back I was especially relieved that we hadn't had accident and needed to jettison vehicle quickly, as I found that my door could only be opened with pliers…

Pat and I went for a meal last night at the home of an Indian colleague – mmmm! Delicious food – shame about the calories! I got very upset on the way: we saw a driver of a horse-cart beating his horse, which was already scarred on his haunches and not in particularly good condition. The horse was jittery, skittish and unhappy, the cart ramshackle as usual and we half-expected the whole thing to collapse. Anyway, the traffic continued to swerve around him without slowing and he beat this poor horse into a canter. I lost my temper and wound down the window and Pat and I shouted 'Shwoyer, shwoyer' (slow down) and 'Haram' which an Egyptian friend has told us to say; it means 'bad/

disgrace/ – it's against your religion'. I was absolutely hopping mad and it took me ages to calm down – even if they don't care for their horses how can they fail to see that if their horse dies, they can't support their family? The local people seem to have literally no concept whatsoever of cause and effect. Very strange.

A friend told us that she'd been driving up to Cairo when her driver started to laugh, and pointed to the driver of a lorry who was smoking a sheesha in the cab as he drove. A sheesha is like a hookah as in 'Alice in Wonderland' and stands between two and three foot high… And then the other night Pat and I saw a car driving along the highway, and two passengers each had an arm sticking out from both the front and the rear window; between them they were holding a large bundle of very long drain pipes…

Pat and I took Titi out for a farewell dinner the other night; two friends came along too and we had a very pleasant evening watching the harbour lights while we had our meal. In spite of the shabbiness Alex has a beautiful harbour, overlooked by an old fort, which stands on the remains of the old Alexandria Lighthouse, one of the Wonders of the Ancient World. By day it was beautiful with all the brightly-coloured boats, and at night it was magical with all the lights from the eight-mile-long Corniche reflected in the sea. We saw a charming sight on our way back from town – a family, obviously moving house, had all their belongs stowed very precariously in two lorries which were bowling along the highway. The mattresses were stacked untidily on the first lorry, and about six family members were sprawled on top as they drove.

On Saturday night Pat and I went to a party at friends just down the road. Very pleasant; most of our friends were there. Super buffet and I'd been asked to sing. Gave them 'Don't be Cross' and 'Prima Donna'. Everyone was complimentary and I was delighted with how it went!

The mouse saga continued: Suffice to say that we now had a photo of him munching away at his jalapeno-flavoured cheese, with the door of the trap still wide open and un-sprung. Then that morning we'd found the door of the trap shut, but with no mouse in trap. Either he'd bumped into the outside of the cage and sprung it, or had made a quick escape before door snapped shut. He would be referred to from now on as Houdini Mouse…

Local Mosque,
Alexandria

Last day in Alex: Houdini continues to thrive, and sends his regards to you all. He continues to evade capture and re-location, and is almost tame now. We often see him in different rooms and have been amused to see him on more than one occasion running all round the edges of two rooms to get to a third, so he doesn't have to go across the exposed part of said rooms. He is so tiny and with a long pointy nose – more like a shrew – and we think he must be a desert mouse. Pat actually found him sitting on top of an avocado earlier...

OK Houdini. We're exhausted by this psychological war. We never know where you're going to turn up next. You've now found the large supply of dog-food in the spare-room cupboard which we're leaving with Menem for Mishou - we heard you scrabbling and we've found the evidence. OK! OK! You win. We give in. We're obviously never going to get the better of you, and we grant you henceforth the Freedom of Villa Mariem. We've given the cage back to Suzanne and we wish you all the best for the future. And Houdini please – stop smirking. Just promise us one thing: if you have relatives in China, please, please, don't tell them we're coming.

Now I know how you all love – and need – my little household tips and hints for everyday living, well, here's a final very important one, literally just before we leave the Land of the Pharaohs: Before you move house, always check under the beds. You never know, you might find a very expensive pair of diving flippers, which could, just could, be squeezed into your already-excess-luggage. You may even also come across a set of dumb-bells which very definitely won't...

CHINA

Arrival in Southern China January 2003

The journey out was interminable; I slept very little but at least had two seats to myself. I flew by Virgin to Shanghai, where I met one of the guys from the Project, then changed to China Southern for the domestic flight to Shenjen. Meal boxes were given out. I expected larks tongues on noodles with side order of frog's intestines but it was much worse than that - synthetic-looking pastries and white jelly with cubes of unknown origin. (Probably bean-curd but I'm just giving you the picture) The driver met us in Shenjen (Pat tied up in meeting) and whisked us here – one-and-a-half hours' away. I arrived tired and starving but in good shape. Well, as good shape as I ever am…

I had my little eyrie in our apartment on the 16th floor, overlooking the bay. Beyond the rusty container port, the container vessels, the mounds of garbage and the decaying smugglers' boats, it was quite picturesque, with almost a hundred little fishing boats going back and forwards. They anchored up at night in semi-circles – in fact on one occasion we saw a complete circle below – first time Pat had seen that – with the prows all touching so the fishermen could walk from one to another along a sort of curved marine corridor. They disappeared in the early morning to fish, returning later. All round the bay there were mountains, which looked like some stylized Chinese brush painting.

The apartments were ok, in the Holiday Inn Aoutou, with minimal modern furnishing and reasonably well-equipped. We had an exceedingly generous settling-in allowance but it was difficult when you were new to find everything in the shops. Only problem with the apartment was that it was very dark in the lounge and positively sepulchral in the small guest-room, with dark brown furniture and dark-brown, lined curtains. I rest my case. I missed having a swimming-pool and garden, but these would be in place hopefully by June.

The expats we met seemed very nice; I met up with a new friend I'd made in Beijing when visiting Pat: she introduced me to a few people. Drinks party on Friday night, informal drinks and meal yesterday to meet the Deputy Consul. We had people coming in for dinner twice that week, and I had a musical soiree lined up for an afternoon(!!), so I guess you could say I was settling in. I did my painting and worked on my music most days; some of the wives didn't have hobbies and were bored to bits – some had already given up and gone home.

The local people were absolutely charming, little English was spoken but they were very anxious to please, and of course to make money…Shopping was very good for electrical goods and bedding and so on but it could be really difficult to know what you were buying 'cos of the language barrier. Food-wise, there were excellent fruit and veg but very poor meat locally we were told, though we hadn't tried that yet, and some shops sold Western foods, understandably at a price. We'd stocked up on those. There was a shopping trip every day to different places but I hadn't been yet as all the shopping trips were day-long and I wasn't keen to spend whole days shopping just for the sake of it.

Pat and I took a local bus, nearly an hour's journey, over to the golf resort one day to the shop there which sells Western foods. Stocked up with loads of goodies – only to find they couldn't take credit cards. A charming Chinese lady told us to pay next time we were in – we'd spent about a hundred pounds sterling, and she didn't know us from Adam! Trust or what – needless to say we sent the money over almost immediately.

I'd already had a job interview but hadn't made my mind up whether to go ahead with it or not – it would be teaching local businessmen and would be very interesting but evenings, for initially about eight weeks, three evenings per week and it was a new project – would be interesting to help get it off the ground.

The Chinese were heavily into keep-fit. Every morning, from our vantage point in the bedroom, we watched the little figures below going to work in the Customs sheds, and doing Tai Chi before work commenced. One individual, obviously an exhibitionist (it takes one to know one!) insisted on doing Tai Chi on a flat roof while his colleagues did so on terra firma below. We saw about twelve Customs men marching on duty, each carrying a brightly coloured plastic stool and later in the day with bright plastic (?) lunch containers. At least two of them were in step. Even funnier was the dozen or so ladies working in some anonymous concrete block near the car park. (We found out later it was supposedly a brothel…). They seemed to be doing some sort of manic ritual, all in perfect synchronization, with an indeterminate three-legged black dog philosophically looking on. Anyway, we happened to open the window one morning, heard the strains of rock and roll, and realised it was a dance troop practising; one morning there were two of their number unselfconsciously fox-trotting around amongst the rock-and-rollers.

One Tuesday I went on one of the afore-mentioned shopping trips. Long day out – almost eight hours – just to get a few groceries. Good shopping, and good prices, but it was so difficult to find what you wanted, particularly with one eye on the time so you didn't miss the bus. Wouldn't be doing it very often, 'specially as excitement, excitement, the new shop had opened in the hotel complex. The scenery en route was interesting, and in places really beautiful...

Country Scene

Once again I was beavering away at Pat's office machine as we couldn't get the necessary cable for his lap-top – his boss had tried in Hong Kong with no success so I was still having to limit my e-mails to evenings whenever I could. I'd tried working on his lap-top during the day, but my efforts were thwarted (doesn't that sound old-fashioned?) when I discovered it kept typing in Arabic: we remembered that Pat had some work done on it in Alex, but when we tried to change the language to English, it kept reverting to Arabic. Pat changed it finally to English, only to find that the cursors still moved the Arabic way, so striking the 'end' key for end of line kept taking me back to the beginning, and right cursor went left and vice versa. Gave it up as a bad job in the end...

Pat and I were fine and settling in socially: we'd had two colleagues from Batangas days to dinner one evening, and our second small dinner party that week swelled to ten of us, which was quite a large number for the apartments. However, both meals were fine – different, three-course meals each time – in spite of catering constraints. I loved cooking anyway (still do!) but particularly relished trying out new ideas and the challenge of limited ingredients.

One Saturday we had an irritating day: hired a car with a friend and went to Shenjen, armed with long shopping list for household items we hadn't managed to track down - including single bedding for the spare bed, sewing threads so I could do some dressmaking with the suitcase-full of fabric I'd brought with me, a standard lamp for the lounge as it was so dark, and kitchen scales – or even a measuring jug like the Yanks use. Even baking bread with my precious new Panasonic was a trifle complicated: I had to find three bowls the same size, divide a bag of flour equally into three and use one part, replacing the other two parts in a plastic container, and remember to divide by two only the next time…

Anyway, back to Shenjen: we spent £25 on our share of the car, £20 on three bottles of water and three fruit-juices in a nice hotel, and all we got were groceries we could have bought in the local town; we couldn't find any of the other items. Plus it wrote off a day – it's a three-hour round trip plus shopping.

It was common to see bicycles with one or two children perched behind the cyclist or balanced on the handlebars, but also cycles, frequently three-wheelers, pulling small carts which carried an interesting assortment of goods. We saw bamboo poles or flexible metal pipes carried at right angles to bike, usually several metre across – it's a wonder they didn't sweep everyone along with them. We saw a bike one day with sort of base-board, on which were several aquariums? aquaria? complete with water slopping and goldfish. We've seen mattresses stacked up precariously and huge piles of cardboard, which caused the whole edifice to sway alarmingly, also large boxes of electrical goods…

Recently a photographer friend took Pat and me, and another expat couple, to visit an old Hakka village some miles away, out in the countryside. It was semi-derelict, but the few people who lived there were friendly and welcoming – it was a huge help that Ian spoke the local language. Many of the houses were crumbling and derelict, overgrown with weeds – some of them even had faint pictures and exhortations of Mao over the lintels. One little house was particularly poignant: there was an old bed, a small table, and a faded photo of the elderly couple who had lived there…

We saw two little girls, maybe 3 and 6 years old, doing the family washing—by hand, crouched down over a bowl of soapy water. After our visit Ian, his girlfriend, Pat and I had lunch in the hotel together: in the restaurant we spotted a small girl, very pretty if a bit precocious, and with a very little-girly dress and necklace, preening and posturing. Ian pointed out that she was probably about the same age as one of the two little girls we'd seen actually doing the laundry...

Phone Phobia...

The staff in the hotel, and the local people, were lovely, but I dreaded answering the phone to anyone Chinese. I found them difficult to understand even face-to-face, but on the phone it was sometimes impossible. So I'd answered the phone the previous day and heard 'Thi' Choy from Sieve a Parrot'. Mind went into overdrive and I started thinking 'Sieve a Parrot?' This is terrible – should I ring RSPB or International Fund for Animal Welfare?' The line was as clear as a bell but I kept saying 'Sorry, it's a terrible line'. Caller repeated message several times and penny finally dropped – it was one Joy, from the Silver Palate shop at the golf resort, about a delivery of dish-washer powder for me...

Had a musical afternoon one Tuesday. There were eighteen of us, and it was fun—quite an innovation for here: I just did three numbers and gave 'em a music-based quiz with afternoon tea. Good fun, everyone left laughing ...

There was literally nothing to do here for expat ladies in the day, apart from the daily shopping trips I told you about – most destinations were about one-and-a-half hours' away. I simply refused to do it unless I had to. Some ladies went out most days, but I'd heard some of them say they were getting fed up with it. I had a coffee with several ladies in the local village hotel one day– hotel clean but a bit drab – coffee best I'd had yet out here, and I heard someone else say the same. The small village/town where we were based was incredibly boring and there was no-where nice to walk. Suffice to say that I had painted for eight hours the previous day, alternating with reading while the painting was drying! There was a small choir being formed, a bit shambolic, but I was giving it a try anyway, and someone was trying to get together a variety show. That was more my scene – Pat's too so we were checking that one out.

Remember I told you about the keep-fit activities in the mornings? Well, you may be interested to hear that the ladies wot dance are doing well, and send their regards to you all. Besides the rock 'n roll and ballroom they do Chinese dancing too (surprise surprise!) and were spotted the other morning doing an elegant do-se-do to a tinkling Chinese tune – all twenty of them in two neat lines. And the exhibitionist doing Tai Chi on the roof? Remember him? Well, little Mr Precious has been joined by two friends. They all, obviously, vant to be alone, Garbo-style – just like teenagers all wanting to be different and ending up all being different the same...

In the mornings we used to see the Customs officers going on duty. Sometimes they marched, sometimes attempted to march, sometimes just walked. One day it was the latter as it was raining and they were all carrying umbrellas, two pale green, two violet and two pale blue. So pretty!

We'd been living on a building site, but the hotel was due to be finished mid-April so there would be at least somewhere we could meet up for coffee. They were working hard on the gardens below our windows – hard being the operative word, as it was bed-rock and had to be hewn by hand. It was taking shape and would be nice when it was finished. Couldn't wait for the swimming pool! Gangs of hard-working guys were man-handling mature palm-trees into place – twelve feet tall or taller. (The palm trees, not the men…)

The hotel staff, and many Chinese who deal with Westerners, often gave themselves Western names. So, we had a Jimmy, a James, an Anna, a Freda; one of them was called Lolita. She was one of the Night Managers (well, she would be, wouldn't she, with a name like that?) and we had a Clive, who'd introduced himself, in broken English, as 'Cleeve'…

Great excitement! Pat and I'd spent the three weeks since I'd arrived trying to get our new DVD player to work so we could stock up with DVDs—in China they were less than £2 each. Also the video player we'd brought with us, as we'd also brought lots of videos, old and new, to watch – including three art-instructional ones which I'd been dying to see. We'd had at least three lots of engineers in, and loads of advice from expats and had almost been tearing our hair out. Then, having brought seven DVDs locally, determined to try again, we asked a new little hotel engineer to have a go – he succeeded! Hooray!!

You can't imagine how happy we were: it'd be great to see a video in the evenings. (Pat had been talking to one of the young Chinese guys in Reception and even he'd said that, basically, Aoutou was a dead loss.) We got: *Harry Potter* one and two, *The Sound of Music* '(don't laugh; I hadn't seen it for years but love the music), *Chicago, Catch me if you Can, My Big Fat Greek Wedding,* and *The Hours.* They were all mixed up in the shop with the soft porn, New Year concerts from Vienna, and *Songs from a Tea-House.*

Here's a film review from one of the new DVDs to keep you up-to-date with the cultural scene: **Ha Li's baud is an orphan, and in he just from childhood lives in the virtue this between the stairs that the aunt family is dark continuously, being laughed by vicious aunt and the husband of mother's sister, being bullied by the schoolmate neighours of vicinity, the world that he lived is complete darkness, miserably chilly simply. But in that day of 11 years old birthday Ha Li's baud is got the one's life experience of cicada oneself, and his life has also occurred the earthshaking change at the same time just** etc. etc. etc… Just in case you're not sure which film was being reviewed, it was of course one of the Harry Potters, but we're not sure which. Don't you just love the 'Ha Li' bit??? And what have cicadas got to do with it? Your guess is as good as mine.

Pat and I went into the small town nearby one Sunday, where the Project bus stopped outside a local hotel. We'd been amused to see a couple of 'door-persons' there – young ladies – in incredible outfits – navy, long, great-coats with scarlet lapels, navy and scarlet kepis on their heads, broad white belts, tight, wrinkled black ankle-boots and lashings of gold braid. Straight out of 'White Horse Inn', 'The Student Prince', or some similarly Ruritanian musical...

In town we'd found some flashcards in Pinyin (simplified Mandarin) - one set with fruit and veg, and a transport set, with words such as 'train' 'racing car' 'road roller' etc. but in the same set, 'tommy gun' 'grenade' 'tank' 'pistol' 'nuke' 'bow and arrow' (huh?) 'missile' 'sword' 'machine gun' 'rifle' 'battle-plan' 'warship' and, believe it or not, 'tumbrel' which, correct me if I'm wrong, was the sort of truck which transported people to the guillotine in the French Revolution. Also spelt 'tumbril' for your information. Useful to trot out these interesting facts at dinner parties…

Mountain Road

Hula Hoop Anyone?

So, what with the lack of exercise, I'd had a brilliant idea. Not. Spying some hula hoops in a shop up the road, I'd thought, 'Aha! Just the thing. Could whittle away what I laughingly called my waist, to music' – at school I'd used to be rather good at hula-hooping. Pat and I duly had trotted up t'road for said hoop, and I'd chosen what I thought was the right size – there were several – in rather natty purple, yellow and white. Must confess that I'd never thought of myself as a purple, yellow and white person but then beggars can't be choosers. Back we came, no doubt causing caustic comments in Chinese from the locals, but I was already gloating about my imagined reduced waistline. However, I somehow seemed to have lost the knack, and as it was actually very heavy, it bashed my legs on its inevitable way down, duly aided by gravity, and finally landed with a crash on my toes. I kept trying, but got most of my exercise from nimbly skipping aside as it descended and then bending to pick it up. Ideas, anyone?

Had a jaunt to the local post office to post Mum's Mother's Day card. Entered the Stygian gloom and queued at one of the two windows open. Wrong one. Seeing the 'strange' writing on the envelope, the clerk directed me to the other window where pleasant lady indicated that I'd used the wrong envelope. Ah. Kindly gave me the right envelope, so I transferred card, re-wrote address, and attempted to stick it down. No adhesive strip. Pointed this out to lady who then produced pot of old-fashioned paste – flour and water variety by the look of it, with brush, with which she carefully sealed envelope. However, still no good. I obviously shouldn't have written in English – in fact, don't think she understood the word 'England' – 'cos if she had she could have written it in Chinese. Finally got through to her by saying 'Queen Elizabeth' and 'Tony Blair'.

She still looked worried and quite unconvinced (would anyone be able to read this peculiar scribble on the front of the envelope?) but she took my money and consigned the envelope to what I hope was the right sack for Strange, Uncivilized, Faraway Lands. Well, I tried, Mum. Very hard…

Here is today's film review competition for you all: **'The United States of story occurrence at 1964 until 1966, leave a 17 years old young man flank abener (Leonardo DiCaprio) by dint of the falsification technique of his charming face, his, with the strength of eloquence successfully 'impersonation' e very kind of** dignity person of doctor, professor, airplane pilot. **Cheated to take the innumerable's money, more of is, he go as far as to pretend to be the airplane pilot of the airline the free week to visit the worldwide locations**... etc. etc..

And the answer, of course, is 'Catch Me if You Can' with DiCaprio as Flank, sorry, Frank, Abgagnale...

March 2003. Yes, we're fine, thank you, to those of you who have expressed concern about SARS. This is the area it started, and of course we're near to Hong Kong. We have no problems on the expat front, but certain places, like Hong Kong and Shenzen are out of bounds to us at the moment, as is one particular market area, and also we're advised not to use public transport for the time being. The situation is being monitored and we've all been well-briefed. In spite of that, most of the Shell wives, Dutch ladies who live on Palm Island Resort, have gone home, but I suspect that that could be an over-reaction. We'd planned to go to Hong Kong for a few days at Easter but will now be staying put in downtown Aoutou instead. Oh joy! Unconfined transports of delight!

Should have started giving English lessons week before to workers from the hotel up the road, but because of SARS decided not to do so pro tem. I didn't feel comfortable going to teach unknown people, maybe in badly-ventilated classroom; said I'd review the situation soon. Better safe than sorry...

Pat was coming along the main road one day and saw the whole of the local traffic Police manning a large roundabout. All eight of them. Only problem was that, because they were not actually trained in what to do, they were so busy arguing, gesticulating and pointing that they failed to notice two motor-cyclists watching them, who then collided with each other...

Had two Mandarin lessons with friends, but like our Arabic, it was badly taught by a local lady – lovely lady but with no teaching aids, whose only qualification, I suspect, for the job was that she was Chinese. The expat lady organising lessons before had left to have a baby, so I took the opportunity to butt out and I doubted if I'd start again. It would have meant less time to do my music, which I practised each weekday, and my painting, which I did all day every day if I was at home. I'd got really hooked on it!

One of the American ladies was a professional artist back in the States: she'd worked directly with the famous Jean Dobie, and was much in demand with wall -to-wall commissions. She was kind enough to set up art classes here, and it was such a privilege to study with her – I learnt more in the few months available than I would have thought possible – we started with basic exercises in light, shade and form, did a lot with watercolour, and also had a life drawing group. We were all very keen but with different levels of ability. We thoroughly enjoyed our sessions with Margaret, and I'm so grateful to her…

At this time the apartment complex was still a building site, but there was light at the end of the tunnel, and I caught a glimpse of the hotel foyer one day – it would be really nice when it was finished. Oh! To have a coffee shop to meet up in! And we no longer had to clamber over piles of builders' rubble to get out of the hotel drive – there was a cleared space for us to walk. The latest date for the swimming pool was July, but I wasn't holding my breath…

One of the ladies was telling me they'd been over to Palm Island Resort on the local bus. It wasn't luxurious but it wasn't too bad, and they had a DVD on board which showed Chinese programmes, music and films to entertain the passengers. They were certainly entertained that day, 'cos it was a porn movie!

Progress: the hotel garden was half-turfed; they'd started planting flower beds, and they were still planting mature trees – three lorry-loads of palms one day, each over twenty foot tall, took eight men shifting and striving to lift each one – and there was a sort of pavilion half-finished which we thought would be seating in the shade. Not, unfortunately, that we needed it at that moment: the weather had been mostly poor – at best – since I'd arrived. We had lots of fog still, real, old-fashioned pea-soupers, and Pat and I had been very amused the evening before to see people sitting outside one of the local restaurants over the little jetty, in such a fog. You could hardly see your hand in front of your face! We'd had heavy rain on a number of occasions, which made us think the rains must have been coming early, so I reckoned the gardens might just about be finished by the rainy season and we wouldn't be able to use them anyway.

Our expat social events around this time included a party, a baby shower party, and an appallingly mediocre buffet supper with other Brits to meet the Consul at the Palm Island Golf Resort. It was nice to chat to everyone but that was all.

Mountain Retreat

Old Sea-Dog

Music and Medicals..

We still had our small choir practices and I'd taught everyone the delights of Schumann's 'Orchestra Song', in which there are six parts, each singing a sort of motif which represents an instrument. Anyway, two little Chinese gentlemen had been elected to represent the horns section (not specially groomed for stardom, it was just that they couldn't hold a part, and the horns sing on only one note.) We coached them and coached them, and finally got them singing out so we could hear them. Pronunciation wasn't their strong point either: it transpired that they were singing lustily 'The whores, the whores, they shout it out...'

We all had to have quite stringent medicals to get our residency permits, which included ECG's, chest x-rays and blood tests to mention but a few; the Chinese Government insisted on all these tests, and on using the correct forms for said medicals. Pat's boss went for an ECG, and as he had a hairy chest, (he may still have, I wouldn't know) the Chinese doctor couldn't get the electrodes to stay on. She had several tries without success, but in the end just shrugged and ran the ECG anyway. It came out in long straight line – normally an indication that the patient is dead. The doctor stapled all the papers together with said ECG and sent it off. Drew's permit duly arrived...

A Chinese lady was walking down the road the other day pushing a long fruit and veg stall on wheels before her. Sitting atop the apples, mangoes and whatever, was a plump Chinese baby in typical padded jacket, looking inscrutably at us as they passed. A veritable cherub with cherry-bum...

The ladies continued to dance every morning outside the brothel; they met up just after 6 a.m. On one occasion the dog was there first and sat waiting in what was to be the front row. Nay, the only row. They did mainly Chinese dancing and what appeared to be American Line Dancing, but the other week, while the usual routine was going on we noticed two ladies solemnly doing an old-fashioned waltz around the courtyard of the brothel. Also we'd recently seen two men un-self-consciously walking backwards down the road. I was told that it was supposed to add years to your life, - always supposing you didn't walk into a lorry. I don't suppose that would do too much for your life expectancy.

It was quite a challenge getting all the grocery shopping done: we had most of ours brought in by a charming Philippina lady and husband, who ran a shopping service for expats. Not cheap but efficient and we could get most things, albeit at an exalted price. Still, it saved the hassle of trying to make out what you were buying. Before I came out Pat had bought a tube of what he thought was toothpaste. It may well have been, though we couldn't tell from the taste as it was certainly not peppermint. Maybe we were cleaning our teeth with shaving foam. What was worse, I asked myself, that, or Pat shaving with toothpaste?

Seen the other day: young lady (will give her the benefit of the doubt) waiting at bus stop, wearing miniscule mini-skirt and thigh boots held up by a suspender belt. Obviously on her way to her Chinese traditional dancing lessons.

One bright spot on a recent shopping trip, was the sight of a man coming out of the shop to his scooter. He had on his head a well-fitting contraption which at first looked like an inverted basket but which turned out on closer inspection to be a woven wicker safety helmet. No chin-strap, but it was a veritable work of art, beautifully crafted and highly varnished. I think perhaps his Mum had made it for him and he didn't want to offend her. You can just imagine the conversation: 'Our Fred, have you got your safety-helmet on?' 'Ah, Mum, I'm only popping down to the shops...' 'You put that helmet on, our Fred – I wove that special-like from your Auntie Mavis's pattern...'

Here are two red-hot fashion tips: firstly, make two long cylinders of suitable fabric of your choice, insert elastic in casings at either end of each tube and slip over each arm, from wrist to upper arm. These will protest your arms from fierce sunlight when riding side-saddle, or any other saddle for that matter, on bicycle, scooter or motor bike. It's très a la mode my dears, here in Aoutou: all the best people are wearing them... The other tip also concerns sun-wear: if you don't have a sun-hat, no problem. Just take one round washing-up bowl, make holes at opposite points (maybe a heated skewer, might I suggest?) and thread string through. Place inverted bowl on head, tie string under chin, et voilà! A sun-hat to be proud of. Spotted by Pat recently...

Back from seven-hour shopping trip: all we had to show for it were two carrier bags of food and some CDs; a Chinese lady on the bus had kindly showed us round two Chinese tea-houses. The much-vaunted 'beautiful lake' turned out to be man-made, surrounded by the concrete tower blocks which dominated the landscape. Drove through beautiful mountain scenery to get there—we'd have preferred to have found somewhere nice to walk in the country-side. Said CDs are 'classical' and include 'Handel: ten famous golden music of Tchaikovsky', 'Mendelssohn: ten famous golden music of Tchaikovsky' 'Everlasting Classics, the Most Enchainted Melodies' which includes 'Old Black Joe' 'American Patrol' 'Oh my darling clemaeine' and 'Moscow noghiis'. (What?).

On another trip we were on the bus to go shopping, and were getting close to the border (Shenzen is a duty-free zone) so we all started to get out, as required, passport or resident visa at the ready; I happened to have both with me. One expat husband with us had forgotten his, so I duly gave him my visa. The photo was taken ten years before when I sported a long, dark, curly pony-tail of the pre -Raphaelite variety, and large dark horn-rimmed spectacles. Ian, said guy, who was about twenty years younger, was over six foot tall and had short spiky hair. He popped on his dark-rimmed spectacles and was waved through…

Went across the road to one of the little shops which cater for expats, to buy flour. Couldn't see it in the usual place, so assistant came up to help. 'Flour?' she asked, 'Come with me.' She took me round the back to a row of freezers (not so silly, as in the Philippines we kept the flour in the fridge because of the weevils) and asked 'What sort of flour do you want?. 'Self-raising' says I. 'For cakes'. 'Sorry', she says 'We don't have any flour at all…' Silly me, I should just have asked 'What sort of flour don't you have?'

Pat had a lovely birthday over the Easter weekend. I bought him a brass telescope which he had admired in a local shop some time before, and painted a water-colour of Hamilton Road (our home in UK) which I'd then had framed. The wrapping paper, which I'd found locally with great difficulty, had various messages on it, including: 'show wishs who who, the greatest happiness to possess what can be cherished in life one should cherish his friends. Among friends he should cherish the most intimate ones'. Quite right too. And then there was: 'life is grotesque and gaudy like a kaleidoscope, may you have a colourful world in your life!' Well, that just about sums it all up.

So, life was even quieter than before here, but at least we were no longer living on a building site. The hotel part of the complex finally opened and the restaurants, but believe me, their prices were West End prices, and few of the expats would be eating there. There were tiled drives up to the hotel now so we no longer had to climb over piles of rubble, as we did up till this week. The garden was finished but was totally and completely disappointing: it was mainly grass and some trees and a couple of flower-beds. No shade (though we were hoping for garden furniture and umbrellas in the near future) – it was far too hot and humid to sit out in the sun. Also, it was not private: set in the container port, it was a busy area with cranes and lorries coming and going all day, and metre-wide gaps in the boundary wall every ten or so metres where people could peer through, plus being extremely noisy and dusty.

As I say, life was quiet but we had a very nice party for Pat – about thirty people came, and I'd been to a couple of 'do's' for the ladies. At weekends we usually went for a walk towards the mountains and after the first mile the builders' rubble was left behind (literally) and it was a very pleasant walk. As the road curved round the bay there was a dilapidated, disused, sinking boat, which somehow looked very pretty.

Saw a delightful sight the one day: it was normal to see parents and one or two children on one motor-scooter, but that day we saw Dad riding the bike with child one in front of him, and child two behind, then Mum followed by child three all squeezed up together…

Forgot to say the other week when we'd had an exciting trip to B & Q, that we'd invited our hired driver to have a snack and drink with us at the coffee bar. He opted for a pizza and coke, and when his pizza arrived he attacked it with chopsticks. We thought that he probably didn't know how to use a knife and fork—why should he? - and obviously felt embarrassed, as he moved the menu across to screen himself from our expat eyes. We excused ourselves, and drifted off, ostensibly to look at some shelving…

Had lunch in a local Chinese restaurant the other day with a group of Pat's colleagues and young Chinese students, who'd been doing work experience. Found it laborious serving one mouthful at a time into tiny dish about the size of a small coffee cup, and although the food was fresh and hot I didn't really enjoy it much. The most exciting part of the lunch was when the waitress tipped a bowl of soup into my lap.

Typhoons and Tables

The shopping in China was fantastic – inexpensive and good quality – and the haggling was fun. Most of the time, that is; sometimes we just wanted to buy something without all the preamble. In the Long Market in Beijing, Pat picked up a Chinese hat with long black pigtail attached (to go with his newly-purchased French navy silk jim-jams). So he tried it on and looked so ridiculous with this long pigtail tossed nonchalantly over his shoulder, that I got the giggles. I ended up bent double crying hysterically with tears running down my face, whereupon the stall-holder started to laugh at me, and literally people all down the market were craning their necks and laughing too. It created absolute mayhem, and all the way back to the hotel we kept laughing.

We went on a shopping trip to a furniture and antique warehouse, and saw there a beautiful table which would have looked perfect in our dining room – added to that, it was a most ingenious design so that it split into five irregular pieces, each one of which could be used as an occasional or coffee table. It was a veritable work of art, and really unusual. We both loved it and asked the assistant could she please take it apart so that we could see the smaller tables. This she did, and we were seriously thinking of buying it, until, that is, said assistant tried to put the pieces back together into the larger format. She couldn't. We tried, very hard, but we couldn't. The assistant called over a colleague. He tried. No luck. Enter supervisor, ditto. By this time we were all giggling – everyone trying to help put the pieces back together. Absolutely no joy, so, sorry furniture warehouse, no sale. We left giggling and left them giggling too and still trying to solve the puzzle…

Have had two visits to Beijing: first one a short visit before coming out. Both times it was cold and foggy most of the time, but it was good weather for our day on the Great Wall. We went up in a ski-lift, walked along the Wall for a couple of hours, and came down in a bob-sleigh. I went down first, more than a trifle

Walking the Great Wall

nervously I have to add; Pat followed. I arrived at foot of slope and waited for Pat. And waited. And waited. Was beginning to think that he'd had an accident, when he came into sight, slowly, inch by laborious inch. He'd got leaves in his runners (ooh, missus!) and had to propel himself down using a punting action with his hands. So much for sweeping down in style! In Beijing we went to Mass at the Cathedral, and were most amused to hear the organist playing, apart from the usual hymns, 'Way down upon de Swanee River' and even better, softly and soulfully – honestly – 'Two lovely black eyes'...

Out and about one day we saw a guy on a bicycle pulling small hand-cart, a bit like a wheel-barrow, in which his wife was sitting. She looked uncomfortable, undignified and downright disgruntled, a sort of Chinese Ena Sharples. You can imagine the conversation: 'Ee up our Ena, tha looks a bit peaky... wah... I'll tek thi' fer a drive this afternoon – get thi- some roses in thi' cheeks... wah' 'That'd be luverly our Fred, wait while I change mi hair-net... wha...'

This has been an exciting week: we had a ladies' lunch here, and a fire-drill! The most exciting week for ages! Be still my beating heart... Spent the whole morning pre-fire-drill wondering what to wear – what does one wear on these occasions? Must be comfortable enough to walk down sixteen flights of stairs, but don't want to let the side down. Settled finally on cream safari skirt and sand-coloured linen blouse with cream sprigs; sand-coloured sandals and painted toe-nails completed the ensemble, with just a touch of my favourite lipstick. I like to think it struck just the right note...The lunch was fun! Ten of us – loads of delicious food: we had a friend in to dinner to help with the left-overs...

With an expat friend, Susan, I'd been teaching oral English skills a couple of mornings per week at a local private school; Lucy one of Pat's Chinese colleagues had been asked to find someone who could help with English lessons, not necessarily a teacher (I was) but someone 'who loved children'. Lucy spoke fluent English but spelling wasn't her strong point – the email to Pat said 'Surly Mary could help with this?' The first time I'd gone along to meet the staff and children, the children had sung me a charming little song, but I literally hadn't understood a word. I asked about the song and was told it was Engrish!

Although the teachers in the English department spoke some English, obviously, it wasn't English as we know it; they were frequently incomprehensible and couldn't hold an English conversation in any depth... Just before my first class I was asked by the Chinese teacher to teach 'orange'. 'What?' says I being a bit thick. 'Orange' he repeated. Three times in all he said it, and I still didn't know what he meant so regretfully couldn't oblige. As stated elsewhere, Chinese people frequently gave themselves western names, so I wasn't surprised to hear the Head of English was called Simon. At least, so I thought—I called him 'Simon' the whole time I was there, and when I'd left he said to Susan 'Why did Mary call me Simon? My name is Sam.'

The children were delightful, and seemed to enjoy their lessons. The Chinese system of learning a language was to learn given conversations by heart, so the children didn't know the meaning of individual words, and couldn't actually use them. One day, bored as much as the children by the incessant chanting of stilted irrelevant English phrases, and without suitable textbooks, I introduced a word search game on the topics in question. We did it in teams on the blackboard, and they were just galvanised into life, which was very gratifying to see – me too – I was practically jumping up and down with excitement... After that it was games all the way. Susan and I spent a lot of time devising games for our lessons which the children enjoyed, although the Chinese teachers remained unconvinced by my methods...

On the way to school one day (they always sent a car and driver) we saw a charming sight: a young mum had her baby in a sort of woven wicker backpack, like a little laundry-basket, moulded into a tiny bum-shape to fit a tiny baby bum. Said baby was head and shoulders only visible, impassively surveying the scene. He was wearing a bright yellow anorak with red trim, and a delightful little lilac hat shaped like a solar topee.

Looking out one day from an upstairs window in the school, I saw hundreds of students from the secondary school next door doing military drills in the school grounds. When I say it was regimented that just doesn't describe it. It was like watching robots. I found it chilling...

The art stuff on the walls in the school was superb, but some of it may have been a tad misplaced: the teachers had lovingly and skilfully cut a large climbing bamboo out of paper and pasted it all over a window to a cupboard on one of the staircase landings, with pandas clinging to it. Only problem was, and please forgive me for bringing it to your attention – the cupboard in question was where the fire hydrant was stored, and ahem, well, wouldn't it be a good idea to have said hydrant visible in a fire??? Speaking of which, Susan had twice seen the new boilers in the kitchen on fire. No-one had batted an eyelid...

I finished there as demob time drew near. After lessons on my last day I was mobbed by little girls hanging onto my arm, skirt, and anything else they could get hold of, all saying 'Mary, we'll miss you' and working each other up into a state of mass hysteria. Kisses and compliments were flying, but the latter I could well have done without: one of the teachers in the English Department commented that I was 'a very lively teacher for one so old', then a little girl had lovingly pinched my my arm and said 'fat' and later that day one of my adult students had said that I must have been beautiful when I was young...

The Project organised a boat trip and picnic one Sunday – unfortunately it started to rain just as we set off, which no doubt saved me from a few more wrinkles. It was very pleasant. Did a little pen and wash sketch on the boat. Rain had stopped but started again and the ink ran on the painting, so nothing daunted, I went with the flow (literally!) and called it 'Fishing in the Rain'... We had a swim with some of Pat's colleagues and a walk—a really good day!

I used to go to the new purpose-built gym several times a week, in the newly-opened swimming pool building, where my preference was for the cross-trainer. (Swimming pool was not ready for use). State of the art equipment. Brilliant! In said gym TV screens were all duly erected, connected and operational. Ah, problem: Correct me if I'm wrong, but aren't the TV's supposed to be facing the equipment, rather than away from it? Maybe I've got it all wrong, but I just sort of assumed that they were for watching while you exercised. Silly me!

On a recent visit to the original tiny gym in the apartment building, I was encouraged to watch the 'calories used' display on the screens. After earning my first half-slice of dry bread I couldn't decide whether to go for the other half, or butter the first... Having 'cross-country skied' for fifteen minutes (not easy in downtown Aoutou) I 'walked' two kilometres. Only problem is, as I pointed out to Pat, is that, had I actually walked that distance, I'd have been at the small local supermarket, and could actually have done some shopping...

Crossing the road to the gym I saw a group of elderly ladies exercising to Chinese music, dancing a traditional dance in perfect synchronisation. Twenty metres away, just at the limit of the music, was a solitary elderly gentleman, also in perfect sync, but facing away from them like a mirror image, obviously trying to make out that he wasn't sharing their music. One morning, as we watched the ladies dancing outside the brothel, we saw two couples jitterbugging: we opened the window to listen to the music and heard the plaintive strains of a very gentle little traditional Chinese song, 'The Jasmine song'...

The other week, amongst all the keep-fitters doing their own thing in and around the container port was a gentleman brandishing a large sword, and a lady, completely alone, doing intricate movements with a large red fan. Day before, we'd seen the ladies outside the brothel all doing a flag-dance, waving large red flags. No wonder the little three-legged spectator dog looked so lugubrious! One day I saw nine hotel employees, smartly dressed in their dark suits, marching solemnly to the Holiday Inn flagstaff, each carrying a flag – Holiday Inn, China, UK, USA etc. Each flag was carefully attached to flagpole and ceremoniously hoisted. One had to observe the niceties...

There was a lovely china shop in the village which we sometimes visited for a little stroll; we bought lots of pieces of very typical table-ware for peanuts. We also found there two huge Chinese vases, blue and white, very traditional, which we bought for our lounge in Reading. They were each almost four feet high and were absolutely gorgeous – would have cost a fortune in the UK. They were duly delivered to our apartment block – on a motor bike! The mind boggles...

Also during the summer brother Mike, my sister-in-law Jan and nephew Andy came for a few days during a holiday trip to China. It was lovely to see them. They'd been doing lots of travelling around, and had more scheduled after us, so we didn't do anything strenuous while they were with us, just catching up with the gossip, and a lovely afternoon swimming at the Palm Island Resort...

We had a break near Gweilin during the summer, which is that beautiful place on the river with the strange-shaped mountains you see in all the tourist literature. We had a lovely cruise down the river on a small boat, and watched cormorants fishing, though I think that was mainly for the tourists. We hired a very nice driver and he took us around. Did some serious shopping too. We stayed in a small, traditional guest-house which had been a temple, in a small, pretty village outside the main tourist area. The scenery was spectacular and breakfast outside was marred only by the hawking and spitting from a near-by table…

One Saturday morning we went to Guangzhou with friends, came back Sunday evening. The town itself is a large, sprawling, unattractive city on the Pearl River, but there's a small island over the river-bridge, just literally yards away, with a strong Western influence. Shamian Island was the only place where 'foreign devils' were allowed to settle during the time of the Emperors. It was originally just a sandbank, but the settlers developed it and it's a really peaceful, pleasant place. The streets are wide and quiet, the buildings very French.

Sunday morning the place was alive with Chinese people doing physical fitness activities. A badminton net was stretched across one street, with a row of people either side hitting shuttlecocks back and forth; there were about forty ladies doing a Chinese Hat Dance (!) and best of all, there was a large adults" playground' with about twenty different pieces of brightly-coloured gym equipment. There were twenty or more elderly ladies and gentlemen swinging, twizzling, hanging, see-sawing, foot-massaging, and back-rubbing in a sort of manic circus. They take their keep-fit very seriously, which is very creditable, and there seemed to be no joking or light-hearted banter of any sort., apart from two middle-aged ladies, sitting astride their piece of equipment, skirts hiked up over their knees, handbag hanging from appropriate hook, doing back-rubbing against rollers while they chatted and gossiped.

Back in Aoutou it was amusing to see the buses arrive each day with the Chinese office workers, many wearing cocktail dresses, frilled, flounced, fishtailed, beribboned, full-length or ballerina length, - all in synthetic fabrics – in this hot, humid climate…

We had a fearsome double-eyed typhoon during a spell of bad weather; had to close all the curtains and vacate our apartments because of the danger of broken windows; couldn't use the lifts. Hacked down 16 flights of stairs and joined all the other expats in the dining room behind the bar, which was window-less. The storm raged outside: we saw mature palm-trees up-rooted and flying through the air. The hotel staff were magnificent: they barricaded the huge plate-glass windows and doors with heavy furniture, and someone was on duty at each door all through the storm- which lasted several hours, literally just hanging on so they couldn't be blown open. The force of the wind was incredible. Some of the children were understandably quite nervous: one little girl, Francesca, sat on my lap for a cuddle, and I explained to her that this was a typhoon, so we had to have a typhoon party, because 'you always have to have a party when there's a typhoon.' One of the expats brought a DVD player down with some children's DVD's and the hotel gave ice-creams to all the children.

A bit later, as I saw her rushing past, playing with some of the other children, she saw me, did a double-take, skidded to a halt, and said breathlessly to me before she rushed off again: 'I like typhoon parties!' At one stage during the evening someone living in the penthouse on the eighteenth floor or so was worried whether they'd secured everything properly, so Pat went up to see. The windows had all been smashed and there was glass all over the floor…

Note on hotel lift door: 'Lift out of order. We are sorry for the incontinence'…

…turning out the cupboards the other day I found several items, the names of which I must share with you: there was 'Ugly Girl' hand cream (yes honestly), Fuku soup, and maybe best of all was the dried orange peel which came free with something else. It was coated in a sort of sugary, vaguely spicy powder, and it tasted absolutely vile. Which didn't surprise me really when I looked at the brand name on the packet. It was 'Old skin'. I rest my case…

We received a flyer one day advertising mountain bikes: apparently China is a particularly good place to buy them. Flyer was impressive, with list of bikes and everything which a keen cyclist might need, but the effect was somewhat spoilt by the legend at the bottom which read 'also maid service, storage, manicure and pedicure'; I've heard of diversification but this was ridiculous…

Wash-day, Hakka Village p.270

Below: A Different Use for Lego!

Christmas

Here I am in the Land of the Pagodas, sitting at my desk looking out over the bay, and surrounded by packers. Yes folks, we're off again, but this time, initially at least, back to UK. Pat's contract was officially due to end in October 04, but the powers-that-be have decreed that we, along with a number of others, should demobilise early. Pat will report back to the Company after Christmas and find out what they have in mind for us. Anyway, back to the present: The packers have just finished: the estimated two-hour stint has turned into six hours, and with forty-one packing cases packed (that's two less than the Philippines!), we're only just over double our permitted allowance.

Aoutou itself is not exactly the hub of the universe, in fact, when we arrived it was like the back of beyond, but there have been enormous changes: the complex where we live is no longer a building site; we don't have to climb over piles of bricks and rubble to go in and out.. The garden is finished, the tennis courts are in constant use, as is the children's playground. The small grocery shop in the hotel has brought down its astronomical prices (standard packet of cornflakes £8) and now frequently stocks bananas! We have a new state-of-the-art gym, and the swimming pool is newly operational. Just too late for us!

Just over a year ago, the main road was unpaved; now it's a proper, busy road, with pavements, street lighting, and lots of new buildings. The row of tiny shabby shops has disappeared – some of them virtually overnight. Doubt if their owners necessarily think that this change is a Good Thing, but we'll never know. The path around the bay, which was lined with rubbish tips, is now tarmacked and has street-lighting. There are a number of small bars and restaurants. The workers have left the barracks round the back of the hotel, as have the rats, and the barracks have been demolished. The narrow pathway cutting through the rock-face to the fish market has been widened and levelled, giving access to the new building site around the corner. Aoutou is booming – as is China.

Some things haven't changed: the Customs men still amble across the square with only one in step, the twenty-odd ladies (as distinct from twenty odd ladies) still dance outside the brothel from 6 to 7 a.m. and the little lame dog still keeps them company: we see the ladies arrive in semi-darkness and strut their stuff. In a dancing contest I'd give them 101% for enthusiasm, reliability, and precision, and 3% for choreography... The ladies outside the Bank still do their strange dance/Tai Chi? which consists of hand and arm-washing movements, interspersed with synchronised hair-smoothing. To music. 'Why?' I hear you ask. The answer is, I haven't a clue. This is the Mystic East, remember?

Here it's been more difficult to get under the skin of the place than in the Philippines or in Egypt: in both of those places we were actually living amongst the local people. Being on the sixteenth floor of a block of flats makes that much more of a problem, and also the language here poses a huge problem for most Europeans – I love languages, speak French and German and can get by with key-words in Arabic, but Mandarin? Sadly it has proved far too difficult.

The powers-that-be were obviously determined to put Aoutou on the map: we had an invasion of a thousand potential investors visiting. Twenty-five luxurious yellow and blue coaches filled the newly-surfaced car-park, with more due the next day. The hotel was buzzing; derelict buildings had huge, brightly-coloured banners hanging down as camouflage; hundreds of workers had planted thousands of trees and plants along the roadsides; there were massive gas-filled balloons about seven foot in diameter suspended from large buildings, there was bunting everywhere, and small vans delivering and/or collecting flags which lined the roads for miles. In fact, I'd wondered whether a team was following the cavalcade, removing them and then nipping up side roads and planting 'em again up front so that you wouldn't need so many. We'll never know...

We had an excellent carol service on Sunday evening: our small choir was joined by another expat choir and together we made really good music – I felt proud to be involved! The Christmas tree was beautiful and it was so refreshing to start thinking about Christmas on the First Sunday of Advent, and not in September. Hard to believe it was communist China when you heard the old traditional carols, and saw the polystyrene angels singing from the Holy Bible! We celebrated afterwards with canapés and mulled wine, and some more mull' wine, and hic, some more wulled mine, and huc shome mo' wun mile...

Had a nice farewell lunch with the ladies, where they gave me a lovely jade necklace, and Margaret, my American artist friend gave me a beautiful large framed pencil picture of our house in Reading, which we'll treasure. I sang one of my usual numbers, plus the following version of 'A Policeman's Lot Is Not An 'appy One' which I'd written specially for the occasion: I can't think of a more apt way of winding up this journal than to re-produce it here:

Oh our friends at home all tell us just how fortunate we are,
To lead a pampered life here in the sun.
But they just don't understand that things are really not like that,
Or why we're all so tired when day is done (day is done).

Oh yes, we may have apartments with a view out to the bay,
But with trucks that shift containers by the ton,
And the thumping and the crashing and the bright lights night and day,
Oh an expat life is really not much fun (not much fun).

Now the shop has no potatoes and there're weevils in the flour
You need mega bucks for coffee and a bun,
And fresh veggies are like gold-dust and the fridges are too small
And the cookies cost a fortune. Chinese pun (Chinese pun).

Oh the engineer has fixed the waste-disposal yet again
It's fortunate that I don't have a gun,
The light fitments are unstable, maybe dangerous as well,
I'm tempted to go off and be a nun (be a nun).

But we're here to help our husbands and that's what it's all about
We play at silly games and have a lot of fun,
Yes our systems may be gummed-up but with loads of friends we've chummed up,
Oh an ex-at life can be a happy one!

YES, AN EXPAT'S LIFE CAN BE A HAPPY ONE!!!

Post-script.

Pat and I returned to UK at the end of 2003. Pat's contract with FW having finished, he worked for them on an ad hoc basis before being head-hunted by Bechtel for a major project in Rumania, the building of a new highway – the first of its type there. Pat was preparing for posting to Rumania when he was diagnosed with prostate cancer and was therefore unable to take up the position.

Whilst he was waiting for surgery, we travelled to New Zealand for son Ben's Graduation from Video and TV school in Auckland. We loved New Zealand and travelled on a backpackers' bus round South Island.

Pat recovered very well from the surgery, remaining his usual positive cheerful self throughout his convalescence, but sadly he developed oesophageal cancer, supposedly unconnectedly from the original cancer; he died in 2007. He was, and is, much loved and missed by the family. RIP.

Several years after Pat's death, I re-married, one Alan, whom I met on-line. We've been married nearly three years at time of writing, and we both have two children and two grandchildren. We keep very busy with families, friends, and a good social life. I still paint whenever I have time, and am grateful to my long-suffering dentist, who until recently hung my paintings in the waiting-room for several years, and even sold a large number of them! I sing in two choirs, and am a volunteer with the Police, role-playing for the Police trainees. Alan and I have also organised eight regular holiday breaks for a group of friends.

Now that this book is finished, I think I might have time to try something I've heard people mention: it's called 'housework' – I'm not sure what it is, but, anything for a laugh, I might just give it a try…

What the reviewers say:

Highly recommended - you absolutely must buy this book!	Author
Aaaaaaw Mum!	Author's children
Nanny, we like the pictures!	Author's grandchildren
So now can we have home-made cake again please?	Author's husband

Scallop Shell Press

Ever since the Middle Ages the scallop shell has been the symbol of those going on pilgrimage to the shrine of St James in Compostela, Spain.

Today the pilgrimage is even more popular than ever as people of all faiths, and none, seek a meaning for their journey through life.

The shell became a metaphor for the journey, the grooves representing the many ways of arriving at one's destination. At a practical level the shell was also useful for scooping up water to drink or food to eat.

Scallop Shell Press aims to publish works which, like the grooves of the shell, will offer the modern pilgrim stories of our shared humanity and help readers arrive at their own meaningful interpretations of life. We hope that our books will be shells within whose covers readers will find an intellectual and spiritual source of sustenance for their own personal pilgrimages.

If you would like to find out more about Scallop Shell Press please visit our website

www.Scallopshellpress.co.uk

or email us

Email: Scallopshellpress@yahoo.co.uk